THE JESUS PAPYRUS

THE JESUS PAPYRUS

The Most Sensational Evidence
on the Origins of the Gospels
Since the Discovery of the
Dead Sea Scrolls

Carsten Peter Thiede

AND

Matthew d'Ancona

GALILEE
DOUBLEDAY
New York   London   Toronto   Sydney   Auckland

A GALILEE BOOK

PUBLISHED BY DOUBLEDAY

a division of Random House, Inc.

1540 Broadway, New York, New York 10036

GALILEE, DOUBLEDAY, and the portrayal of a ship with a cross above a book are trademarks
of Doubleday, a division of Random House, Inc.

Book design by Julie Duquet

The Jesus Papyrus was originally published in hardcover by Doubleday as
Eyewitness to Jesus in April 1996.

The Library of Congress has cataloged the 1996 Doubleday hardcover edition
of Eyewitness to Jesus as follows:

Thiede, Carsten Peter, 1952–
Eyewitness to Jesus: amazing new manuscript evidence about the origins of the Gospels
Carsten Peter Thiede and Matthew d'Ancona. —
p.   cm.
Includes bibliographical references and index.
1. Magdalen papyrus.   2. Bible.   N.T.   Matthew XXVI, 6–7—Authorship—Date of
authorship.   3. Bible.   N.T.—Manuscripts, Greek.   4. Bible.   N.T.—Manuscripts
(Papyri)   5. Bible.   N.T. Gospels—Authorship—Date of authorship.   6. Magdalen
College (University of Oxford).   Library.   7. Huleatt, Charles Bousfield, 1863–1908.
I. Thiede, Carsten Peter.   II. Title.
BS2570.5.M343   1996
226.2′048—dc20   95-48987
CIP

ISBN 0-385-48898-x

To my three-year-old son, Frederick, who said that he would like as many heaps of paper on his desk when he has grown up as I had while writing this book.

Carsten Peter Thiede

To my darling wife, Katherine, who explained to me why the papyrus mattered. As on our wedding day, I still "count the ways."

Matthew d'Ancona

PREFACE

Any scholar or journalist who enters the extraordinary terrain of this book needs all the friends he can get. This has been a collaborative venture between the two of us, spawned by a series of interviews in late 1994 and subsequent meetings in London, Paderborn and Oxford. But our work has been made easier and more stimulating by the support of others.

In New York, our editor Mark Fretz was a patient and sympathetic shepherd to a project that was often logistically complex. In London, we received energetic help from our nonpareil agent, Giles Gordon.

At *The Times,* Editor Peter Stothard was extremely generous in his support, while Executive Editor Martin Ivens provided welcome intellectual encouragement.

Pursuing Charles Huleatt through the Victorian mists would have been much harder without guidance from his descendants Captain Julian Williams, Thomas Huleatt-James and Vere Wilcher; the historian of Wycliffe Hall, the Reverend J. S. Reynolds; and Jill Lomer of the Thomas Cook Archive. In Egypt, Dr. Mary Masoud and Nael El-F“arargy of Wena Hotels were very helpful in our quest for the origins of the Magdalen Papyrus.

In Oxford, Anthony Smith, CBE, the President of Magdalen College, gave freely of his time and intellectual energy. We owe him a great debt of gratitude. Dr. Christine Ferdinand, the college's Fellow Librarian, and Sally Speirs, the Assistant Librarian, were untiring and self-sacrificing in their patient assistance.

Among those who have offered indispensable criticisms, advice and help are Joseph Zias, Curator at the John Rockefeller Museum, Jerusalem; Dr. Ulrich Victor, Reader in Classical Philology at Berlin's Humboldt University; Professor José O'Callaghan of the Seminari di Papirologia at Sant Cugat del Valles; Professor Dieter Hagedorn of the Institute for Papyrology at the University of Heidelberg; and Professor Georg Masuch of the German Institute for Education and Knowledge, Paderborn.

Neither of us would have been equal to the task without his family's love and support. Above all else, this book is meant for them.

Paderborn/London, St. Matthew's Day, 1995

CONTENTS

THE GREEK ALPHABET

UPPER CASE	LOWER CASE	NAME	LATIN EQUIVALENT
A	α	*alpha*	a
B	β	*beta*	b
Γ	γ	*gamma*	g, n
Δ	δ	*delta*	d
E	ε	*epsilon*	e
Z	ζ	*zeta*	zd, z
H	η	*eta*	ē
Θ	θ	*theta*	th
I	ι	*iota*	i
K	κ	*kappa*	k
Λ	λ	*lambda*	l
M	μ	*mu*	m
N	ν	*nu*	n
Ξ	ξ	*xi*	x
O	o	*omicron*	o
Π	π	*pi*	p
P	ϱ	*rho*	r, hr
Σ	σ, ς	*sigma*	s
T	τ	*tau*	t
Y	υ	*upsilon*	u (u, ü)
Φ	φ	*phi*	ph (f)
X	χ	*chi*	ch
Ψ	ψ	*psi*	ps
Ω	ω	*omega*	ō

FOR TRULY, I SAY TO YOU, TILL HEAVEN AND EARTH PASS AWAY, NOT AN IOTA, NOT A DOT, WILL PASS AWAY FROM THE LAW UNTIL ALL IS ACCOMPLISHED.

—ST. MATTHEW 5:18

THE JESUS PAPYRUS

1

THE MAGDALEN
COLLEGE PAPYRUS:
AN INTRODUCTION

JESUS WAS AT BETHANY IN THE HOUSE OF SIMON THE LEPER, WHEN A
WOMAN CAME TO HIM WITH A SMALL BOTTLE OF FRAGRANT OIL, VERY
COSTLY; AND AS SHE SAT AT TABLE SHE BEGAN TO POUR IT OVER HIS HEAD.

—ST. MATTHEW 26:6–7

WE MAY START WITH THE FACT, WHICH I CONFESS I DID NOT APPRECIATE
BEFORE THE BEGINNING OF THE INVESTIGATION, OF HOW *LITTLE* EVIDENCE
THERE IS FOR THE DATING OF *ANY* OF THE NEW TESTAMENT WRITINGS.

—JOHN A. T. ROBINSON, *REDATING THE NEW TESTAMENT* (1976)

O N CHRISTMAS EVE, 1994, *The Times* of London reported on its front page an astonishing claim made by the German biblical scholar Carsten Peter Thiede. "A papyrus believed to be the oldest extant fragment of the New Testament has been found in an Oxford library," the newspaper said. "It provides the first material evidence that the Gospel according to St. Matthew is an eyewitness account written by contemporaries of Christ."

The story concerned three tiny scraps of paper belonging to Magdalen College, Oxford, the largest of which is only 4.1 cm × 1.3 cm (1⅝ in. × ½ in.). On both sides of the fragments appeared Greek script, phrases from the twenty-sixth chapter of St. Matthew, which describes Jesus' anointment in the house of Simon the leper at Bethany and his betrayal to the chief priests by Judas Iscariot. Though the verses concern a crucial moment in the life of Christ, the scraps looked unremarkable in themselves. Yet Thiede—Director of the Institute for Basic Epistemological Research in Paderborn, Germany—argued that they were of astonishingly early origin, dating from the mid-first century A.D. He was shortly to publish his claims in the *Zeitschrift für Papyrologie,* a specialist journal for papyrologists (scholars who study ancient manuscript evidence on papyrus).

The argument was complex, based upon expert analysis of the Greek writing on the fragments and upon extensive comparisons with calligraphy on other manuscript fragments. A scholarly controversy was bound to follow, since Thiede was challenging the orthodox view that the tiny second-century fragment of St. John's Gospel in the John Rylands Library in Manchester was our earliest Gospel text. He was also making a claim which would have radical implications for our understanding of the Gospels and their origins. And—most important—he was doing so on the basis of physical evidence rather than literary theory or historical supposition.

The new claim clearly deserved a much broader audience than the comparatively small guild of papyrologists to whom Thiede's learned article was addressed. Here, it was alleged, was a fragment of the twenty-sixth chapter of St. Matthew—remnants of a book perhaps 150 pages long—which might have been written in the lifetime of the apostle himself. If true, Thiede's argument had far-reaching implications. As one senior fellow of Magdalen put it at the time: "It means that the people in the story must have been around when this was being written. It means they were *there.*"

In its editorial column, *The Times* noted that many historians, theologians and linguists had speculated in the past that the New Testament was written by contemporaries or near contemporaries of Christ. "What separates Thiede from his academic predecessors," the editorial went on to say, "is that he has identified an artefact—albeit a tiny one—which seems to prove his point . . . This bold contention moves the debate on the antiquity of the New Testament into new territory."

None of this might have come to light had Thiede, whose wife is English, not found himself in Oxford for a family celebration in February 1994. As a routine act of scholarly curiosity, he asked the assistant librarian at Magdalen College if he could take a look at the St. Matthew papyrus. He was struck and perplexed by what he saw—particularly that such an intriguing fragment had been so neglected since last being dated, to the second century, in the 1950s. Four visits to Oxford followed, in the course of which Thiede was able to study the papyrus in detail and refine his thesis.

When Anthony Smith, President of Magdalen, learned what Thiede was planning to argue, he made it his task to find out more about the fragments and how they had fallen into the hands of the college. How had this mysterious papyrus reached its twentieth-century home at Magdalen? The college records listed the donor as the Reverend Charles Bousfield Huleatt (1863–1908), a onetime undergraduate about whom almost nothing was known. Who was he and what was his part in the story of the papyrus?

Not since the discovery of the Dead Sea Scrolls in 1947 had there been such a potentially important breakthrough in biblical research. Thiede appeared to have found evidence that the St. Matthew Gospel was written only a generation after the Crucifixion—or even earlier. The papyrus itself, unearthed in Upper Egypt and bequeathed to Magdalen in 1901, might conceivably have been read or handled by one of the "five hundred brothers and sisters" (1 Corinthians 15:6) whom St. Paul declares to have seen the resurrected Jesus with their own eyes. It was a claim that nobody with an interest in Christianity—spiritual or scholarly—could possibly ignore.

Aware of the story's significance, *The Times* put its vast production halls in east London on security alert during its press run to prevent the news from leaking to a rival publication overnight. Only a handful of the newspaper's staff knew the details of what was to be published. But discreet soundings in the scholarly world had already suggested to them how much interest was likely to be generated by Thiede's claim and how fierce the scholarly debate would be.

So it has proved. In the days after *The Times* ran the story, it was picked up by news publications all over the world, from Los Angeles to New Delhi, while in Britain, the ITN news channel ran the story prominently on its prime-time bulletin. On January 23, 1995, *Time* magazine's Religious Editor, Richard Ostling, reported the new research under the bold and evocative headline "A Step Closer to Jesus?"

As expected, Thiede's argument provoked a powerful response, not least a vigorous correspondence in the letters columns of *The Times*. Some academics were hostile, arguing that the papyrus had been dated quite satisfactorily in 1953 to the late second century A.D. and that

Thiede had done nothing to alter that consensus. In *The Sunday Telegraph,* the distinguished politician and scholar Enoch Powell dismissed Thiede's argument about the handwriting on the fragments as unfounded and "arrogant." Many others, however, commended Thiede's approach and wanted to learn more. "The problem is, this upsets the whole theological establishment," Ulrich Victor, a distinguished German classical philologist, told *Time* magazine. Hugh Montefiore, the normally measured columnist of *The Church Times,* described the story breathlessly as a potential "bombshell."

It was not only in academic circles that the new research inspired strong emotions. Thiede and Matthew d'Ancona, the author of the original *Times* piece, were overwhelmed with telephone calls and letters seeking further information about the Magdalen fragments. In his scholarly travels around the world, Thiede discovered that his research had made an impact upon ordinary people, fascinated by the questions it posed to them about the relationship between history and faith, religion and empiricism. They were enthralled that the fragments might have been read by men and women who had walked with Jesus through Galilee and wept as the storm gathered above the Cross on Golgotha. But they were also intrigued by the methods used to reach the new date and its implications for contemporary approaches to religion. It seemed at times that everybody had a view on the Magdalen Papyrus, ranging from fanatical fundamentalism to almost pathological liberal skepticism. Never before had a scholar produced forensic evidence that St. Matthew's Gospel was written not long after the events it described. It was hard to be indifferent about such a find.

The experience of Magdalen College itself was similar. Three tiny scraps of paper which had attracted little attention for almost a century were suddenly being treated by outsiders as a uniquely sacred artifact, of interest to people around the world who had never heard of the college. The papyrus had long been stored in a display cabinet in Magdalen's Old Library with other memorabilia such as Oscar Wilde's ring and Joseph Addison's buckles. Now it required completely different care and far tighter security. Overnight, a college treasure, one of hundreds of precious manuscripts in Magdalen's custody, had apparently become a relic of awesome significance. For the first time, Sotheby's was asked to place a value on the fragments. For an academic institution to discover that it owns what may be the first Christian document, a tiny but crucial foundation stone in the literate culture of the West, is a momentous experience. But it is not without its challenges, some of them burdensome.

This book is a response to the flood of interest in the Magdalen Papyrus. It is neither a religious tract nor an exercise in Christian persuasion. Instead, it seeks to make accessible to the general reader a major papyrological discovery and its implications for the dating of the New Testament and our knowledge of early Christianity. It seeks to bridge the gap between scientific investigation and the questions which every thinking person must ask about the Gospels and their significance. It seeks to promote debate as much as to answer questions definitively.

Indeed, such a book was overdue long before the Magdalen Papyrus was redated in 1994. Since the great philosopher and historian Albert Schweitzer wrote his groundbreaking work *The Quest of the Historical Jesus* in 1906, there has been a relentless effort by modern scholars to cross what the German thinker Gotthold Lessing (1729–81) called the "ugly ditch" between history and faith. The New Testament itself and the question of its origins have occupied center stage in this debate. When were the Gospels written, and in what order? And what exactly is a gospel? What were Jesus' aims and would he have recognized and approved of early Christianity? From Schweitzer and Rudolf Bultmann— the most influential biblical critic of the twentieth century—to more recent writers such as E. P. Sanders, John Dominic Crossan and John Meier, scholars have tried in countless ways to assess the relationship between Christ's divinity and his humanity, between the Gospels as faith documents and their disputed role as historical sources.

It is central to our argument that the science of papyrology has played too small a part in the answering of such questions. To prove their theories about the life of Jesus and the early Church, scholars have produced archaeological, numismatic, inscriptional and literary evidence. They have happily imported the methods of interpretation offered by literary criticism, sociology and anthropology to support their own claims about the nature of the Gospels or the social structure of the early Church. A 1988 bibliography on the use of the social sciences in New Testament studies, for instance, listed more than 250 items. It has become fashionable to speak of the "interdisciplinary quest for the his-

torical Jesus." Yet the rich seam of papyrology has yet to be mined in
the same imaginative way by biblical scholars. This omission has been an
intellectual loss for all who have an interest in these fundamental issues.

In the chapters which follow, we demonstrate the dramatic effect
which papyrus evidence may have upon our understanding of Christianity's origins. The Magdalen Papyrus is a key document in the long
history of New Testament dating—a scholarly argument which has raged
since the time of Papias, Bishop of Hierapolis, who lived in the second
century A.D. But it also has much to tell us about the first decades of
Christian life; the multicultural, Greek-speaking society to which the
papyrus was addressed; and the precocious development of the Church
before A.D. 70—the pivotal year when the Roman army crushed the
Jewish rebellion in Palestine and sacked Jerusalem. What can we know
of the early Christians, such as those described in Acts 2:44–46, who
"went as a body to the Temple every day but met in their houses for the
breaking of bread"; or the followers of "Chrestus" in Rome mentioned
by the Roman historian Suetonius? These fragments are important evidence of the institutional sophistication and ambition of the Church
before the destruction of the Temple and even suggest a well-developed
ecclesiastical strategy already at work in the mid-first century A.D.

Above all, this is a series of interlocking stories about the papyrus and
the men whose lives it has affected. It explores the life of St. Matthew
and asks whether he might indeed have written the Gospel which takes
his name and of which the papyrus is an early copy. It looks at the kind
of men and women who might have been the first readers of this ancient
codex and how they would have used it.

It follows the trail of the Reverend Charles Bousfield Huleatt, the
Oxford graduate, amateur scholar and devout missionary who found the
papyrus in Egypt but tragically perished in a 1908 earthquake in Sicily,
leaving almost no trace of his life and work. Like the fragments he
discovered and bequeathed to his beloved college, the story of Huleatt's
life, scholarship and desire to spread the Word has remained obscure for
almost a century. His is the enigma at the heart of the tale, a strange
Victorian story of frustrated intellect and unequivocal faith rewarded by
virtual eradication from history. It is also the story of Carsten Peter
Thiede, whose modern search for answers to academic questions echoes
Huleatt's own private pilgrimage.

Finally, our book examines the papyrus in the twentieth century, the last dating in 1953 and the redating four decades later. Much has been said and written since the original *Times* story about Carsten Thiede's research, and Chapter 5 of this book responds to the criticisms which have been made, explaining in greater detail than ever before the scholarly argument behind the new date in terms that those with limited familiarity with the subject can understand. We conclude by speculating upon the place of the Magdalen Papyrus in our own age, and its significance to believer and nonbeliever alike.

At first sight, this fragment could scarcely be less prepossessing. It amounts to little more than three tiny pieces of old paper, clasped between two slides of glass and labeled. History does not obviously cling to it, let alone faith. Yet this ancient papyrus, we contend, is one of the most important documents in the world. It is this bold claim which our book sets out to prove.

2
DATES AND DEBATES: ST. MATTHEW AND THE CONTROVERSY OVER THE ORIGINS OF THE NEW TESTAMENT

"By the way, Sherlock," said he, "I have had something quite after your own heart—a most singular problem—submitted to my judgement. I really had not the energy to follow it up, save in a very incomplete fashion, but it gave me a basis for some very pleasing speculations. If you would care to hear the facts—"

"My dear Mycroft, I should be delighted!"

—Sir Arthur Conan Doyle, "The Greek Interpreter" (1894)

There is a world—I do not say a world in which all scholars live but one at any rate into which all of them sometimes stray, and which some of them seem permanently to inhabit—which is not the world in which I live . . . In my world, almost every book, except some of those produced by Government departments, is written by one author. In that world almost every book is produced by a committee, and some of them by a whole series of committees. In my world, if I read that Mr Churchill, in 1935, said that Europe was heading for a disastrous war, I applaud his foresight. In that world no prophecy, however vaguely worded, is ever made except after the event. In my world we say, "The first world-war took place in 1914–1918." In that world they say, "The world-war narrative took shape in the third decade of the twentieth century."

—A. H. N. Green-Armytage, "John Who Saw" (1952)

T HE WARNING SIGNS against intellectual trespass are all around
us. Thomas Hobbes, the great political philosopher of the seventeenth
century, acknowledged as much in 1646. Recognizing the jealousy and
territorial claims of tenured academics, he wrote to his French colleague
Samuel Sorbière: "Their public reputation demands that in the subject
in which they teach no one should have discovered anything which they
have not already discovered." With a few exceptions, this melancholic
observation still holds true. For only during the past few years has there
been some movement toward open-minded, interdisciplinary research
and debate on the subject of this book. Martin Hengel, the internationally respected theologian from Tübingen University, former President of
the Society of New Testament Scholars, was one of the first to point the
way. At the end of his magisterial book, *Studies in the Gospel of Mark,*[1] he
reprinted an essay by one of the leading classical philologists and Homer
experts of our time, Wolfgang Schadewaldt. In "The Reliability of the
Synoptic Tradition," Schadewaldt demonstrated the reliability of the
three closely related Gospels of St. Mark, St. Matthew and St. Luke,
leaving St. John's quite different approach aside. He never pretended to
be a theologian, let alone a New Testament scholar. He wrote as a
classicist, as one thoroughly schooled in the study and analysis of classical
texts. Needless to say, the New Testament, if judged as literature as well
as Holy Scripture, is very much part of classical antiquity. It is, in other
words, part of the natural domain of the classical philologist.

After a detailed comparative study, Schadewaldt states: "As to the
substance of the narratives and sayings, I would say that if, as often in
philology, we make a comparison in terms of good tradition, bad tradition, and very good tradition, on this scale of values we would say that
the Synoptic Gospels are very good tradition." This does not mean that
every single word in the Gospels is to be taken at face value. They are,
profess to be, proclamations of the good news (the *eu-angelion,* or "good
spell," gospel) about Jesus the Christ. The historical facts are presented,
shaped and ordered with a conscious purpose, so that some sermons are
omitted or set in different places in different Gospels. The same applies

to St. John, who selects and uses entirely different speeches, the inti-
mate, very personal ones, rather than the major public ones. The first
compilers of the four-Gospel canon and those who decided to preserve
four Gospels rather than just one—such as a purified version of St.
Luke, as suggested by the second-century heretic Marcion—well appreciated that four partially or wholly independent testimonies would assist
historical recollection in the future rather than make it more difficult.[2]

Myths of New Testament Criticism

Insights of this kind have largely been ignored, and Martin Hengel was
not always thanked by his colleagues for taking them back to basics.
Does it really require the forensic experience of a legal scholar like the
late Sir John Anderson, with his many publications on the reliability of
the Gospels, or of a classical philologist like Wolfgang Schadewaldt to
put things in perspective? Here is just one example of Schadewaldt's
applied approach. One of the most persistent myths about the origins
and transmission of the Gospels concerns the length of time it took for
them to be received and digested and used. For over a century, it has
been assumed that it took the recipients of the first Gospel at least ten
years to produce a sequel. Thus, it has been taken for granted that St.
Matthew's Gospel must have been written in the eighties of the first
century, assuming an approximate date of c. A.D. 70 for St. Mark.
Schadewaldt acknowledges that this "error in the history of tradition,"
as he calls it, was also quite common in classical scholarship until its
exponents, unlike New Testament scholars, mended their ways.

One such error also occurred in Homeric scholarship, Schadewaldt
writes:

> People have always acted as though it took years for the Ionian epic
> to cross to the mother country. In Homer Achilles said: "The day
> after tomorrow I will be at home in Phthia, on the third day." I
> have checked this out with old ships' logs, and it is true: ships went
> as fast as that. But according to earlier Homeric criticism the epic
> took centuries to find its way gradually. It is always a good thing

for scholars—I put this quite generally—to use common sense as well as their methods.[3]

Another popular myth of New Testament criticism, used to argue that the Gospels were written later rather than earlier, is the myth of the anticipation of an early Second Coming of Christ. According to this scholarly myth, the first Christians expected the risen and ascended Jesus to return sooner rather than later, to herald "the end of the Age" during their lifetime. As long as they expected the end to be nigh, they would have seen no reason to preserve, collect and publish the narratives about his life and works. Only later, when the first generation of eyewitnesses had passed away, and when embarrassment and disappointment at the failure of Christ to return had given way to a different theological assessment of the situation, would there have been a need for longish documents—or so it is claimed. Perhaps this is a subtle way to arrive at late dates, but there is no conclusive trace of such an expectancy. Sometimes Jesus himself is quoted in defense of this theory. In St. Mark 9:1, he says: "Truly, I say to you, there are some standing here who will not taste death before they see that the kingdom of God has come with power."[4] But let us follow the line of argument of those who prefer to date the Gospels later rather than earlier. Sheer logic suggests that precisely such a saying would have been *omitted* later if it really was a reference to an early Second Coming and if, by implication, Jesus had been in error. But this saying does not refer to Jesus' own Second Coming at all. It is, as the structure of the Gospel makes quite clear, a reference to the Transfiguration of Jesus, which is reported, in the following verses, "six days later." Here, Jesus is revealed as God's unique son, in the full glory of God's power invested in him. With St. Peter's authority, this very incident is later recounted once again:

When we told you about the power and the coming of our Lord Jesus Christ, we were not slavishly repeating cleverly invented myths; no, we had seen his majesty with our own eyes. He was honored and glorified by God the Father, when a voice came to him from the transcendent Glory, "This is my Son, the Beloved, he enjoys my favor." We ourselves heard this voice from heaven,

when we were with him on the holy mountain. (2 Peter 1:16–18,
New Jerusalem Bible)

Others have focused on St. Matthew 10:23: "In truth I tell you, you
will not complete the towns of Israel until the Son of Man comes."[5]
True or false, unfulfilled prophecy or misunderstanding? Again, such a
saying would have been deleted had the Gospel been written at a time
when this would have looked like an erroneous prophecy. And again, we
realize that its meaning is less clear-cut than people have assumed. If we
take the Greek text seriously, then it refers not to "go the rounds of the
towns," as the New Jerusalem Bible translates it. Ambiguous as it is,
and therefore anything but a definite allusion to the Second Coming, it
far more probably refers to an event which St. Paul also strongly wished
for, without expecting its immediate or even distant fulfillment: the
conversion of the whole of Israel.[6] The first Christians were being expelled and prosecuted, and as they fled from town to town—how bit-
terly realistic this prophecy was to prove!—Jesus expected them to use
the opportunity to preach and evangelize. This was duly done and reported on in the Acts of the Apostles.[7]

This very passage, St. Matthew 10:23, is in fact compelling evidence
for a very early date for this Gospel. Describing the towns of Israel as an
escape circuit would exclude the non-Jewish town of Pella in Trans-
jordan, to which the Christians did flee in A.D. 66.[8] This can mean only
one thing. As Theodor Zahn, a classicist and professor of New Testament studies at such renowned universities as Erlangen, Göttingen and
Leipzig, pointed out in his commentary on St. Matthew's Gospel, written in 1903 and often reprinted since: "Mt would hardly have written
v. 23 if the escape of the Christians [to Pella] had already taken place at
the time of his writing. Our gospel is written before A.D. 66."[9]

While the first Christians certainly did expect the Second Coming as
much as their modern counterparts do today, no one who had a voice in
the primitive Church regarded this event as imminent. Nor would the
sense of expectation have been considered a reason not to record Jesus'
sayings and structure them into gospels. St. Paul himself, whose early
letters precede all four Gospels, according to the present majority opinion of scholars, makes this quite clear—first by writing early letters at

all, and second by stating in the earliest of them, 1 Thessalonians, what should still be regarded as a warning against speculation:

> About times and dates, brothers, there is no need to write to you, for you are well aware in any case that the Day of the Lord is going to come like a thief in the night . . . God destined us not for his retribution, but to win salvation through our Lord Jesus Christ, who died for us so that, awake or asleep, we should still live united to him. (1 Thessalonians 5:1–10)[10]

A third popular myth about the origins of the Gospels concerns Jesus' divinity. "I and the Father are One" (St. John 10:30) is the most poignant utterance; some of his fellow Jewish audience clearly understood this as a claim to divinity. Preparing to stone him, they declare that "we are stoning you, not for doing a good work, but for blasphemy; though you are only a man, you claim to be God" (St. John 10:33). The whole prologue to this Gospel (St. John 1:1–14) stresses this claim to divinity, only more elaborately. The point here is that Jesus existed before the creation of the world, that he partook in the creation; he and the father were, and are, one in action. The claim to divinity is also present in the other Gospels—St. Matthew 16:19–20, in which Jesus gives the keys of the kingdom of Heaven to St. Peter, is only one example of this and there are many more. But are they late additions, made long after the destruction of Jerusalem in A.D. 70 and the reorganization of Christian life and mission? Far from it. There is no evidence that the "deification" of Jesus was a late development. Belief in his divinity was prompt and unequivocal. In a letter written as early as c. A.D. 55, 1 Corinthians, St. Paul says very much the same thing, clearly based on a much older teaching he himself had received and authenticated: "For us there is only one God, the Father from whom all things come and for whom we exist, and one Lord, Jesus Christ, through whom all things come and through whom we exist" (1 Corinthians 8:6). In fact, the editors of one of the standard editions of the Greek New Testament are so convinced of the extremely early, even pre-Pauline nature of this statement that they have it printed like a quotation.[11]

Many other myths continue to influence New Testament criticism, some of which will be discussed later in this book. One is the claim that Jesus could not have made accurate prophecies and that the Gospels which quote him as predicting the destruction of Jerusalem and the Temple in A.D. 70 must have been written after this date. According to this skeptical thesis, words were put into his mouth by later writers to make him look like a prophet.[12] Another such misassumption concerns the organization of the early communities, their administrative structure and, indeed, the very existence of a "Church." Could Jesus have foreseen, let alone have supported, such an institution? Could he have spoken about it himself? St. Matthew 16:18 says he did: "So now I say to you: You are Peter, and on this rock I will build my *ecclesia.*" *Ecclesia*—there we have it. Some translations, the traditional ones at any rate, render the word as "church"; other, more liberal translations prefer "community." Could the historical Jesus really have said such a thing in A.D. 28 or 29 for it to be written down during the lifetime of the eyewitnesses? The answer, of course, is yes. The Greek word *ecclesia* occurs—often and without exciting attention—in the Greek translation of the Old Testament, the Septuagint, which originated in the third century B.C. There, it means the community of God's people, the congregation of God—a translation of the Hebrew word *qahal*. To Jesus, using this word (whether in Hebrew, Aramaic or Greek) would not only have been natural; it would also have been the self-evident extension of his role as the Messiah.[13] It is quite different to ask if Jesus hoped for an institution to develop in his name, as the Church—or, rather, the Churches—did in later centuries. But it is one thing to deplore the Churches as they have come to be, and quite another to project a modern distaste for these present structures back onto what the historical Jesus is reported to have said about the *ecclesia.* Understandable as such a projection may be, it is dubious scholarship.

We could go on. There are virtually no limits to what people have attempted to do in order to rule out early dates for the Gospels. Historians and classical philologists, however, and a growing number of New Testament scholars have shown repeatedly that none of these arguments is watertight. In Chapter 7, we discuss the cultural and philosophical context in which these attempts to sustain the myth of late Gospel origins have prospered, and why this approach is still so popular at universities and colleges, in textbooks and introductions to the New Testament.

What We Know

In this chapter, we set the scene for the more technical aspects of papyrology and Gospel origins, which we deal with later. If we take the sources seriously, what can we know? What can we say about St. Matthew and his Gospel if we examine the evidence anew? One example from papyrology serves to illustrate what can be achieved. And although it is taken from this specialized field, it was a famous New Testament scholar who made use of it first.

Martin Hengel of Tübingen University noticed that the following well-documented technique customary in the making of scrolls at that time ensured the very early preservation of authors' names:[14] Scrolls with literary texts had tags glued to them. These were strips made of parchment, papyrus or leather, which were affixed to the handle or were in some other way attached to the back of the scroll so that they projected from that side which was facing the bookseller or reader.[15] They fulfilled the same purpose as the spine of a modern book: one does not have to open a book in order to find out who wrote it and what its title is. In the same way, rather than unrolling the beginning of a scroll to obtain this information, scroll users simply looked at that tag, called *sillybos* or *sittybos* in Greek. Hengel points out that such a tag would also have been attached to a Gospel scroll. Theoretically, the very first Gospel's *sittybos* could just have said "Gospel," or *Euangelion* in Greek. As long as there was no second Gospel, this would have been sufficient to find and identify the scroll. But, as Hengel observes:

> [A]t the latest when the communities had two different copies of the Gospels, titles had to be used to distinguish them, in order to avoid confusion. Where the author was well-known to the community, a verbal reference would have been enough, but as soon as his work was copied, sent to other communities and put in an archive there, a title was absolutely necessary to distinguish it from other works. We may assume that at least the larger communities got

hold of the newly composed Gospels relatively quickly because of the lively interchange between the communities . . . If, as is usually argued today, the earliest Gospels were anonymous or lacked titles, because of the pressing need to distinguish them in community libraries, a variation of titles would have inevitably arisen, whereas in the case of the canonical Gospels (in contrast to that of countless apocryphal writings) we can detect nothing of this.[16]

Now, if we grant, for the sake of argument, that the orthodox dating of the Gospels is acceptable, we would have to date St. Mark to c. A.D. 70, St. Matthew and St. Luke to the eighties, and St. John to a date near A.D. 100. Even in the eighties, no one could have blatantly invented authors' names contrary to the factual recollection of the apostles and other first-generation Christians. When the moment came to write the *sittybos* for the second Gospel, the tag for the first one had to be enlarged as well; at this stage, at the very latest, both had to carry the names of their authors in order to avoid confusion. It is unthinkable that anyone would have dared to invent such unlikely, less prominent candidates as Mark and Matthew (or Luke, for that matter) if they had not indeed been the correct authors' names—or had not been in some way directly associated with the books. And what is true for a date in the eighties is, needless to say, even more true of the sixties. During this decade, as we have seen and shall see throughout this book, the first two Gospels, St. Mark and St. Matthew, not only existed as scrolls but had already been copied onto codices.

We have already observed that the arguments in favor of an early date for St. Matthew are stronger than orthodoxy suggests. But who was St. Matthew? The oldest available tradition identifies him as Levi-Matthew, called upon by Jesus while he was sitting at his customs post near Capernaum (St. Matthew 9:9; St. Mark 2:14; St. Luke 5:27–28). He was much more than a mere "tax collector." He was a *telones,* which in Greek could be used to refer to an official who was in charge of a customs station. In his case, he was in charge of a major border crossing. At Capernaum, two forms of levies were involved. One was the sea tax which fishermen had to pay in Roman times.[17] The other was the land border tax levied on goods traveling along the Via Maris, the important

trade route between Damascus (90 km/56 mi. inland) and the Mediterranean Sea. This road crossed the domain of Philip the Tetrarch and
touched the border with the Galilean territory of Herod Antipas adja-
cent to Capernaum, where there was also a junction leading toward Tyre
and Chorazin. Recent research has been able to establish that Levi-
Matthew was an influential customs official, perhaps even the leaseholder
or tenant of the station, in accordance with the bureaucratic practice of
the time.[18]

St. Luke, less reticent in his description of the man than Matthew
himself would have been, underlines the status and wealth of Levi-
Matthew in a cameo describing the scene after his calling (5:29): "Then
Levi held a great banquet for Jesus at his house" (New International
Version), or, in the refined, stately terminology preferred by the Revised English Bible: "Levi held a big reception in his house for Jesus."
Such a man had to have both professional qualifications and financial
resources. It goes without saying that he was fluent in Aramaic and
Greek, and some scholars have suggested that shorthand writing was
another of his skills (we shall read more about this in Chapter 6). It will
suffice, for the moment, to quote one of those British New Testament
scholars whose research remained refreshingly untrammeled by trends
and theological correctness, the late C. F. D. Moule of Cambridge
University. The disciple Matthew may well have painted a kind of self-
portrait by quoting a particular saying of Jesus in chapter 13:51–52 of
his Gospel ("Well then, every scribe who becomes a disciple of the
kingdom of Heaven is like a householder who brings out from his store-
room new things as well as old"). Moule suggests that this "scribe" was
not a "teacher of the law," as many translations have it, not a rabbinical
scribe in other words. Instead, the Greek word *grammateús* here suggests
the well-trained writer. For, as Moule comments:

> [T]he writer of the gospel was himself a well-educated, literate
> scribe in this sense. But so must also have been that tax-collector
> who was called by Jesus to be a disciple. Is it not conceivable that
> the Lord really did say to that tax-collector Matthew: You have
> been a "writer" (as the Navy would put it); you have had plenty
> to do with the commercial side of just the topics alluded to in the
> parables—farmer's stock, fields, treasure-trove, fishing revenues,

now that you have become a disciple, you can bring all this out
again—but with a difference.[19]

Because of his position, Matthew, like his fellow *telones,* was despised
and rejected by orthodox Jewish society. Jesus himself was attacked
because he was mingling with such people: "When the Pharisees saw
this, they said to his disciples, 'Why does your master eat with tax
collectors and sinners?'" (St. Matthew 9:11). Even so, Levi-Matthew
was himself a Jew by birth. Unlike, for example, the names of the
disciples Andrew (Peter's brother) and Philip, who were Jews with
entirely Greek names, the two names of this disciple betray very old and
highly honored Jewish origins. As Levi, he was a member of the tribes of
the Levites, who had control over the conduct of Temple worship in
Jerusalem. Having chosen the disreputable but profitable profession of a
customs official or "tax collector," he remained proud enough of his
origins to retain the name at the moment of his calling. Later, St.
Matthew's Gospel, like the others, prefers his second name, Matthew,
which is no more humble than his first: the Hebrew word *Mattya* means
"Gift of God."

What else can we say about the man who is the shadowy figure behind
the Magdalen Papyrus? We know the name of his father, Alphaeus (St.
Mark 2:14); some scholars have tried to argue that this Alphaeus was the
same one identified as the father of "James the son of Alphaeus" (St.
Mark 3:18). Matthew did not apparently belong to the "inner circle" of
disciples—the two pairs of brothers, Peter and Andrew, John and
James—and after the Resurrection, his further career is not followed in
the New Testament. The last time his name is mentioned is in Acts 1:13,
when the core group of apostles, diminished by the suicide of Judas,
meets in an upper room in Jerusalem. Some forty years after the composition of Acts, the theologian and historian Papias is the first to mention Matthew again. And here we encounter, for the first time, the
attribution of the Gospel to this man,[20] which was never doubted in the
early Church. But even as a Gospel author, St. Matthew would have
remained a helper, "a servant of the word," as St. Luke so aptly put it
at the beginning of his own Gospel, where he talks about his predecessors and fellow authors without naming names (St. Luke 1:2). A servant, not a master: thus, there was no "hero worship," there was no

public acclamation, once the completed Gospel had reached communities all over the Roman Empire, nor when the success of this new Gospel began to overshadow St. Mark's earlier publication. No one wrote Matthew's biography, and we simply do not know what happened to him later. A second-century author, Heraclion, claimed to know that the apostle was not martyred but died a natural death.[21] And that is that.

Sketchy as this portrait is, it is decidedly more than we know about many classical authors. It is a combination of archaeological and circumstantial historical evidence—the standard fare of classical scholars, who are expected to piece together a tattered mosaic from scant remains. In any case, those tesserae, those small pieces of the Matthean mosaic, fit the information we have so far gathered about the Gospel and its context. But this is not a book about St. Matthew and St. Matthew's Gospel.[22] It is a study of a particular papyrus, its origins and its implications. What we can say with confidence is that there is no sound philological, archaeological or historical evidence to challenge the thesis that the fragments date from before A.D. 70. We do not have to rewrite any rules to redate the papyrus—on the contrary.

Fortunately, there are two sides to recent scholarly debate in this field. On the one hand, there is the old-fashioned liberal consensus which finds late dates academically comforting. This school continues to question the authenticity of the Gospels and—in one or two cases— even suggests that the gnostic writings of the second, third and fourth centuries are more reliable than the canonical Gospels (Crossan, Lüdemann). But progress has also been made thanks to common sense and rigorous scholarship. Many will remember the furor caused by John A. T. Robinson's *Redating the New Testament* in 1976. It was a breakthrough, a thrilling intellectual bolt from the blue. For who would have expected the archliberal author of *Honest to God* to propose dates prior to A.D. 70 for all New Testament writings? The book stimulated many academics in Anglo-Saxon countries, but it did not change the tide. In fact, German New Testament scholars all but ignored it. Not until 1986, ten years later, did Robinson's work appear in Germany, when two publishing houses (one Catholic and one Evangelical) joined forces to translate and publish the book. Even so, the provenance of these two houses encouraged the community of New Testament scholars to pursue their stubborn refusal to take notice of *Redating the New Testament*. Robinson's sequel, the posthumously published *Priority of John* (1985), based on his Oxford University Bampton Lectures, has still not found a German publisher. And it has hardly had a major influence on scholars elsewhere. Why? Is it incompetent scholarship? The sheer brilliance of Robinson's two introductory chapters on applied methodology is unsurpassed; their clear-sightedness remains impressive, even if one does not agree with every single conclusion.[23]

Can New Testament scholarship risk isolating itself from other disciplines dealing with ancient texts—classical philology, history, and papyrology? Can it risk not learning the lesson of Homeric studies, so succinctly described by Wolfgang Schadewaldt? No one interested in the future of New Testament scholarship and its contribution to a better understanding of Scripture can take pleasure in such arbitrary and unnecessary isolation. But there are grounds for optimism in the efforts of both younger and more established scholars to combine sound interdisciplinary research with mold-breaking analysis. Richard Bauckham at St. Andrews, Rainer Riesner at Tübingen and Craig L. Blomberg at Denver are three protagonists of the younger generation; Martin Hengel at Tübingen, I. Howard Marshall at Aberdeen, E. Earle Ellis at Dallas, Harald Riesenfeld at Uppsala, Klaus Haacker at Wuppertal and Klaus Berger at Heidelberg are six who have been battling longer. Less than two years after its publication, Berger's latest major contribution to the discussion is still proving hard for many of his colleagues to swallow: improving on Robinson's thesis, he argued for a date of c. A.D. 66 for St. John's Gospel, and of A.D. 68/69 for Revelation. And he did so not in a commentary or introduction, but in a detailed and closely argued monograph which deals with the history of early Christian theology and with the methods needed for its proper analysis.[24]

Literary Criticism

To end this introductory chapter on a lighter—but equally pertinent—note, let us take a glance at yet another academic discipline, literary criticism. One of the most celebrated authors of detective novels is Dorothy L. Sayers (1893–1957). Her stories about Lord Peter Wimsey have remained classics, and her series of radio plays about Jesus, *The Man Born to be King* (1943), has been produced time and again and been reprinted nearly thirty times. But she was also a literary historian, one of the first women to receive an academic degree at Oxford. In her scholarly capacity, she wrote a number of essays on Aristotle, the use of language, and the Bible. Her introduction to *The Man Born to be King* has remained as readable as her "Vote of Thanks to Cyrus" from the collection *Unpopular Opinions* (1946). Focusing on St. John's Gospel, she writes about the "notorious dispute" surrounding it:

> Into the details of that dispute I do not propose to go. I only want to point out that the arguments used are such as no critic would ever dream of applying to a modern book of memoirs written by one real person about another. The defects imputed to St. John would be virtues in Mr. Jones, and the value and authenticity of Mr. Jones's contribution to literature would be proved by the same arguments that are used to undermine the authenticity of St. John.
>
> Suppose, for example, Mr. (George) Bernard Shaw were now to publish a volume of reminiscences about Mr. William Archer: would anybody object that the account must be received with suspicion because most of Archer's other contemporaries were dead, or because the style of G.B.S. was very unlike that of a *Times* obituary notice, or because the book contained a great many intimate conversations not recorded in previous memoirs, and left out a number of facts that could easily be ascertained by reference to the *Dictionary of National Biography?* Or if Mr. Shaw (being a less vigorous octogenarian than he happily is) had dictated part of his material to a respectable clergyman, who had himself added a special note to say that Shaw was the real author and that readers might rely on the accuracy of the memoirs since, after all, Shaw was a close friend of Archer's and ought to know—should we feel that these two worthy men were thereby revealed as self-confessed liars, and dismiss their joint work as a valueless fabrication? Probably not; but then Mr. Shaw is a real person, and lives, not in the

Bible, but in Westminster. The time has not come to doubt him.
He is already a legend, but not yet a myth; two thousand years
hence, perhaps—.[25]

Dorothy L. Sayers was aware of Rudolf Bultmann and his powerful
campaign to "demythologize" the New Testament. Her essay was an
early reaction to this trend, which was becoming popular in Britain after
the Second World War, when she wrote her piece. But its message
remains true today. Many scholars should and will recognize their own
flaws represented in her humorous critique. But the errors she carica-
tured are not set in stone. As we have seen, we have the academic tools
to make real progress in this area, in a concert of the sciences. This book
is meant to be read as a contribution to the tuning of the instruments
and the search for a full accord. With the Magdalen Papyrus, papyri and
papyrology may become the initial drum roll in the new symphony.
Imagery apart, the motto for our procedure in the following chapters
can be found in St. Paul's first letter to the Thessalonians (5:21): "Test
everything. Hold on to what is good." And so, we proceed to an
investigation of the Magdalen Papyrus itself—the unlikely cause of
heated debate.

3

INVESTIGATING THE
MAGDALEN PAPYRUS

HUNT: PETITION CONCERNING REPAYMENT OF LOAN
PETITION COMPLAINING OF . . . NON-PAYMENT OF LOAN.
GRENFELL: LETTER ON BEER TAX TO THE *TARACHEUTAI* "MUMMIFIERS."
HUNT: BUT *TARACHEUTAI* MIGHT MEAN "SALT-FISH SUPPLIERS."
GRENFELL: IT MIGHT! IT MIGHT! IT MIGHT! IT MIGHT! IT MIGHT!
GOD! I DO WISH SOME *LITERATURE* WOULD COME TO LIGHT.
—TONY HARRISON, *THE TRACKERS OF OXYRHYNCHUS* (1990)

DESPITE ATTEMPTS BY ARCHIVISTS TO GET HIM TO USE MICROFILMS OR FAC-
SIMILES OF DOCUMENTS IN HIS RESEARCH, HORATIO ALWAYS INSISTED ON
WORKING WITH THE ORIGINALS. ANYTHING ELSE, HE USED TO TELL ARCHI-
VISTS, WAS LIKE BEING ASKED TO MAKE DO WITH PHOTOCOPIES OF ONE'S
LOVE LETTERS.
—ANDREW ROBERTS, *THE AACHEN MEMORANDUM* (1995)

The Science of Papyrology—An Introduction

Papyrology is a complex, specialist field, requiring many years of train-
ing. But even before the Magdalen Papyrus made the headlines, the
history of this academic discipline had been peppered with anecdote and
adventure. One thing is certain about papyri: they smell nice when they
burn. This, at any rate, is the story told by an antiques dealer who, back
in 1778, bought a papyrus scroll dating from A.D. 191/192 from some
Egyptian peasants and had to look on helplessly as they set fire to fifty
further scrolls, visibly enjoying the fragrance of the smoke.[1] There are
no comparable stories about the side effects of parchment or vellum, but
Konstantin von Tischendorf, the man who discovered one of the two
most valuable codices of the whole Greek Bible, the Codex Sinaiticus,[2]

at St. Catherine's Monastery in Sinai in 1844, found the first 129 parchment sheets of that codex in a room full of combustible rubbish. Even in the twentieth century, the methods used to preserve papyri have left much to be desired. Kando, the famous shoe salesman in Bethlehem, kept some of the most important Dead Sea Scrolls hidden under the floorboards of his shop until he sold them—or, in some cases, until they were requisitioned by the Israelis after the conquest of the Jordanian occupied territories in 1967. And sometimes, accidents can befall papyri in the few decisive moments before the manuscript is preserved after discovery—as in the unfortunate experience of the Qumran scholar who found a scrap, looked at it against the sunlight ("Could be a fragment from Genesis!") and then saw it crumble into dust.

Discovery, preservation, identification and publication of ancient manuscripts are the papyrologist's task. Sometimes, others can lend assistance—archaeologists who discover the material, or classical philologists who are experts in the technique of editing ancient texts. On other occasions, outsiders can cause difficulties, which happens from time to time when a New Testament scholar, burdened with scholarly assumption, assumes that he knows more about New Testament papyri than the papyrologist. The debate about the Magdalen Papyrus has prompted many examples of such academic presumption.

To the average person, if it rings a bell at all, papyrology is understood to be a kind of "paper-ology." But papyrology is not about paper—a medieval Chinese invention—at all. And it is of course more than just the art of dealing with ancient papyri, sheets manufactured from the stem of an aquatic plant cultivated mainly in Upper Egypt.[3] For convenience' sake, the name stands for the study of all ancient texts written on all sorts of material—papyrus, parchment, vellum, leather, linen, slivers of wood, wax tablets, potsherds (so-called *ostraca*) and so forth. Only inscriptions on stone, marble, and similar material have brought forth their own distinct discipline, epigraphy. As it happens, the earliest New Testament manuscripts are indeed papyri, which justifies our reliance on the discipline of papyrology in our investigation.

If we trace the origins of the term in ancient sources, we find that "papyrus" even occurs in the Bible. The Greek translation of the Old Testament, the so-called Septuagint of the third century B.C., refers to the papyrus plant three times: Job 8:11 and 40:16 and Isaiah 19:6. "Can papyrus grow except in marshes?'' Job 8:11 asks rhetorically. It is a helpful question, as it underlines the special conditions needed for the cultivation of this plant. Centuries later, the Roman scholar Pliny the Elder (A.D. 23–79) described the production of papyrus sheets and began his treatise with this remarkable praise: ''On its use as scrolls human civilization depends, at the most for its life, and certainly for its memory.''[4] Beyond doubt, papyrus scrolls were the single most important vehicle for the transmission and safekeeping of human knowledge. From the oldest known Egyptian papyrus manuscript (P. Berlin 11301, c. 2700 B.C.), to the oldest extant Hebrew papyrus—found in a cave at the Wadi Murabba'at near the Dead Sea and dated to c. 750 B.C. (P. Murabba'at 17)—to New Testament times (the period when Pliny the Elder himself was writing) and beyond, this fragile reed plant provided the material for documents of every kind.

The production of papyrus sheets and rolls was the privilege of Egyptian workshops, most of them situated near the delta marshes of the Nile. They exported the finished product all over the Mediterranean basin, and farther north, south and east. Because of this regional monopoly and because the vast majority of papyri were found at Egyptian sites like the Fayyûm and Oxyrhynchus, there is occasionally a misconception concerning the scope of papyrology. Even in a recent introduction to the field, papyrology is limited to texts from Egypt, and at some universities, such as Trier in Germany, it is taught in the Egyptology Department. But, as we point out in Chapter 5, since papyri were exported from Egypt even during the Roman Empire, the scrolls or codices with literary texts—poems, epics, plays, gospels and letters—could have come from virtually anywhere in the Empire at that time. The discovery of such a text somewhere in Egypt does not imply that it was written there or that a copy could not be found elsewhere in the region. In addition, there are, after all, several non-Egyptian sites where Hebrew, Greek and Latin texts on papyrus, leather, wood, and potsherds have been found—from the Wadi Murabba'at, the Nahal Hever, Masada and Qumran at the Dead Sea, to Petra in Jordan, Dura-Europos in Syria, the Avroman Mountains in Kurdistan, Pompeii and Herculaneum in Italy, up to the northern border of Roman Britain at Vindolanda. Papyrology should be considered a subdivision of Egyptology only when the texts are composed in one of the Egyptian languages or dialects.

As for the general scope of the field, it is the study of all ancient texts regardless of local origins. The papyrus like the one at Magdalen College, Oxford, is an ideal introduction to investigation of a range of techniques that we can and must apply to such manuscripts. Let us look at the Magdalen Papyrus from this viewpoint, and do so in a proper historical context. The story of its acquisition at Luxor by the Reverend Charles Huleatt, and of its remarkable journey to Oxford, follows in Chapter 4. Here, we discuss the "detective story" of its textual analysis and of the attempts to find other papyrus fragments in other collections which might match the three pieces at Magdalen College. We begin our investigation with a brief introduction to the tools and findings of papyrology.

Even the first step is not as straightforward as might be imagined. At first glance, it seems obvious that the three Magdalen fragments do not come from a scroll. To begin with, they have text on both sides, which is a characteristic of the codex, the precursor of our modern book. But in this context, one must not jump to conclusions: as any observant reader of the Bible knows, there were exceptions to this rule. For example, a scroll with writing on both sides is mentioned in Ezekiel 2:9–10: "When I looked, there was a hand stretching out to me, holding a scroll. He unrolled it in front of me; it was written on, front and back; on it was written lamentations, dirges and cries of grief." The one example in the New Testament is slightly more ambiguous; it is in Revelation 5:1: "I saw that in the right hand of the One sitting on the throne there was a scroll that was written on back and front and was sealed with seven seals." It is ambiguous because at the time when Revelation was probably written, Christian scribes had already introduced the codex with text on both sides of the sheet. Is the Greek word *biblíon* in Revelation 5:1 a break with tradition and the first reference to such a codex book rather than a reference to the old scroll? The technical implications of such a break can be understood by anyone who has handled a book and has access to a fax machine. A fax roll looks very much like an ancient scroll, and if the machine does not cut the pages, the user ends up with meters of communications on his roll—with the text on the outside of course rather than inside, as was the case with scrolls. Conversely, any modern hardback still closely resembles the old codex. It reflects the same principle of production, with print having taken over from handwriting since Gutenberg's invention of printing by movable type in the fifteenth century.

The question of the change from scroll to codex is much less theoretical than one might think. As we shall see in Chapter 5, this watershed is important for the purpose of dating Christian manuscripts in general, not just the Magdalen Papyrus of St. Matthew's Gospel. It is also of considerable importance for the development of the canon, the official collection of New Testament writings. When Christian communities and churches decided to go from scroll to codex, this was an opportunity to select their favorite texts. Inevitably, not everything was likely to be copied from one format to the other. If publishers today decided to cease producing hardbacks and to switch to paperbacks, not every existing hardback would be reprinted in the new format. Instead, the opportunity would be exploited to choose and discard texts. Even today, not every hardback makes it to the mass market paperback format. Likewise, if a particular scroll was left uncopied, it would fall out of use once that scroll had fallen apart. In terms of New Testament origins, this order of precedence—scrolls first, codices next—is important to our approach to the origins of the texts themselves. There are still a few influential scholars who would have us believe that the Christians never used the scroll, and that they started by using the codex straightaway. With or without the initial scroll, if papyrologists are correct in assuming that the Christian codex was introduced before the year A.D. 70,[5] then even Revelation 5:1 could already refer to a codex. But is this passage, interpreted in this sense, signaling the first or the second stage of the transmission of Christian documents?

Revelation was, at any rate, written at a time when the traditional scroll was still very much an integral part of practical experience or, at the very least, part of living memory. The vivid imagery of Revelation 6:14 is a perfect example: "The sky disappeared like a scroll rolling up and all the mountains and islands were shaken from their places." This verse would have been completely incomprehensible to the communities who were expected to read the book of Revelation if they had not seen and used scrolls themselves. And indeed, the scroll was of paramount importance to early Christianity. Jesus himself read from a scroll of Isaiah in the synagogue of Nazareth (Luke 4:17); and even much later, a late-second-/early-third-century fresco in the Roman Domitilla Catacombs documents the ongoing awareness of the scroll's importance: it portrays St. Paul with two *capsae,* containers of scrolls, each filled with five scrolls. These *capsae* are probably meant to signify the equal value of the five scrolls of the Torah—the first five books of the Old Testament—and the five historical writings of Christendom—the four Gospels plus Acts.[6] In the same catacombs, we encounter a mural of St. Petronilla, depicted with a *capsa* at her feet and an opened book, a codex, at her left shoulder. The relationship between these two frescoes is more revealing than one might assume.

A long time after the transition from scroll to codex, the artists—and those who commissioned them—knew exactly how to differentiate between the two stages of Christian literary transmission. St. Paul, who was martyred in A.D. 64 or, according to a different interpretation of the sources, in A.D. 67, is shown with scrolls only. St. Petronilla, martyred—according to tradition—in A.D. 98, already has both formats beside her, scroll and codex: a perfect illustration of a period when the new format had taken over, while the old, traditional scroll was still a part of shared memory and may even still have been in use here and there.

The turning point is in fact already visible in the New Testament, leaving aside the controversial interpretation of Revelation 5:1. One of the so-called Pastoral Epistles, 2 Timothy, tells the story in 4:13: "When you come, bring the cloak I left with Carpus in Troas, and the scrolls, and especially the parchment notebooks." Most modern translations avoid the problem of terminological precision, but the original Greek text is unambiguous: The two decisive words in this passage are *biblia* and *membranas. Biblia,* literally "books," should be understood as a reference to "scrolls." This, at any rate, is the common usage of the word prior to the introduction of the codex.[7] These scrolls may well refer to Old Testament books in Greek translation, or indeed to the first Christian scrolls preceding 2 Timothy. We do not know. The second technical term, *membranas,* is more illuminating. First of all, it is a *Latin* word, transcribed into Greek. There is a consensus among experts that the author of 2 Timothy is talking about parchment notebooks, which is, so to speak, a literary first. Commenting on this passage, the British papyrologist C. H. Roberts noted that "St Paul" is in fact "the only Greek writer of the first century A.D. to mention the parchment notebook."[8] It was just a small step from notebook to book, from *membrana* to codex. But its theological and sociological implications were momentous.

Christians had used the scroll not merely because it was convenient. As the mural of St. Paul in the Domitilla Catacombs shows, it was more than that; it was a statement of identity. The very first Christians, after all, were Jews or of Jewish origin. Among the Gospel authors, St. Luke may be the only exception, and even this is far from certain. Until missionary activities among non-Jews became the norm rather than the exception, spreading the good news of the Gospel was almost an inner-Jewish affair. Quite a few writings of the canonical New Testament, such as the Epistle to the Hebrews, the Epistle of James and, indeed, St. Matthew's Gospel, betray this deep immersion in Jewish thought and tradition to such an extent that non-Jewish readers would have found it difficult to understand them without explanation. The scroll was the natural means of expression in this context. Any other, "new" format would have signaled a counterproductive break with the common tradition. Even the Babylonian Talmud, polemical and aggressive wherever it refers to Christianity, acknowledges this state of affairs. It refers to the existence of Christian scrolls in Jewish possession and decrees that they shall not be saved in case of fire, even though the name of God is mentioned in them.[9] The Babylonian Talmud, a collection of texts of post–New Testament times, is an irreproachable source precisely because it is comparatively late and generally anti-Christian. The information about the existence of early Christian scrolls could not have been invented at a later stage; it is historically reliable.

Scrolls and Codices: Qumran Cave 7 and the Dead Sea Scrolls

We can see that the Magdalen Papyrus of St. Matthew's Gospel, which appears to be a codex fragment, may be very early indeed, older than anything we possess from the New Testament. But it cannot be the original Gospel manuscript or a "facsimile" descendant of it: St. Matthew's original was a scroll. This poses two intriguing questions: What happened to all those Christian scrolls, and are there no traces of them?

And what was it that made Christian scribes change to the codex, of which the Magdalen Papyrus is very probably the oldest known example?

The answer to the first question is fairly straightforward. As we have already seen, early Christian scrolls did not survive because they were transcribed onto the new format, the codex. Whenever a scroll became tattered or otherwise illegible, it would be copied as a codex, not as a scroll. Thus, the last scroll exemplar of, say, St. Matthew's Gospel would soon have disintegrated and disappeared without trace—unless of course there was a place where Christian texts were stored and left before the takeover of the codex. Surprisingly, such a place exists. It is a cave at Qumran, and its contents make a unique contribution to our quest for the historical background of the Magdalen Papyrus.

The very peculiar Cave 7 at Qumran has aroused the pugnacious attention of scholars ever since the Spanish papyrologist José O'Callaghan, the renowned editor of the Palau-Ribès papyrus collection, suggested in 1972 that some of the papyrus fragments found in that cave are New Testament texts.[10] Cave 7 is unique among the Qumran caves. Like all Qumran finds, its eighteen fragments (to which one has to add a nineteenth fragment of inverted writing preserved, in the form of an imprint from a lost papyrus, on hardened clay) are scroll fragments— but in Cave 7, they are exclusively in Greek and exclusively on papyrus. Elsewhere in Qumran, there are only six further Greek texts—all in Cave 4—among hundreds of Hebrew and Aramaic scrolls; and only two of the Greek Cave 4 texts are papyri (the other four are leather fragments). The importance of Cave 7, as of any other Qumran cave is heightened by the fact that there is an archaeological date after which the scrolls could not have been deposited: A.D. 68.[11] This was the year when the settlement, the *khirbet* of Qumran, and the nearby area of the caves were overrun by the Tenth Roman Legion "Fretensis." Should any of the fragments from Cave 7 turn out to be Christian, then we would indeed possess physical evidence of the existence of a Christian scroll before the introduction of the codex.

Obviously, the latest possible archaeological date, certain as it is, must still be checked against two conflicting theories. First, Qumran inhabitants or, if Cave 7 was Christian, those interested in Christian papyri of the first generation, could have returned at some stage after A.D. 68. Alternatively, they could have gone there for the first time and deposited these documents over sixty years later, during the Bar Kokhba Revolt (A.D. 132–35). Thus, the Austrian scholar Kurt Schubert, convinced that the papyrus 7Q5 from that cave is a fragment of St. Mark's Gospel, came up with this "second stage" suggestion.[12] But the results of all serious archaeological investigations rule out any reinhabitation or reuse of the Qumran caves after A.D. 68 (unlike caves in different Dead Sea wadis, such as the Wadi Murraba'at and the Nahal Hever[13]). Even more important, the very fact that these Christian scrolls are scrolls—an assessment accepted by Schubert—rules out either the cave's reopening after A.D. 68 or the scrolls' later deposition in c. A.D. 132–35. In the thirties of the second century, it would obviously have been Christian codices, not scrolls, that would have been placed in Cave 7. And, archaeological evidence aside, a reopening after A.D. 68 can be ruled out for related reasons; the scrolls would then have come into use again, and they would, at some stage of wear and tear, have been exchanged for codex copies. But the fragments in Cave 7 are scroll fragments. They cannot have been deposited after A.D. 68. In addition to all these criteria, the paleographic dating of the handwriting argues against both reopening Cave 7 and redepositing scrolls at Qumran. Long before O'Callaghan had identified fragment 7Q5, it had been ascribed by Colin H. Roberts, acting on behalf of the editorial team, to the so-called Zierstil (decorated style), which peaked in popularity at the turn of the first century. Regarding 7Q5 as a late example of the style, one would say, with Roberts, that it could be no later than A.D. 50. Given the possibility that the style fell out of use more slowly, one might even be prepared to add a few years—as we shall see in Chapter 5, dating an undated hand is a complex business. But the archaeological end date of A.D. 68 then limits the time frame one might theoretically be prepared to allow.

The Papyrologist at Work: How to Identify a Papyrus

So far, so good. But are Kurt Schubert, José O'Callaghan and many others right in their other conclusion—that there really are Christian scroll fragments among the finds in Cave 7? The controversy has been going on ever since 1972, with an apparent consensus that the scrolls are not Christian. After a lull in the late seventies and early eighties, Carsten Thiede reopened the debate with a 1984 paper in the scholarly journal *Biblica*.[14] Publication after publication entered the fray—in German, English, French, Dutch, Italian, Spanish—in opposition as much as support.[15] Many New Testament scholars, convinced that St. Mark's Gospel could never have reached the Essene community of Qumran at such an early date, were opposed by other academics, who were equally sure that this was not only possible but also quite plausible. Leading papyrologists argued in favor of the Markan identification of fragment 7Q5. Even one of the Jewish members of the editorial board of the Qumran scrolls, Shemaryahu Talmon (Jerusalem), has publicly supported the idea that the Cave 7 fragments are Christian.[16] And in 1994, the last word on the identification seems to have been the statement of one of the great papyrologists of our time, Orsolina Montevecchi, Honorary President of the International Papyrologists' Association. She summarized the results of her analysis in a single unequivocal sentence: "I do not think that there can be any doubt about the identification of 7Q5."[17] And yet, some scholars still refuse to acknowledge that the fragment is part of St. Mark's Gospel. For the most part, these are New Testament scholars rather than papyrologists who continue despairingly to deny that 7Q5 is the only extant papyrus scroll fragment of St. Mark's Gospel, written shortly or even some time before A.D. 68. Graham Stanton of King's College, University of London, dedicates a whole chapter of his latest book to papyrus 7Q5—and another one to the Magdalen Papyrus—in one such attempt to exclude early papyrological evidence from gospel studies.[18] Why?

Here we enter an area of the papyrologist's work which applies as much to the Magdalen Papyrus as it does to the Qumran scroll fragment. It is the task of getting the text right, of reconstructing a fragmentary snippet of material in such a way that the lines make sense and yield a satisfying, acceptable whole. José O'Callaghan had almost accidentally identified the tiny fragment 7Q5, with its twenty letters (ten of them fragmentary) on five lines, as St. Mark 6:52–53. Working on an annotated edition of Greek Old Testament manuscripts, he came across the third volume of the official series of Dead Sea Scrolls editions,[19] which included the finds from Cave 7. The editors had managed to identify two of the fragments: 7Q1 = Exodus 28:4–6 and 7Q2 = Baruch

[Letter of Jeremiah] 6:43–44; hence, O'Callaghan's justified interest in this cave. None of the other sixteen fragments, or the reversed imprint on clay had been identified by the original editors; one of them, however, the fifth fragment, 7Q5, offered a rare and intriguing combination of letters in line 4: *nu/nu/eta/sigma*. To the first editors, this combination had suggested the possibility of the Greek word *egennēsen* ("gave birth") and thus, possibly, a genealogical text. The problem with this suggestion was that such a text, which would then have to allow for all the other letters preserved on 7Q5, does not exist in extant Greek literature, biblical or nonbiblical. This is where José O'Callaghan's remarkable powers of deduction came into force. He thought of other Greek words with the *nu/nu/eta/sigma* sequence and, having excluded words which did not fit the context, finally had the instinctive idea of trying out the Greek name of that famous lake in Galilee, *Gennesaret*. It was a vintage example of academic detective work: exclude the improbable, and the probable will emerge.

In any case, O'Callaghan's problems had only begun. For, astonishingly, there is only one passage in the whole Greek Old Testament, the Septuagint, where the name of the lake is written in such a way that the combination *nu/nu/eta/sigma* occurs: the deuterocanonical book of 1 Maccabees 11:67, where it appears as *Gennesar*. Elsewhere, the lake is called *Chenereth* or *Chenara*. However, none of the other legible letters in fragment 7Q5 would fit 1 Maccabees 11:67. Fortunately, O'Callaghan was and is a papyrologist rather than a New Testament scholar. He would not rule out textual discoveries because they conflicted with other scholars' academic presuppositions. A papyrologist worthy of his craft would not be influenced by hypothetical arguments such as the claim that a New Testament text could not possibly have been written at a date that would place it at Qumran before A.D. 68, and that it could not have reached the Qumran Essenes, in any case. Since the New Testament belongs to the body of existing Greek literature, it was a necessary step for O'Callaghan to investigate its texts. And indeed, there it was: a passage where *Gennesaret* occurred and where everything else on the fragment seemed to match—St. Mark 6:52–53. "They were utterly and completely dumbfounded, because they had not seen what the miracle of the loaves meant; their minds were closed. Having made the crossing, they came to the land of Gennesaret and moored there." Herbert Hunger, the famous Austrian papyrologist, mischievously alluded to the irony of these verses, anticipating the twentieth-century reaction to O'Callaghan's discovery: "their minds were closed."[20]

The modern English translation quoted above is taken from the New Jerusalem Bible. The editors of this version, realizing that one story ends with verse 52, and another one begins with verse 53, left a blank line between the two verses and added a title link, "Cures at Gennesaret." Ancient scribes had no such devices at their disposal. Instead, they projected one letter into the left margin, as in the Magdalen Papyrus, or two, as in the Paris papyrus 𝔓⁴, or they left a gap between the two relevant verses, a so-called *spatium*. In such cases, there would also have been a horizontal line underneath the beginning of the line, a so-called *paragraphus*. Needless to say, this can only be detected where the beginning of the line has survived intact; in the case of 7Q5, it has not. But with or without *paragraphus*, the *spatium* indicates the beginning of a new sequence, a new "paragraph." In other words, the gap in line 5 fulfills the purpose of the blank line and the subtitle in the modern Jerusalem Bible. Thus, together with the occurrence of *Gennesaret*, this *spatium* fits St. Mark 6:52–53 like a glove. All the more so as the first word after the gap, the clearly legible Greek word *kai* ("and") is indeed the first word of St. Mark 6:53. Helpful in a more indirect way is the further observation that sentences beginning with "and," the so-called paratactical *kai*, are a typical Markan structure. Finally, the one letter just legible before the gap, although half destroyed by a tear in the papyrus, is an *eta*—a fact never disputed even by O'Callaghan's detractors. And St. Mark 6:52 ends with an *eta*—it is the last letter of the perfect passive *peporomene*, "(their hearts) were hardened," or, in the English of the New Jerusalem Bible, "[their minds] were closed."

Observation and Deduction: A Papyrus and Its Context

Can the case rest there? Not quite. Justice has to be done to the *whole* fragment. As Sir Arthur Conan Doyle put it, in his Sherlock Holmes story "The Sign of Four": "So much is observation. The rest is deduction." Three significant problems remain. The first problem is related to textual reconstruction. The reconstruction of complete lines is a matter of stichometry, calculating the average number of letters per line. Every scribe, and by definition every manuscript, is characterized by such a "measure," and variations are permitted only within a certain range of letters. For example, the Magdalen Papyrus with its three fragments and text on both sides has a total of twenty-four lines. They offer a beautifully regular number of letters per line:

Fragment 1, verso: 16/16/16/15
Fragment 2, verso: 16/16/15/
Fragment 3, verso: 16/17/17/18/17
Fragment 3, recto: 15/15/17/15/16
Fragment 1, recto: 15/17/15/17
Fragment 2, recto: 16/16/15

The exact average thus is sixteen letters per line, with a maximum of eighteen and a minimum of fifteen. On the basis of this average measure, one is able, as we shall see later on, to correct the first edition of the Magdalen Papyrus. By excluding the possibility of the grammatically superfluous word *humeis,* which exists in all other Greek manuscripts of St. Matthew 26:31, we achieve the optimum line length: with it, line 1 of fragment 1, recto, would have twenty letters; without it, fifteen.

Stichometry is of course a decisive instrument in reconstructing a text. Only if the end of one fragmentary line and the beginning of the next fragmentary line "match," and are in agreement with the visible text "in the middle" (and in the case of the Qumran fragment 7Q5, both ends are missing), can we achieve an acceptable result. The comparative yardstick for New Testament texts is one of the standard editions of the Greek text, with all its manifold variants. What happens when the reconstructed or seemingly reconstructible text of a given line does not comply with the established stichometry or with any of the other known New Testament manuscripts? In the case of the Magdalen Papyrus, a superfluous *humeis* can easily be accepted; after all, the identification of the three papyrus fragments as segments from the twenty-sixth chapter of St. Matthew is undisputed. But in the case of the small single fragment 7Q5, it is the very identification which is at stake, so that any deviation from the "standard text" would have to be closely scrutinized. Now, the stichometry of 7Q5 is, in itself, as regular as that of the Magdalen Papyrus: 20/23/22 (including the *spatium* of the length of two letters) /21/21. An average just above twenty-one, with twenty and twenty-three as the extremes. Since this is so, and if it is applied to the visible letters on the fragment, then there is no room, in St. Mark 6:53, for the three Greek words *epi ten gen* ("on to the land"). They would have belonged either to line 3 or to line 4. With them, line 3 would have had thirty-one letters; or line 4, thirty. Could there have been a version of St. Mark 6:53 without these three words?

If we remember our starting point, the fact that the papyrus scroll fragments from Cave 7 must be older than A.D. 68, the answer is as simple as it is historical: yes. The only reason why *epi ten gen* is in the standard text editions of the Gospel—a standard text, after all, based on second-, third- and fourth-century manuscripts—was that cataclysmic event of the Jewish revolt against the Romans, which ended in the destruction of Qumran in A.D. 68, of Jerusalem with its Temple in A.D. 70, of Masada in A.D. 73/74 and of many other parts of the country during that period. One of the places destroyed by the Romans was the town of Gennesaret, or Kinneret, only recently rediscovered and excavated by archaeologists in the very region presupposed by St. Mark's account. This particular phrasing, *epi ten gen . . . eis Gennesaret* ("on to the land . . . of Gennesaret"), became necessary after the destruction of the inhabited area which had had the same name as the lake, so as to avoid uncertainty and confusion. Before the destruction (A.D. 70), these three words would have been pure pleonasm, all the more so as the place Gennesaret was within daily range of people living at Capernaum, where Jesus and his disciples had lived and worked for some time. One should therefore turn the tables. In a papyrus written before A.D. 70, we would even expect these words to be missing. The fact that they are absent conforms to the sociotopographical framework of the story told in St. Mark 6:53. Had they been included in the text of papyrus 7Q5, then this would have had to be explained, rather than the other way around.

Beyond archaeology and history, we also have of course the textual, the philological argument: the later addition of *epi ten gen* yields a very awkward Greek, a "tormented text," as one commentator has called it, which suggests a less than ideal attempt to correct the problem. Even the parallel passage in St. Matthew's Gospel betrays this uncertainty, and so do early translations like the second-/third-century Bohairic and the fifth-century Latin Vulgate. In brief, classical philologists do not doubt that the text without *epi ten gen* is not only the shorter but also the better original version. Our analysis of "the case of the missing words" has led us to a constructive result. Without them, the stichometry of St. Mark 6:53 confirms rather than undermines the identification of Qumran fragment 7Q5 with this Gospel.[21]

Problem number two is completely different, but equally fascinating in its corollaries. It concerns the first letter of the word after the *kai,* the "and," in line 3. In St. Mark 6:53, this word is *diaperasantes* ("[they,] having made the crossing"). As anyone can see, it begins with the Greek letter *d* (*delta*). But it is equally obvious that on our papyrus, the first letter after the *kai* is not a *delta* but a *tau,* or *t.* Quite a few opponents of the Markan identification have concentrated on this variant, in spite of all the cumulative evidence that establishes the identification anyway. Is it an unanswerable riddle? On the contrary, a close and serious analysis provides an answer which further corroborates the identification.

To begin with, we have to remember that this papyrus was written before A.D. 68. Any comparative evidence must take account of this fact. And secondly, the identification of the papyrus with St. Mark 6:52–53 has already been reached by other means. We are looking at the question of whether the *d/t* phenomenon underlines—or undermines—this identification. Is it a simple misspelling, or are there more serious reasons for this variant? In such a small fragment as 7Q5, with text on a mere 3.3 cm × 2.3 cm ($1^1/_4$ in. × $^7/_8$ in.), slightly larger than a stamp, every completely legible letter counts. One cannot frivolously explain away such a variation as a simple spelling error. Things are different in the case of the Magdalen Papyrus, where a genuine spelling mistake certainly does occur. On the recto, or back side, of fragment 2 (St. Matthew 26:32–33), the Greek word *galilaian* ("Galilee") is spelt *galeglaian.* Here, the scribe had been thinking in terms of common, so-called itacism, a spelling variant based on the identical pronunciation of different letters or combinations of letters: for example, the letter combination *ei* was pronounced like the letter *i* alone; and thus, it was quite possible and legitimate to write *ei* instead of *i.* However, the scribe then made a mistake. Instead of *i* after the *e,* he wrote *g,* coming up with *galeglaian* instead of the acceptable *galeilaian.* For whatever reasons, he

added the horizontal bar that turns a *iota* into a *gamma*. Even ancient
scribes were only human. A harmless mistake in the context of the
Magdalen Papyrus. So, again, what about the potentially much more
serious shift from an initial *delta* (*d*) to *tau* (*t*) in the Qumran papyrus
7Q5?

Our first answer comes straight from Jerusalem, the home of the first
Christian community. When Herod the Great rebuilt the Temple, he
had an inscription placed on the second wall prohibiting entry to (non-
Jewish) strangers on pain of death. The inscription is mentioned by the
Jewish historian Flavius Josephus (*Jewish Antiquities* 15.417), and it is the
background of an incident in Acts of the Apostles 20:27–36, where St.
Paul is threatened with execution because he has been seen entering the
holy precincts of the Temple in the company of the non-Jew Trophimus.
In fact, the text on that barrier stone is unequivocal enough: "No
foreigner is to enter within the balustrade and embankment around the
sanctuary. Whoever is caught will have himself to blame for his death
which follows." Two verbatim copies of this stone have been found by
archaeologists, a complete one, now in Istanbul, and a fragment, now at
the Rockefeller Museum in Jerusalem. The spelling is striking: in line 1,
the Greek word *medena* ("nobody") is spelled *methena;* and in line 3, the
word *dryphakton* ("barrier stone") is written *tryphakton*. Quite obviously, the scribes had a problem with the soft *d*. In both cases, they
turned it into a hard *t* or *th*. In our investigation, the change at the
beginning of the word *tryphakton* is more revealing, as it corresponds to
the initial change at the beginning of *d/tiaperasantes*. It cannot have been
an accidental spelling mistake—in ancient Greek, *delta* and *tau* (or *delta*
and *theta*) look as dissimilar as *d* and *t* do in English. As Christian
Clermont-Ganneau, the first editor of the complete stone, had already
noticed in 1872, the variants faithfully reflect a characteristic way of
pronouncing the letter *d* in Greek-speaking, Second Temple Jerusalem.
Whatever we may think about the author of St. Mark's Gospel—and
many think he is identical with the Jerusalemite John Mark, writing in
Rome with the authority of St. Peter, whose oral teaching material he
used—the "Jerusalem experience" and Jerusalem sources undoubtedly
stand behind this Gospel. Thus the *d/t* shift in a papyrus of this Gospel,
to be dated before A.D. 68—that is, before the destruction of the Temple and the disappearance of the stones in A.D. 70—is a compelling piece

of circumstantial evidence for a local or regional pronunciation and spelling variety which was common, and indeed visible, to anyone in the city as long as it stood.

Understandably, the discovery of this difficult inscription prompted intense debate. In 1905, the German epigrapher Wilhelm Dittenberger pointed out that even much later, the Greek grammarian Herodianus Technicus, writing in Rome toward the end of the second century, still knew about this change and tried to explain it etymologically rather than phonetically. As this does not explain away the fact that it existed in pre–A.D. 70 Jerusalem, more than one hundred years before Herodianus, Dittenberger then argued—against the explicit evidence of the contemporary historian Josephus—that the stone was not Jewish at all, but erected by the Romans. This is a classic non sequitur, of course: even if non-Jews had put it up (which they did not), it does not follow that nonlocal masons would have been employed. A few years ago, in 1989, the Israeli scholar Peretz Segal finally settled the matter by establishing the local origins of the inscription.[22] Dittenberger did not perhaps like the linguistic consequences of the inscription, but writing almost seventy years before O'Callaghan's identification, he had no theological axe to grind. However, the extent to which some scholars will still go to deny the importance of the inscription—nowadays, of course, in the context of the Markan Qumran papyrus—is remarkable. One German patristic scholar, for example, not only resuscitated Dittenberger's comments long after their shelf life had expired; he also thought nothing of making the somewhat off-hand remark that the discovery of the stone was "accidental."[23] There could hardly be a more versatile way of rejecting unwelcome archaeological (or papyrological) finds: describe them as accidental, ignoring the fact that many such discoveries are accidental by definition. Thus the unpalatable evidence disappears as though it had never existed. Fortunately, the world of serious scholarship does not respect such sloppy argument.

Once again, as with the case of *epi ten gen,* the solution to the *d/t* phenomenon hinges on more than archaeology and history. As far as papyrological evidence is concerned, there are no fewer than twenty biblical manuscripts which have such a shift of consonants. One of them is the $\mathfrak{P}^4$ at the Bibliothèque Nationale in Paris, a codex papyrus of St. Luke's Gospel which will concern us again at the end of this chapter.

Moreover, a text exists which is dated to A.D. 42, almost exactly the date of the 7Q papyrus, with *tikes* instead of *dikes;* in other words, with the change of *d* to *t* preceding the same vowel as in 7Q5, *i.*[24] To sum up, then, it was entirely possible to switch from *d* to *t* before A.D. 70, whether by accident or because of regional customs of pronunciation. Regarding 7Q5, the inscription from the Temple helps us to understand that the peculiar spelling of 7Q5 in St. Mark 6:53 is not surprising at all. It is to be expected and thus, once more, confirms rather than undermines the identification and the very early date of the papyrus.

The papyrologist as investigative scientist has one more problem to solve, which introduces us to yet another technique of papyrology. It is so puzzling a matter that even the Austrian papyrologist and Byzantine scholar Herbert Hunger, the author of many standard textbooks on the papyri and the textual tradition of antiquity, spent twenty-three pages and twenty-two illustrations seeking a first step toward its solution.[25] In line 2 of 7Q5, the reconstructed text of St. Mark 6:52 reads *all'en autōn he kardia pepero [mene],* "their hearts were hard[ened]." The last letter of the Greek word *autōn* ("their") obviously is a *nu.* But critics have insisted on a different reading in the papyrus. The preceding letter, an *omega,* is obvious enough; however, the *nu* is not a *nu* at all, they have claimed, but an *iota.* And if it is an *iota,* then the word cannot be *autōn,* and thus the passage cannot be St. Mark 6:52.

Coincidentally, an almost identical problem occurs in the Magdalen Papyrus. In 1953, Colin Roberts, the first editor of the Oxford fragments, had read *autō* in fragment 3, recto, line 1. Early in 1995, Thiede had corrected this to read *autōn,* with far-reaching consequences for the reconstruction of the text, as we shall see later in this chapter. Here, in papyrus scroll fragment 7Q5, the letter in question is indeed severely damaged. There is a left vertical stroke which could be either an *iota* on its own or the left stroke of a *nu.* To the right of this stroke, no ink is visible for a few millimeters until a curvature appears which moves upward into what appears to be the beginning of another fragmentary vertical stroke, then the stroke moves down again in another curve toward the lower right. What on earth could this be? Remnants of an *alpha,* as some have suggested? Nothing in the one *alpha* which does exist on this papyrus, in line 3, looks remotely like it. Had those traces left and right originally belonged together, when the papyrus was undamaged? Could they have been the lines of a *nu?* The critics would deny this on the grounds that the remnants of ink are just too far apart.

Drawing on numerous examples from contemporary, earlier and later papyri, Herbert Hunger demonstrated conclusively, in his aforementioned essay, that the remaining traces of ink could be reconstructed to form a perfect *nu,* curvatures and all. He and Thiede even measured the length of comparable letters within fragment 7Q5, with a remarkable result. There are two complete *etas* in this fragment, in lines 4 and 5. Measuring their "extremities" in width, which is what matters in our comparative case, one notes a difference from 3.0 mm (*eta* in line 4) to 3.5 mm (*eta* in line 5)—between $1/16$ in. and $1/8$ in. Now, the complete and indisputable *nu* in line 4 of fragment 7Q5 also measures 3.0 mm. And what is the width of the letter in line 2 if reconstructed as a *nu?* The answer, which might be guessed, is 3.5 mm. In other words, the allegedly "impossible" distance between the left vertical stroke and the strange remnants on the right are not remotely inconsistent with a *nu.* They conform perfectly to the flexibility the scribe had in drawing his *etas.* It is important not to forget that the difference in question is only half a millimeter.

The papyrologist at work has solved the problem. And yet, scribes may be flexible in ways that some critics are not. What about the skeptics who refuse to be persuaded by even the most scrupulous comparative analysis? Should one accept the failure to achieve scholarly consensus? Not when technology in the form of a high-power microscope can settle the matter for good. In April 1992, Carsten Thiede took the 7Q5 papyrus to the Investigations Department, Division of Identification and Forensic Science, at the Israel National Police in Jerusalem to have it analyzed under their electronic stereo microscope. And here, for the first time, the remains of a diagonal line became visible, beginning at the upper end of the left vertical stroke (which some thought was an *iota*), moving downward to the bottom right. The line was not complete—the traces broke off after a few millimeters—but it was long and straight enough to be absolutely conclusive: it must have been the diagonal middle line of a *nu.* O'Callaghan, Hunger and others were right, that the letter was and is a *nu*—and thus, the word is *autōn,* as required by St. Mark 6:52.[26]

In an amazing attempt to turn this visual evidence on its head, Gra-

Damaged but
clear *nu*
in line 4

Completed *nu*
in line 4

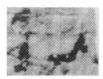

Disputed letter
in line 2

Reconstructed
nu in line 2,
using the *nu*
in line 4 as
yardstick

Eta from line 4

Eta from line 5

Comparison: The two clear but also clearly different
*eta*s in lines 4 and 5

Enlarged Photos of Letters in Fragment 7Q5:
An Example of Paleographic Reconstruction

ham Stanton's recent book *Gospel Truth?* includes a plate with a diagram, attributed to Geoffrey Jenkins, in which the clear and undisputed *nu* from line 4 of 7Q5 has been superimposed on the damaged letter in line 2. Ignoring the difference in width established by Hunger and Thiede and demonstrated as absolutely normal within this papyrus, Stanton claims that the minute difference actually visible on his diagram "shows that the letter cannot be a *nu,* thus undermining the theory that 7Q5 is part of Mark's Gospel." It seems remarkable that a scholar of Professor Stanton's repute would treat the evidence in such a cavalier manner in order to revive a discredited claim. The incomplete drawing of the underlying letter fragment from line 2 is the first distortion; the second one is the willful omission of the diagonal line established by the Jerusalem analysis; and the third one is the conclusion which flies in the face of what even the distorted diagram still shows: the fragment can of course be reconstructed into a *nu,* as Hunger had shown. It goes without saying that Hunger's paper is neither quoted nor mentioned by Stanton.[27]

Errors and Their Detection

The case of fragment 7Q5/St. Mark 6:52–53 shows us what applied papyrology can achieve. It also shows that there are virtually no limits to the scholarly acrobatics which some academics will perform to dismiss a thesis which does not fit their intellectual paradigm. Kurt Aland, the late grand master of New Testament criticism, employed the computer at his institute in Münster, Germany, to "prove" that 7Q5 cannot be St. Mark. Many were impressed by Aland's authority until another German scholar, the New Testament historian and epistemologist Ferdinand Rohrhirsch demonstrated that the grand old man had committed several methodological errors and had programmed his computer in such a way that a result other than St. Mark 6:52–53 was inevitable.[28] Others continue to indulge themselves by inventing alternative identifications.[29] Others keep hanging on to the so-called argument of the tininess of 7Q5, as though a small fragment could not be safely identified.

Certainly, 7Q5 is a small papyrus scroll fragment—twenty letters on five lines, as we saw, and ten of them damaged. That does not make it impossible to identify. Smaller fragments have been identified without objections being raised to the result. Even in the same Qumran cave, fragment 7Q2 has just one more letter—twenty-one on five lines—and yet, no one has ever disputed its identification as Baruch (Letter of Jeremiah) 6:43–44. And this in spite of the fact that the textual variants and deviations over against the standard text of the Greek Old Testament are much more complex and far-reaching than those of 7Q5 compared to the standard text of the Greek New Testament.[30] One might also cite a particular papyrus fragment of the Greek comedian Menander: the Oxyrhynchus papyrus XXXVIII 2831 was identified as a passage from Menander's comedy *Samia,* lines 385–90, even though it measures only 2.4 cm × 3.3 cm ($^{15}/_{16}$ in. × $1^{5}/_{16}$ in.) and has a mere nineteen letters on five lines, and is far from identical to the previously agreed text of the play. On the contrary, it offers "some additional variants."[31] Instead of doubting its identification and rejecting its inclusion in official lists, as happened to 7Q5/St. Mark 6:52–53, classical philologists accepted it, integrated it in new standard editions of the play and supplied it with its own inventory number, 0 16.[32] A third and final example, closer to Qumran, is the Masada papyrus fragment 721a. On that fortress overlooking the Dead Sea, the oldest known papyrus of Virgil was discovered and edited in 1989.[33] Dated to A.D. 73/74, it has just fifteen visible letters on one line, two of which are damaged to the point of illegibility. Despite the meager basis of data, and the fact that it was found on Masada of all places, this fragment is identified as Virgil, *Aeneid* 4.9—an identification which no one has questioned. If papyrologists are allowed to apply their methods without prejudice, they will avoid the trap of double standards. 7Q5 is St. Mark 6:52–53 as surely as P. Oxy. XXXVIII 2831 is from Menander's *Samia* or P. Masada 721a is from Virgil's *Aeneid*—if not more so.

In this context, it is worth noting that the Virgil papyrus from Masada invalidates one of the favorite devices used by those who believe that small scroll fragments cannot be safely identified. Kurt Aland and his followers argued that the text on the back, the verso, facilitates the identification and that such a verso text is a prerequisite for a plausible identification of small fragments. This argument has been used against the identification of the scroll fragment 7Q5, which has no text on the verso, with St. Mark 6:52–53. (Yet the same argument has not been used to dispute the identification of the *Samia* fragment or the Virgil scrap.[34])

The Virgil papyrus from Masada helps us see the fallacy built into the theorem of Aland and his followers: there is indeed text on the other side, on the verso. It is one line, again with fifteen letters, including one complete, rare word: *titubantia* ("swaying" or "stammering"). And yet, this line definitely does not belong to any known work of Virgil's or, indeed, to any other extant work of Latin literature. Does it secure the identification of the front, the recto, with *Aeneid* 4.9? It could not possibly. Small scroll fragments have to be judged on their own terms, and as we have seen, they are quite capable of being so judged.

Finally, it is necessary to make an obvious observation, which seems to have been lost on a number of scholars who have criticized papyrological work on small papyri. A papyrus fragment is a fragment. This means that words and letters on the edges—on all four or on some of them—are fragmentary. Also, unlike damaged, partly illegible letters in the middle of a fragment, such as the *nu* in line 2 of 7Q5, they may not always be completely reconstructible. In many instances, the remaining material is sufficient for a safe assignment. In 7Q5, this is the case in line 3, where the half-visible letter before the gap, the *spatium*, must be an *eta*, because what is left does not allow for any other letter in the Greek alphabet. Or in the Magdalen Papyrus, the first five letters of the half-broken-off fourth line of fragment 1, recto, must read *taute* (with a final *eta*) because nothing else would sensibly match what remains visible. Any reconstruction of partly damaged letters has to make sense; this point is vital. Thus, in the Magdalen Papyrus, one might conceivably imagine a *delta* or *lambda* rather than an *alpha* after the initial *tau*, and a *chi* instead of an *upsilon* after that—the upper parts of these letters look identical. But what would we make of *tdchte* or *tlchte* rather than *taute?* Nothing, of course, because such words no not exist, and even if they did, they would not make sense in the context of what we already know about the rest of the fragment.

Applied to 7Q5, the same basic rule of papyrology holds true. Take line 1. All that remains visible is the bottom curvature of a letter that could be an *epsilon*, an *omicron*, an *omega*, a *theta*, a *sigma*. In the context of St. Mark 6:52–53, it must be an *epsilon*. It is perfectly reasonable to suppose this to be an *epsilon* (and to write it with a dot underneath, signifying its reconstruction from incomplete remains). The basic rule has been observed: a letter must be reconstructed only in such a way that it makes sense within a plausible context. The same is true, of course, elsewhere in this and other fragments. Whatever possibilities there may be from the range of partly similar Greek letters, there is not a single one in fragment 7Q5 which could not be reconciled with a letter fitting the Markan passage. This is a remarkable degree of compatibility, which no other attempt at identifying the fragment has achieved. Nor could it, for as we saw, the identification had been established on the basis of other observations at the start. All the painstaking steps of our investigation were not meant to establish it but, rather, to confirm it and safeguard it against the attacks of critics.[35]

We have come full circle. There is indeed a papyrus scroll fragment of a gospel: it is a fragment from Qumran Cave 7, called 7Q5, containing St. Mark 6:52–53. It must be dated before A.D. 68 and could be as early as A.D. 50.[36] And it is not one of the early collections of sayings which may have preceded the full Gospels—indeed, there is not a single word quoting Jesus in 7Q5, whereas the Magdalen Papyrus has four such sayings. Nor is it a passage from the Passion Story, which again, according to many scholars, may have existed separately before the first Gospel was completed. It is a text with two connected narrative passages from the Galilean ministry of Jesus, which belongs to the final redaction of the full Gospel according to St. Mark—albeit to its first, pre–A.D. 70 text type. A scroll fragment of a full gospel, found at Qumran and deposited there before A.D. 68—where does this take us in our papyrological quest for origins, for the proper context and due evaluation of the Oxford (and Barcelona) codex fragments from St. Matthew's Gospel? Why the codex rather than the scroll? Something must have happened, and it may lead us straight to the Magdalen Papyrus.

The Codex Comes of Age

We already know that the first Christians had good, strategic reasons to use the scroll initially. After all, it was the common Jewish format for literary works and for everyday communications. Any break with this practice would have caused unnecessary irritation rather than assisting the claim of Jewish-Christian evangelists that faith in Jesus as the Messiah was a direct continuation of prophecies shared by all Jews and now fulfilled in the Jew from Nazareth, Jesus. However, a growing and finally unbridgeable rift between Jewish Christians and other strands of first-century Judaism emerged as early as A.D. 62. In that year, the leader of the Christian community of Jerusalem was executed by a group of Jews acting on the orders of the High Priest Ananus. This Christian leader was none other than James, "the brother of the Lord," as he is called by St. Paul (Galatians 1:19). James was known and revered as a devout Jew who continued to pray on his knees in the Temple every day so fervently that he earned the nickname "camel knees."[37] His execution was an illegal act; as it happened in A.D. 62, outside the historical scope of the New Testament, it is not mentioned there, but we have a reliable report from the Jewish historian Flavius Josephus in his *Jewish Antiquities* 20. 197–203:

> The younger Ananus, who, as we have said, had been appointed to the high priesthood, was rash in his temper and unusually daring. He followed the school of the Sadducees, who are indeed more heartless than any of the other Jews, as I have already explained, when they sit in judgement. Possessed of such a character, Ananus thought that he had a favourable opportunity because Festus (the Roman procurator) was dead and Albinus (his successor) was still on the way. And so he convened the judges of the Sanhedrin and brought before them a man named James, the brother of Jesus who was called the Christ, and certain others. He accused them of having transgressed the law and delivered them up to be stoned. Those of the inhabitants of the city who were considered the most fair-minded and who were strict in observance of the law were offended at this. They therefore secretly sent to King Agrippa urging him, for this was not the first time that Ananus had acted unjustly, to order him to desist from any further such actions. Certain of them even went to meet Albinus, who was on his way from Alexandria, and informed him that Ananus had no authority to convene the Sanhedrin without his consent. Convinced by these words, Albinus angrily wrote to Ananus threatening to take vengeance upon him. King Agrippa, because of Ananus' action, deposed him from the high priesthood which he had held for three months, and replaced him with Jesus the son of Damnaeus.

Certainly a dramatic chain of events, for the Jewish community of Jerusalem (and beyond) as much as for the Christians. The Christians had to realize that their efforts at conducting an inner Jewish dialogue were stonewalled, quite literally, with the stoning of their leader "and certain others" by the Jewish court, the Sanhedrin. It is true, of course, that there were many other Jews who took action against Ananus and the Sanhedrin, but the message had got across: we killed your leader, now stop evangelizing. By then, the mission among the Gentiles had already taken off, started long before by St. Peter (baptizing the Roman centurion Cornelius and his household, Acts 10) and vigorously continued and expanded by St. Paul. The turning point of A.D. 62 would have strengthened the hand of those who were looking beyond the confines of Jewry.

Only two years later, another catastrophe occurred—this time in Rome. On the night of July 18/19 in A.D. 64, Rome went up in flames. Ten out of fourteen boroughs were destroyed. Rumors soon spread that Nero himself had started the fire, and when they persisted in spite of his remarkably prompt and generous rebuilding program, he had to look for culprits who were unpopular enough to look convincingly guilty. He found his scapegoats in the Christian community of Rome.[38] Some Roman Christians may themselves have attracted the attention of the authorities. An apocalyptic strand of early Christianity flourished in Rome, and some of its adherents could well have praised the city's destruction. The conflagration of the decadent capital of the Empire, the "Whore of Babylon," might easily be said to be the predicted beginning of the final cosmic clash. Indeed, it seems that there were conflicts of attitude and interpretation among Roman Christians. When the persecution finally started, probably in the following spring of A.D. 65, the climate was right for the cruel outdoor evening spectacles so bluntly described by Tacitus and others—Christians even denounced and betrayed other Christians. Tacitus tells us as much, and the Christian author Clement of Rome confirms it when he writes that divisions and jealousy were the reasons for the capture and execution of St. Peter and St. Paul in the course of the persecution (1 Clement 5:1–5), which probably lasted until Nero's death in June of A.D. 68.

Whatever happened, all our sources make it abundantly clear that Christians and Jewish Christians were distinguished from Jews. In the early years, Jewish Christians and Jews were often mixed up by outsiders. This benefited the Christians, who would have profited from the privileged status enjoyed once again by the approximately fifty thousand Jews in Rome after the end of Claudius's expulsion of Jewish and Christian leaders, between A.D. 49 and his death in A.D. 54.[39] But with Nero's persecution, this confusion ended. The authorities punished the Christians, and only the Christians, leaving the Jews alone. At this juncture, therefore, a wall between the two communities was erected in the largest city of the Empire, and the dialogue was never resumed.

Again, only six years later, in A.D. 70, after nearly five years of military conflict and a siege of the city, Jerusalem fell to the Romans, the city and the Temple were destroyed, and the Jews were expelled. With the destruction of the Temple, the last natural place of contact between Jews and Jewish Christians disappeared. And more than that, while the Jews had to remain outside Jerusalem, the city's Christians (most of them of Jewish origin, of course) who had not participated in the revolt against the Romans were soon allowed to return, settling once more on the southwestern hill, today's Mount Zion. There, they built their first church, which is still visible in the room mistakenly called the "Tomb of David" (David's tomb was actually in the east, on Mount Ofel). Still standing there are the signs of a synagogal building, among them the niche for the Torah scrolls (which Jews venerating David's tomb in this room once again use for this purpose). But it was not a synagogue: even though the builders were evidently preserving some of their architectural traditions, they added a subtle but important change. This niche is not directed toward the site of the Temple, as it should have been, but toward Golgotha and the Empty Tomb, as anyone with a compass can check.[40] And the niche is in fact not quite large enough for more than the Torah scrolls—it could hardly have served the double purpose of keeping some Christian scrolls as well. Since the Torah was still the common scriptural foundation for all Jewish Christians, this was acceptable until a shift took place—as evidenced by the mural in Rome's Domitilla Catacombs which we have already discussed—whereby the Torah and the five historical Christian writings came to be seen as having equal authority. Initially, existing Christian scrolls were stored elsewhere, but it is quite conceivable that the niche was later used to house an ordinary bookcase for codices, which could have stored both the Old Testament and the writings of the New in one and the same place. Whatever happened there on Mount Zion, it was a period of transition and fragmentation. Jews had to remain outside Jerusalem. They proceeded to act on their own terms, and they did so from a place to the west of Jerusalem, some 6 km (3³/₄ mi.) from the Mediterranean Sea: Jamnia, a town also called Jabneh or Jabneel, which still awaits excavation.

According to a story told in the Talmud, Vespasian permitted Johanaan ben Zakkai to establish an academy, or yeshiva, at Jamnia. After the destruction of Jerusalem by Vespasian's son Titus in A.D. 70, the Sanhedrin was expelled along with all other Jewish inhabitants and moved to the place of the Jamnia Academy. It soon became a center of spiritual activities and reforms, and it also dealt with the Christian question. After A.D. 62, 64/65 and 70, what could be an official, "post-Temple" attitude toward the spreading denomination which claimed to embody the new, the true Covenant? In A.D. 80 at the latest,[41] the academy formally accepted the so-called *Birkat hammînîm,* the curse on the Christians from the "Eighteen Benedictions." The Talmudic treatise *Berakot* 28b/29a, attributing the "Benedictions" to the authority of R. Gamaliel and the academy, provides the chronological framework. A version of the text was discovered at the end of the nineteenth century in the genizah of the synagogue in Cairo:

> May apostates have no hope and may the kingdom of impertinence be uprooted in our day. May *the Nozrim and Minim* [i.e., the Christians] disappear in the twinkling of an eye. May they be removed from the book of the living and not be inscribed among the just. Bless you, Lord, you who casts down the proud.

And the tract *Berakot* 28b/29a from the Babylonian Talmud has this to say:

> The eighteen benedictions are in fact nineteen. Rabban Levi says: The benediction against the "Minim" was established at Jamnia . . . Our teachers have taught: Simon ha peqali [the flax heckler] formulated the eighteen benedictions at Jamnia in the traditional order, in the presence of Rabban Gamaliel. Rabban Gamaliel said to the sages: "Is there someone capable of formulating a benedic-

tion against the 'Minim'?" Then Samuel the Small got up and did it. The following year, he forgot the benediction and had to meditate two or three hours without being asked to come up [from the lower place of the prayer leader]. How could it be, that they did not let him come up? Did not Raw Juda ben Ezechiel say in the name of Rabbi Abba Areka: The one who has made a mistake in any of the other benedictions is not asked to come up, but if it is the benediction against the "Minim" one asks him to come up, because it is feared that he did it on purpose, being a "Min" himself? The case of Samuel the Small was different, for it was he who had decreed the benediction [against the "Minim"]. But one might have feared that he had retracted.

In such a severe social context, the curse on the Christians had everyday consequences, not least the expulsion from the synagogues of those Christians of Jewish origin who still went to these common places of worship. The last remaining places of contact after the destruction of the Temple had become inaccessible. And with them, the most natural sites of dialogue, or indeed missionary activity, had vanished for good. Jamnia only sealed a development marked by those four momentous episodes which had begun in A.D. 62 with the killing of James. The cumulative effect resulted in a complete break, which the (Jewish) Christians were unable and probably also unwilling to mend. As early as A.D. 62, but certainly by A.D. 68/70 at the latest, Christians were free to abandon the scroll and to convert to the codex, which they themselves were helping to develop out of the *membranae,* the notebooks already used in the circle of St. Paul (1 Timothy 4:13). It is probable that the change did not take place overnight; as we saw, scrolls and codices would have coexisted for some time to come, until the last existing scrolls fell out of use. The final break was certainly facilitated by the helpful fact that the Romans were familiar with the notebook format even at a pre–New Testamental stage.[42] As we saw above, the word *membrana* for "notebook" is a *Latin* technical term for which 1 Timothy 4:13 is the first *Greek* reference. Obviously, therefore, the Romans were already experimenting with the codex at this time. Martial's publicity-seeking epigrams are the best evidence for this trend.

The stage was set. All the practical advantages of the notebook and its book-form development, the codex, could now be brought to fruition. We can easily imagine a bookseller extolling the virtues of the codex: there was the economical use of papyrus, with text on both sides of the sheet; it came in a compact and often pocket-sized format; it was easy to handle, easy to skip through for quick reference; easier to store, or to hide in times of persecution. The codex was also a convenient means of disseminating collections of texts. Just one codex rather than five scrolls was needed for the Gospels and Acts, for example, making it easier to dispatch Christian texts throughout the Roman Empire.[43] Against this background, the Magdalen Papyrus of St. Matthew's Gospel could technically have existed in or soon after A.D. 62. The paleographic date of that papyrus, c. A.D. 66, which we shall discuss at length in Chapter 5, not only corresponds with the tenets of Italo Gallo and Colin Roberts, who have argued that the codex was in use prior to A.D. 70; it also corresponds with the historical data which we have about the shift from the scroll to the codex in early Christendom.

Comparing the *scroll* papyrus fragment 7Q5 = St. Mark 6:52–53 to the *codex* papyrus fragment P. Magdalen Greek 17/$\mathfrak{p}^{64}$ and its Spanish counterpart, P. Barc. inv. 1/$\mathfrak{p}^{67}$, we should also allow for the possibility that they are closely related in time. For all we know, St. Mark's was the first complete Christian Gospel, preceding St. Matthew's extended version by a few years. A scroll of St. Mark, therefore, had the advantage of being distributed first, not least if it had St. Peter's authority behind it.[44] But St. Matthew's Gospel soon surpassed it in popularity. It simply had more excitement, immediacy and stimulation to offer the reader—more action, more and longer sayings of Jesus (the whole Sermon on the Mount, for example) and the resurrection appearances of Jesus right up to the moment of his great commandment to evangelize all peoples to the ends of the world.

Not surprisingly, there are many more early papyri of St. Matthew than there are of St. Mark. It just so happens that St. Mark had beaten him to Qumran, and that there is no similar place where an early *scroll* of St. Matthew has come to light. A fragment may still be found, among the unopened and unexcavated scrolls at Herculaneum, for example, where a Christian community did exist before the destruction of the town under the lava of Vesuvius in A.D. 79. We do not know, and it gets us nowhere to speculate. What we do have is what counts. And in that sense, the Magdalen Papyrus may be even more important to our understanding of early Christianity than the scroll of St. Mark from Qumran. On the one hand, the Markan scroll confirms what we should have expected anyway—the beginnings of the literary tradition about the history of Jesus during the first generation of disciples and eyewitnesses, and on scrolls. On the other hand, the Magdalen Papyrus is living proof of the maturity of the early communities, the early Church, its concentrated, coordinated decision-making, its innovative spirit of enterprise, drawing on the experience and knowledge of those who had been with Jesus. The first Christian codex, with its early date, documents a decisive moment in the recording, preservation and dissemination of the historical Christian record. The value of this treasure is heightened by the many important characteristics of the Magdalen Papyrus, with its distinctive syntax, its sayings of Jesus and its "holy names." Let us now continue our quest by looking at it in detail.

The Magdalen Papyrus Examined

The basis for any serious study of the Magdalen Papyrus had been created by Colin H. Roberts in his first edition of 1953.[45] Surprising as it was that it had taken papyrology over half a century after the papyrus's arrival at Oxford to get it published, Roberts's edition was both committed and succinct. He needed a mere five pages to establish the text on all six sides of the three fragments, and to add his editorial comments. Roberts stated right at the beginning that "only belief that Hunt's dating in 1901 (i.e., to the fourth century) was substantially incorrect would excuse a detailed study of such minute fragments." We shall see in Chapter 5 that Roberts's belief was justified beyond his own expectations; furthermore, in this chapter we show that he underestimated the importance of the fragments quite irrespective of their date. But let us follow him for a moment as he describes the Magdalen Papyrus.

Roberts begins with a physical description: "There survive three pieces from the same leaf of a codex: frag. (a) 4.1 × 1.2 cm, frag. (b) 1.6 × 1.6 cm, and frag. (c) 4.1 × 1.3 cm. As there are two columns to a page and as verso precedes recto it follows that on the recto frag. (c) precedes frag. (a) and (b).'' (It also follows, as we may add, that these are definitely codex fragments.) He then notes what is written in the fragment:

> There were 15–16 letters to a line and approximately 35–36 lines to a column; the area of writing on the page would have measured roughly 10.5 × 16.8 cm; the proportions of the complete page would probably have been much the same. The double column format is noteworthy since, contrary to common opinion, in the earliest codices the single column format is much more common; it may be significant that in early Christian codices (i.e. those assigned to the second century or to the borderline between second and third centuries) the only examples hitherto known of the double column format have been those of books of the Old Testament.

This last comment is an interesting observation, not least in the light of what we discussed above. Even according to Roberts, the option to choose between single and double columns per page was apparently there from the very beginning—copying the Greek Old Testament was, of necessity, one of the initial tasks of the first Christians, since they based their preaching on the Old Testament and its prophecies; thus, they acquired some of their copying and writing expertise in the early years, before the first indigenous Christian texts became available.

Roberts goes on to extrapolate from the evidence in front of him: ''To contain the entire Gospel of St. Matthew the book must have run to about 150 pages; we may conclude that in all probability it contained nothing else. As verso precedes recto in the second half of the Gospel it is almost certain that this was not a single quire codex.'' After this useful and concise description of the format of the codex, Roberts then adds a number of observations, which shall occupy us later:

> Nomina sacra occur on the recto, vv 23 and 31; in neither passage is the line over the suspension now visible but there is no reason to think that it was omitted. Of some interest is the projection into the left margin of the initial letter of autois in v. 31; this line is the first complete line of what is a new section of the text (beginning

with *tóte* in the preceding line) both in Codex Bezae and Codex Alexandrinus (the latter reads *kaí* in place of *tóte*) which mark it in the same way as does the papyrus; the Vaticanus leaves a space before *tóte*. This system of division can now be carried back a couple of centuries if our dating of the papyrus is correct.

Needless to say, this is highly technical language. The *nomina sacra* ("holy names"), mentioned before in this book, will be properly explained and put into context in Chapter 6. As to those systems of division, it should be remembered that we met one of them in our encounter with the Qumran papyrus 7Q5. There we had a gap, a *spatium,* at a place where a new section begins, between St. Mark 6:52 and 53. This method remained popular and recurs as late as the fourth-century Codex Vaticanus. The Magdalen Papyrus can now be singled out as the first known example of the other, alternative option, described by Roberts. As we shall see later on, in a closer look at the papyrus $\mathfrak{p}^4$ of St. Luke's Gospel, another alternative was to use two projecting letters instead of only one. Scribes and their patrons had a number of options for different tasks; but whatever they did, clarity and consistency were of the essence. Without such consistent devices, the characteristic *scriptio continua* of antiquity—that is, the uninterrupted sequence of letters without divisions between words or sentences—difficult as it was for both scribes and readers, would have caused unnecessary confusion and misunderstandings.

Roberts then goes on to spend the next one and a half pages of his edition discussing the date; to this we shall turn in Chapter 5. Finally— or, rather, in the middle of this discussion, on page 236—he prints his reading of the text on the six fragments, adding two explanatory footnotes. And he ends his article with a concluding remark: "The papyrus contributes one unique reading in v. 22, apart from an obvious error in v. 32; it is noteworthy that here and in one other reading in this verse its text diverges from that of two other papyri, p37 and p45."

Sober notes, unlikely, on the face of it, to cause suspicion or stimulate worldwide attention when questioned and partly corrected in the context of a redating forty-two years later. In fact, the technical papyrological language has all sorts of implications of interest to the nonspecialist: observations, deductions and conclusions which take us back to the world of the first Christian scribes. Esoteric as they may seem, the scientific procedures of papyrology lead us to questions of a far more general nature. Let us look at the fragments again and see what we can ascertain in those letters, words and lines, saving the question of date and datability until later.

Roberts, funnily enough, discusses individual verses, but never mentions that they all derive from the twenty-sixth chapter of "the first gospel" (and by "first" he means the order in the canonical New Testament, not its chronological precedence over St. Mark) until he reaches his actual edition on page 236, where the chapter is indicated twice in minuscule Roman letters (xxvi). It may facilitate our stroll through this colorful but confusing thicket if we read the translated English text of these fragments from St. Matthew 26 first, quoting the New Jerusalem Bible:

FRAGMENT 1, VERSO (ST. MATTHEW 26:7–8):
   poured it on his head as he was at table. When the disciples saw this, they said indignantly

FRAGMENT 2, VERSO (ST. MATTHEW 26:10):
   Jesus noticed this and said, "Why are you upsetting this woman? What she has done for me

FRAGMENT 3, VERSO (ST. MATTHEW 26:14–15):
   Then one of the twelve, the man called Judas Iscariot, went to the chief priests and said, "What are you prepared to give me

FRAGMENT 3, RECTO (ST. MATTHEW 26:22–23):
   They were greatly distressed and started asking him in turn, "Not me, Lord, surely?" He answered, "Someone who has dipped his hand into the dish with me

FRAGMENT 1, RECTO (ST. MATTHEW 26:31):
   Jesus said to them, "You will all fall away from me tonight, for the scripture says

FRAGMENT 2, RECTO (ST. MATTHEW 26:32–33):
  I shall go ahead of you to Galilee." At this, Peter said to him

In printing this translation, we have not tried to copy the line divisions of the Greek fragments or the fragmentary character of words at the beginnings or ends of some lines; and, needless to say, since Greek syntax differs markedly from English syntax, the order of words within the sentences is different as well. We shall have to return to some of these instances in a moment, for the translators of the New Jerusalem Bible (or of any other translation, for that matter) were not aware of the unusual features of the Magdalen Papyrus. But this provides a workable idea of what is in these fragments: scenes from the Passion Story of Jesus, at Bethany, at the Last Supper, and the negotiations of Judas with the chief priests. The moment before an indignant outcry of the disciples, a saying of Judas, a question of the disciples, the run-up to a saying of St. Peter and no fewer than five sayings of Jesus himself: not a meager sum total for three small codex fragments.

The remarkable amount of spoken text on the fragment has prompted the suggestion that the Magdalen Papyrus does not stem from a full gospel at all but from a *collection of Jesus' sayings*. This would be an elegant way of accepting the very early date while avoiding the possibility that the fragment belonged to a full gospel text. In fact, such a collection (or collections) may have existed (although none has survived), and most scholars who believe so tend to call it *Logienquelle* (source of *logia*, i.e., "sayings") or simply "Q." But the Magdalen Papyrus fragments are not only a sequence of words of the Lord; there are, as we have seen, several other people speaking. What is more, the different utterances are already finely structured within narrative elements in a systematic order (St. Matthew 26:7–8, the story of the anointing of Jesus; St. Matthew 26:14–15, Judas Iscariot walking off to meet the priests). A second suggested explanation for the early, pre-Gospel date of the Magdalen Papyrus has been prompted by the fact that all six particles come from the Passion of the Lord. As mentioned before, such a text may have been circulated independently and before the composition of any completed gospel. Again, this is pure speculation, as there is no literary evidence for such a theory. Even the Magdalen Papyrus does not advance this thesis. This is clear from its sister codex in Barcelona, which contains St. Matthew 3:9, 15 and 5:20–22, 25–28—the other end of the Gospel, so to speak, the meeting of John the Baptist and Jesus and the Sermon on the Mount.

Not all of the six sides of our three fragments are equally noteworthy. On fragment 1, verso, for example, the first text (St. Matthew 26:7–8) is completely unremarkable, as it conforms to the standard text and offers no particular paleographic highlights. In his first edition of 1953, Roberts omitted several words which could be reconstructed from the stichometry; Thiede merely completed the lines in his second edition of 1995.[46] The second passage, St. Matthew 26:10 on fragment 2, verso, is again fairly straightforward until one reconstructs the complete lines, which Roberts did not do: the stichometry of line 1 strongly suggests that the Greek word *iesous* ("Jesus") was abbreviated to *IS*, the trademark of a "holy name," or *nomen sacrum*—an equivalent modern English Bible would print "Js noticed this and said . . ." The third text, St. Matthew 26:14–15 on fragment 3, verso, at last gives us the first reason to assume that the scribe was keenly aware of what he was doing and how he was doing it.

In line 2, he does not write *dódeka,* the Greek word for "twelve," but the numerical symbol ιβ *(iota + beta)*, comparable to a modern scribe writing the letters "xii" for "twelve": "Then one of the xii, Judas Iscariot . . ." Only the lower half of the *beta* remains visible on the fragment, but this and the completed stichometry of lines 1 and 2 are sufficiently clear to make the conclusion inescapable. Roberts had noticed this, but a second peculiarity had escaped his attention: immediately after the "twelve," a word is missing. One cannot quite express the force of this omission in English, but suppose that instead of the literal "Then went one of the twelve, he who was called Judas Iscariot . . . ," we were to read, "Then went one of the xii called Judas Iscariot." The Greek word missing is the article *ho* before *legómenos*. It is the only known instance of this omission at this place in any papyrus of St. Matthew's Gospel; and elsewhere in the New Testament, it occurs only in connection with place-names—see, for example, St. Matthew 2:23 (Nazareth) and St. John 4:5 (Sychar). Is it a mere slip of the pen, or was this early scribe consciously keeping the style simple so as to avoid any rhetorically effective but otherwise unnecessary accretions? Was he writing his copy for an early community which did not yet expect elegance and refined rhetoric? We shall have to come back to this question.

And then, with the fourth text, the going really gets tough. It is perhaps the most important side among the six of the Magdalen Papyrus. And to solve the problem, to reach a final judgment, Carsten Thiede had to utilize a new microscope: an epifluorescent confocal laser scanning technique which he and his colleague Georg Masuch, a biologist, had recently developed and patented.

St. Matthew 26:22–23 on fragment 3, recto, had already tested Roberts's powers of deduction. Line 1, damaged and partly illegible, preserves one letter which is complete enough to allow for only one reading: it is an *omega*. Of the preceding letter, only a vertical stroke remains, resembling the elongated stroke of a complete *tau* elsewhere in the Magdalen Papyrus. Following the *omega*, there appears to be a high dot; and immediately to the right of it, the beginnings of a letter which could be a *nu* or perhaps, though less probably if compared to other occurrences of this letter in the papyrus, a *mu*. As the rest of fragment 3, recto, necessitates the identification of the passage with St. Matthew 26:22–23, line 1 must contain the remnants of 26:22, and the letters *tau* + *omega* would belong to *autōn* ("of them"). But Roberts was impressed by the high dot; obviously, he thought it was a punctuation mark set before the ensuing question of the disciples, literally "Not me, Lord, surely?" Consequently, he had to assume that the fragmentary letter after the dot was a *mu*, not a *nu*, for the word must then be the interrogative particle *meti*, in the sense of "surely not?" Such a reconstruction would be unique, as Roberts himself duly noted. But it would also be unnecessarily awkward Greek. Indeed, this very verse has gone through all sorts of contortions in later manuscripts, as a look at the extensive footnotes, the critical apparatus in the Greek edition of Nestle-Aland[27rev], page 76, demonstrates. Thiede then recognized that the letter after the *omega* was a *nu* after all. Thus, the sentence was quite different, not only from Roberts's reconstruction but also from the standard printed texts of the Greek New Testament, in two notable respects.

What had happened? If the letter is indeed a *nu*, then the saying of Jesus which precedes the question of the disciples ends with *hekastos autōn* ("each of them"). It is a question of syntax and of intuitive style:

the standard text, as we read it in our Greek New Testament editions
and which ends with *legein auto heis hekastos,* would literally mean "And
very saddened, every [single] one of them said to him . . ." The reading of the Magdalen Papyrus, however, is: "And very saddened, each of
them said . . ." The precise nuance cannot be successfully rendered in
English: the Magdalen text emphasizes that they were all joining in, all
speaking at once—a realistic description of a dramatic moment. The
"standard texts," on the other hand, would have us believe that they
spoke up one after the other, waiting their turn in an orderly fashion. If
anything, the unembellished style of the Magdalen Papyrus takes us back
to a vivid scene of human excitement, while the later variants suggest
the subtle campaign to present the disciples as mature, soberly behaved
apostles-to-be even at this early stage.

In the debate about Thiede's work, Roberts has had his defenders.
After all, there was that high dot next to the right-hand "shoulder" of
the *omega.* Had Thiede tacitly ignored it or assumed that it belonged to
the *omega,* as a broken-off decorated elongation not uncommon elsewhere in all sorts of directions—such as in the *alpha, delta* and *lambda* of
the Magdalen Papyrus? For if it was meant to be a dot, a punctuation
mark, then the *nu* could again, if only tenuously, be interpreted as a *mu.*
We would be back to square one.

The final, clear answer came in June 1995, when the Magdalen Papyrus was brought to Germany by Dr. Christine Ferdinand, the Fellow
Librarian of Magdalen College, Oxford. In her presence, Carsten Thiede
and his colleague Georg Masuch analyzed the fragments under their
epifluorescent confocal laser scanning microscope. Unlike any other
modern microscope, it is able to differentiate between twenty separate
micrometer layers of a papyrus manuscript. It can select individual layers, measure the height and the depth of ink on and within the papyrus
sheet. Furthermore, this new instrument is able to generate the results on a video printout including, if desired, topographical charts
with detailed measurements, which detect the imprint of the scribe's
pen or stylus on the papyrus—even where there is no ink left—and
determine which way an individual letter was drawn. Finally, if necessary, it can collate all this information into a three-dimensional photograph.

Looking at the high dot under this microscope, Thiede and Masuch soon established that there never had been any link with the *omega* to its left or, indeed, with the letter to its right. A punctuation mark, after all? They measured the ink of the letters and of the dot. And here, the result was definitive: while the letters possess a thickness (height + depth) of 12.1 micrometers, the dot has a mere 4.0. It is an accidental ink blot, and nothing more. Such ink blots are frequent enough in ancient papyri; they are perfectly commonplace. It is now certain that this is all there is to say about the Magdalen Papyrus "high point," which has caused so much debate and irritation. Thus, Thiede's reconstruction is correct, including, as we might add, the obligatory *nu* after the *omega*, which was also checked. The result of this analysis was presented at the Twenty-first Congress of the International Papyrologists' Association in Berlin on August 15, 1995, and met with unanimous approval.

The new reading of the text on this line is identical with the reading in another old papyrus, the $\mathfrak{P}^{45}$, and apparently (the passage is fragmentary) with the text of the papyrus $\mathfrak{P}^{37}$, of Codex D (the famous early-fifth-century Bezae Cantabrigiensis at Cambridge University Library).[47] It is consistent with many other manuscripts. The $\mathfrak{P}^{45}$, commonly dated to the early third century but probably considerably older, is our earliest extant codex of all four Gospels *plus* Acts, now at the Chester Beatty Library, Dublin, and, partly, at the Austrian National Library, Vienna. The $\mathfrak{P}^{37}$ is an early-third- or late-second-century codex fragment of St. Matthew 26:19–52, at the University of Michigan, Ann Arbor. There is only one widely acknowledged critical edition of the Greek New Testament which has this reading as the best, most reliable one: the Bover-O'Callaghan *Nuevo Testamento Trilingüe*[48]—a trilingual Greek-Latin-Spanish edition, first published by José Maria Bover and then continued in later editions by José O'Callaghan, the very papyrologist who had correctly identified the Qumran papyrus 7Q5 as St. Mark 6:52–53.[49] It is self-evident that this original reading, preferable on the grounds of internal criteria and now corroborated by the oldest papyrus of St. Matthew's Gospel, must replace the text in the two most widely used versions of the Greek New Testament, that of the United Bible Societies (at present in its fourth revised edition) and the so-called Nestle-Aland, the *Novum Testamentum Graece* (now in its twenty-seventh revised edition). At the Münster Institute, which looks after this text, a rearguard action is being mounted, not surprisingly in view of its vested interest in the controversy. One of its staff members, Klaus Wachtel, recently published an article that refuses to acknowledge the change. He (and his colleagues at Münster) may not have been aware of all the relevant information in the matter.[50] In any case, it is a form of intellectual resistance which can not last; the facts are now beyond dispute.

While the Magdalen Papyrus was under their microscope, Thiede and Masuch also had a closer look at line 2 of fragment 3, recto. This, too, is an important line, as it has a second example of a *nomen sacrum,* a "holy name": the way the disciples address Jesus in verse 22, *kyrie* ("Lord"), is written with only the first and the last letter, *KE,* as if our English translation were to read: "Not me, Ld, surely?" The letters are severely damaged, but enough is left to establish, as Roberts had—even without the new laser scanning microscope, but using the stichometry of the line as an additional guide—that this is the case. Roberts had put tiny dots underneath each of the letters, signifying damaged and only partly legible letters. At the right end of the line, hardly anything looks reconstructible, but he had tentatively suggested *de,* the second word of 26:23, a conjunctive particle which could be rendered as "but" or "now then . . ." but often remains untranslated. In Thiede's edition, the editorial bracket which signals the division between visible letters or fragments of letters and the ensuing reconstruction of the line as it would have appeared when complete, was set after the *delta* and before the *epsilon* of *de.* A conscious attempt at improving the first edition, or a printing error? As nothing really depends on this difference—the text would be the same—neither Roberts nor Thiede had commented on their choice. For Thiede and Masuch, it was just a welcome chance to find out what their microscope was capable of establishing in such a case.

Under a twentyfold objective, a minute fiber of papyrus with specks of ink at the far end became visible. They took a computerized measurement of the maximum length from the clearly visible horizontal stroke at the left to the last of these specks and compared it to the length of the horizontal of a complete *epsilon* on another of the three fragments (fragment 1, recto, line 3). The two measurements were identical. But why is there no complete horizontal stroke, obligatory in any *epsilon?* Thiede and Masuch produced a three-dimensional image, and the answer became obvious: precisely along the line where that horizontal stroke once was, there is a papyrus fiber alongside which ink has flaked off and indeed, as they noticed, is still flaking off. A helpful and timely piece of information for the keeper and restorer at Magdalen College!

If that letter definitely is an *epsilon*, then of course the letter to its left must be a *delta*. But it does not look anything like a *delta*—rather more like a low and smallish *omikron*. The microscope detected three tiny spots, thick enough to be integral parts of a former letter, above the apparent *omikron* circle. A complete *delta*, from fragment 1, recto, line 2, was set underneath, and the computer drew white lines into the inner triangle. This triangle was then transferred to the traces of the *"omikron"* and the dots above it. It fit. The letter to the left of the reconstructed *epsilon* is indeed a *delta*, unlikely as this initially seemed. And thus, the last legible combination of letters, the last word on line 2 of this fragment, is a *de* after all.

The fifth side of the Magdalen Papyrus, fragment 1, recto, or St. Matthew 26:31, is characterized by three notable traits. As Roberts had noticed, and as we quoted from his first edition above, the initial letter, the *alpha* of the first word, *autois* ("to them"), is projected into the left margin. As in the sister papyrus at Barcelona, where it occurs in St. Matthew 5:21 and 5:27, this signifies the first complete line of a new section, which begins in the preceding line. Furthermore, here in line 1, we have our third instance of a *nomen sacrum*, a "holy name." *iesous* ("Jesus") is written *IS,* as if it were to say "Then Js said to them . . ." in modern English Bibles. And for good measure, there is a third peculiarity in this line, one unnoticed by Roberts: after *pantes* ("all"), every edition of the standard Greek text prints *humeis* ("of you"). But there is no room for this word in this line of the Magdalen Papyrus. As we noticed above, comparing it to a similar case in the Qumran papyrus scroll fragment 7Q5, with *humeis* this line would have twenty rather than fifteen letters, four above the average for this papyrus. Here, such an excessive length would be all the more irregular, as the line already has a surplus letter to the left, the *alpha* projected into the left margin. One might of course think that this is petty stuff; but in normal Greek, the *humeis* is quite superfluous, even more so than an English "of you." Its omission—or, rather, its original nonexistence—may well confirm the tendency of the Magdalen Papyrus to keep the Greek correct but as simple and unembellished as possible.

Finally, we come to the last side, fragment 2, recto (St. Matthew

26:32–33). For Christians, it is of particular interest because it contains the first manuscript evidence for the name of St. Peter (*petros* in line 3). Otherwise, its only noteworthy idiosyncrasy is the spelling mistake that we briefly discussed above, in the context of the *d/t* shift in the 7Q5 papyrus: in line 2, the word for Galilee, *galeilaian*, is misspelled *galeglaian*. A double check under the confocal laser scanning microscope confirmed that the horizontal stroke on top and to the right of what should have been an *iota* is neither an optical illusion nor an accident— the scribe really drew that line, turning the *iota* into a *gamma*. As we said before, this error makes this thoughtful scribe seem a little bit more human.

Taking all this into consideration, the Magdalen Papyrus contributes greatly to our understanding of early Christianity, the Jesus tradition and its literary structure. We shall look at it again from another angle, using the "holy names" as a starting point, in Chapter 6. Here, in this chapter, we have one more aspect to consider: the close relationship of the Magdalen Papyrus, $\mathfrak{P}^{64}$, and the two fragments kept at the Fundación San Lucas Evangelista, numbered $\mathfrak{P}^{67}$ in the Gregory-Aland list of New Testament papyri.

The Barcelona Papyrus and the Paris Codex

In 1962, nine years after his first edition of the Magdalen Papyrus, Colin H. Roberts published a "Complementary Note" to Ramón Roca-Puig's second edition of the Barcelona papyrus.[51] In it, he had this to say:

> When in 1956 Professor Ramón Roca-Puig published a booklet entitled *Un Papiro Griego del Evangelio de San Mateo,* with an edition of the papyrus in the possession of the "Fundación San Lucas Evangelista," I suspected that the hand in which the two papyri were written was one and the same, and correspondence with Professor Roca-Puig confirmed this beyond doubt. The Barcelona fragments are part of two leaves covering in part Chapters iii and v of the Gospel. It is unlikely that either leaf was conjoint with the Magdalen College leaf, and it therefore remains uncertain whether

or no the codex was a single quire codex or no. The whole gospel would have occupied some 90 pages.

Roberts then proceeded to give his reasons for a second-century date for both papyri, quoting a number of manuscripts, not a single one of which is itself precisely dated—in Chapter 5, we shall see what this implies. Even so, Roberts acknowledged that "the hand in which the text is written is a carefully written book hand that may be regarded as a *precursor* [our italics] of the style commonly known as Biblical Uncial."

The paleographic characteristics of the Magdalen Papyrus and the two Barcelona fragments are indeed so strikingly identical that no one has ever doubted their common origin from one and the same codex. The Barcelona papyrus has not attracted the same level of attention paid to the Magdalen Papyrus after *The Times* published its Christmas Eve story. But although they are both, obviously, of the same date, it is the Magdalen Papyrus which offers all that intriguing and original evidence about the early Christian scribal traditions. For example, the Barcelona sister papyrus has not a single visible "holy name," or *nomen sacrum*.[52] It includes not a single stylistic prose variant, for, as it happens, those fragments do not have any narrative elements—John the Baptist is speaking, Jesus is replying, and then there is a fragmentary piece from the Sermon on the Mount. Even so, these texts should not be ignored. The Barcelona papyrus is important in its own right; here we have the oldest papyrus evidence of a saying of the Baptist and the oldest known passage from the Sermon on the Mount. Here is the text preserved on the Barcelona fragment, quoted in English from the New Jerusalem Bible and disregarding the fragmentary beginnings and ends of the papyrus:

FRAGMENT 1, VERSO (ST. MATTHEW 3:9):
And do not presume to tell yourselves, "We have Abraham as our father," because I tell you, God can

FRAGMENT 1, RECTO (ST. MATTHEW 3:15):
Jesus replied: "Leave it like this for the time being; it is fitting that we should, in this way

FRAGMENT 2, RECTO (ST. MATTHEW 5:20–22):

> If your uprightness does not surpass that of the scribes and Phari-
> sees, you will never get into the kingdom of Heaven. You have
> heard how it was said to your ancestors, "You shall not kill," and
> if anyone does kill he must answer for it before the court. But I say
> this to you, anyone who is angry with a brother

FRAGMENT 2, VERSO (ST. MATTHEW 5:25–28):

> he may hand you over to the judge and the judge to the officer, and
> you will be thrown into prison. In truth I tell you, you will not get
> out till you have paid the last penny. You have heard how it was
> said, "You shall not commit adultery." But I say this to you, if a
> man looks at a woman lustfully

Let us conclude our discussion of the Barcelona papyrus with Ramón
Roca-Puig's note on a remarkable photographic error.[53] In fragment 2,
verso, line 9 (part of Matthew 5:27), two dots had been discovered next
to the Greek word *hoti* ("for that," "that"). Hubert Greeven of Kiel
University had supposed that they signified a *diairesis*—that is, a separating mark to signify independent syllables or single vowels over against
diphthongs, etc. In theory, this could have made sense, since there is
indeed a word after *hoti* which begins with a vowel, *erréthe* ("it was
said"). But Roca-Puig, after a renewed and careful investigation of the
papyrus *a la luz de sol* ("in the light of the sun"), bluntly declares that
the two "dots" are not points "made by ink," but tiny scratches (*rasgu-
ños*) on the damaged papyrus. He adds that he mentions this so as to
prevent other papyrologists from relying on the "dots" and thus being
misled into trusting the photograph.

This is a noble Spanish way of stating a basic rule of papyrology: Do
not trust a photograph unless you can check the papyrus itself when it
matters. Carsten Thiede once had a related experience when he worked
on the critical first edition of the Papyrus Bodmer L from the Biblioteca
Bodmeriana (Fondation Martin Bodmer) at Cologny, near Geneva.[54] A
photograph of that papyrus which he had received from the library
showed a clear, unmistakable horizontal stroke underneath parts of line
2 (or, if viewed differently, above line 3) of the recto. It might have had

all sorts of consequences for his edition; after all, such lines can be vital to an identification. But rather than indulge in speculation, he went to Cologny and studied the original papyrus itself. There is no sign of such a horizontal stroke on the papyrus—it is nothing but a blemish on the photographic plate. Other papyrologists, needless to say, have had similar experiences. Photographs are useful—indeed, they are often the only way to begin one's study of a papyrus kept thousands of miles from one's own desk. But an analysis which relies solely on photographs can never be accepted without reservation. In all fairness, therefore, any edition or critique of an edition should say so if access to the original was not possible.

Before we conclude this chapter, we have to address a related question which has attracted the attention of scholars ever since the Magdalen and Barcelona papyri were linked: Are there perhaps other papyri elsewhere which could have belonged to the same original codex? One candidate was immediately suggested: the codex $\mathfrak{P}^4$, or P. Suppl. Gr. 1120, at the Bibliothèque Nationale in Paris.

Piecing together fragmentary codices—or scrolls, for that matter—of classical texts which may be spread across libraries all over the world is no idle game. Indeed, it may be vital for our understanding of a whole literary work, its text and context. As we have just seen, the "reassembly" of the Oxford $\mathfrak{P}^{64}$ and the Barcelona $\mathfrak{P}^{67}$ has contributed to a much more reliable assessment of the oldest surviving papyrus codex of St. Matthew's Gospel than either of the two could have done on its own, small as they both are. There are other examples, outside the field of Biblical studies; a recent case in point is the edition of the second-century papyrus of *Acts of Martyrs,* the *Acta Alexandrinorum* at Yale—the P. Yale 1385—which belongs to a previously known papyrus of the same work at Giessen University Library, the PbuG 46, on the other side of the Atlantic.[55] Uncommonly close similarities between the Magdalen and Barcelona papyri and a much larger codex fragment in Paris were first noticed by Peter Weigandt, who passed his observation on to Kurt Aland. Aland wrote about these similarities in a paper published in 1966.[56] Ever since, scholars have assumed that Weigandt and Aland were right. Among others, van Haelst, Roberts and Skeat contributed to the popularity of this view.[57]

This identification was—or, rather, would have been—quite helpful.

The Paris papyrus 𝔓⁴ of St. Luke's Gospel not only appeared to add a
second gospel to this old codex; with four leaves of a larger size than any
of the Oxford and Barcelona sheets, and passages from the first six
chapters of St. Luke, it would also supply valuable additional information on scribal habits, editing techniques and so forth. Initially, Aland
persisted in his belief in the common origin of the three papyri; but as
early as 1967, he expressed first doubts—the reconstructions of the
format of 𝔓⁴ differ from those of 𝔓⁶⁴/⁶⁷.[58] And then, in 1981, without
any detailed explanation, he changed his mind completely. He clearly
differentiated between 𝔓⁶⁴/⁶⁷ on the one hand, whose text type he called
fester Text ("firm or stable text"), and 𝔓⁴ on the other, described as
Normaltext ("normal text"). Thus ruling out any former unity of the
papyri on textual grounds, he underlined the difference by dating 𝔓⁶⁴/⁶⁷
"ca 200" and 𝔓⁴ "III."[59] Although both dates are much too late, as we
shall see, the point is that Aland had become convinced that they were
written at different times. In brief, he had himself provided three compelling reasons for the lack of a connection between 𝔓⁴ and 𝔓⁶⁴/⁶⁷: the
different reconstructed formats, the different text types and the different dates.

This did not deal with the paleographic similarities—the hands really
do look closely related, more so on the photographs than on the original
papyri. Some form of relationship remained plausible. But of what kind?
Unaware of Aland's change of mind, Roberts and Skeat had reasserted
their belief in the connection in 1983 without advancing any new reasons; and the American scholar Philip W. Comfort had done the same in
1992, in an introduction to textual criticism, *The Quest for the Original
Text of the New Testament*.[60] It took until early 1995, when simultaneous,
independent investigations by Comfort and Carsten Thiede, stimulated
by Thiede's re-edition of the Magdalen Papyrus, led to a conclusive
result: 𝔓⁶⁴ and 𝔓⁶⁷ did once belong together, but 𝔓⁴ did not. However,
𝔓⁴—the Paris codex—quite probably came from the same scribal school
or center, commissioned by a different patron, and only slightly later. In
February 1995, Comfort published his results, a noteworthy and closely
argued change of mind, in the same journal with Thiede's report on an
investigation of the original sheets at the Bibliothèque Nationale.[61] The
succinct reasons for the nonidentity, as given by Thiede, are easily summarized:

(1) The separate fragment of a title page preserved with the other papyri in box 5 of P. Suppl. Gr. 1120, *EYAGGELION KATA MATHTHAION* (Gospel according to Matthew), which encouraged some scholars to believe that the Oxford/Barcelona papyri of St. Matthew may at one stage have belonged to the same codex, is written in a hand distinctly different from all three papyri. In particular, it is broader and wider, with a flat *nu* and markedly elongated upper horizontal strokes in the two *gammas*.

(2) There can be no doubt that the material of the papyrus in $\mathfrak{P}^4$ and $\mathfrak{P}^{64/67}$, respectively, is different. The dark brown of the Paris fragments, in contrast to the light hue of the Oxford/Barcelona pieces, is organic and cannot be ascribed to different means of preservation and conservation. This observation alone already seems to rule out the possibility of the Paris fragment originally having belonged to the same codex as the other two.

(3) One of the most striking features of $\mathfrak{P}^{64/67}$, the projection of a letter into the left margin in order to signify the first complete line of a new section which begins in the preceding line, is markedly different in the Paris papyrus: its scribe always used *two* letters, rather than one, for this purpose. The photographs supplied in the first edition of $\mathfrak{P}^4$ are unfortunately not very helpful for any serious analysis—indeed, they are of an absolutely deplorable quality. But even here, anyone can see the unambiguous examples of *ar/chomenos* in fragment B, verso, first column = St. Luke 3:23 (plate iv), and of *el/egen* in fragment D, verso, first column = St. Luke 5:36 (plate vi).[62] While this in itself would not necessarily rule out the possibility that the same scribe was at work— after all, any scribe might change his or her stylistic traits from time to time, not least if asked to do so by a customer—such variation would not occur in the same "book."

(4) The differences between the letters of $\mathfrak{P}^{64/67}$ and $\mathfrak{P}^4$ are less apparent but no less significant than the similarities. For example, the scribe of $\mathfrak{P}^4$ has a tendency to raise *omega* and *omikron* above the bottom line, but to keep his *rho* right on the line. This in fact is much like his *tau,* which in $\mathfrak{P}^{64/67}$ extends underneath the bottom line in the same way as the *upsilon,* and which always has a straight top bar in $\mathfrak{P}^4$, but not always so in $\mathfrak{P}^{64/67}$.[63] Fragment A, recto, of $\mathfrak{P}^4$ offers the clearest examples, even on the photograph.

Taken together with the three reasons given by Kurt Aland for distinguishing between the $\mathfrak{P}^4$ codex and the $\mathfrak{P}^{64/67}$ codex, and adding one more argument advanced by Philip Comfort (the pen strokes of $\mathfrak{P}^4$ over against $\mathfrak{P}^{64/67}$ are noticeably distinct; in $\mathfrak{P}^4$, they are much finer and thinner), we must consider the case closed. The two texts were quite separate. Nonetheless, the remaining similarities and certain coincidences demand an explanation. The Paris papyrus and the Magdalen Papyrus were acquired at the same place, Luxor, albeit at different times and by different people, a fact noted by Comfort. Thiede and Comfort argue that the style is indeed paleographically comparable and that, hypothetically, even the same scribe could have produced all three papyri, at different times. Perhaps the less daring explanation, a common scribal center sharing certain characteristics, is more likely.

On the basis of these results, Thiede has changed the date he had put to the Paris $\mathfrak{P}^4$ in his re-edition of the Magdalen Papyrus. In his first article, he had been content with the status quo, as the date of $\mathfrak{P}^4$ was of no immediate relevance to his work on the Oxford St. Matthew fragments. Having analyzed the original of the Paris codex and taking Comfort's own arguments into account, he now shares the American scholar's assessment: the Paris papyrus of St. Luke's Gospel is not much later than $\mathfrak{P}^{64/67}$. Comfort, who had not yet seen the additional comparative material for a first-century date of the Magdalen Papyrus when he wrote his article,[64] tentatively opted for a more conservative position, suggesting an early second-century date for the Paris papyrus. Even so, it is now recognized as the earliest extant manuscript of St. Luke's Gospel.

What the Investigation Shows

The scholarly challenge of dating and redating ancient manuscripts will be described in Chapter 5. Suffice it to say here that the conclusion to Philip Comfort's paper is rather significant. In spite of the difficulties, he writes:

[S]ome manuscripts have been receiving earlier dates. For example, the Pauline codex P46 has been redated by Kim to *ca*. A.D. 85. To this day, Kim's early dating of P46 to the later part of the first century *has not been challenged on palaeographical grounds* [our italics]. And the Johannine codex P66 has been dated to *ca.* 125 by the papyrologist Herbert Hunger. Other manuscripts have been pushed back from the third century to the second century— namely, P32 (*ca.* 175), P45 (*ca.* 150), P77 (*ca.* 150), P87 (*ca.* 125), P90 (*ca.* 150).[65]

Comfort only states what should be obvious: papyrology is anything but a static science. Things move ahead steadily all the time. Sometimes the science itself needs a "sensational" claim to draw the issues to a head and move on. But could we not take a short cut and subject the Magdalen Papyrus to radiocarbon dating? That would surely settle the matter to everyone's satisfaction. Early in 1995, the Fellow Librarian of Magdalen College took the three fragments to the famous Oxford laboratory where the Turin Shroud—among many other objects—had been radiocarbon-dated. What we had assumed before was quickly confirmed at the laboratory: the fragments are too small and too light. Even the new technology of accelerator mass spectometry requires a minimum weight of 20–25 mg, which is used up in the course of the analysis; in other words, the material is destroyed. And even then, the date arrived at is accurate only within a range of +/− fifty years. The three Oxford fragments have a weight of 45, 25 and 21 mg, respectively. It would be impossible, and indeed counterproductive, to subject any of them to a radiocarbon dating analysis. More refined methods would still be de-structive, as there are letters and remnants of letters everywhere, to the very edges of all fragments. No curator, restorer or papyrologist would allow the destruction of even the minutest trace of writing on such a precious papyrus. The Barcelona fragments are excluded for the same reasons; although fragment 2 is larger than the largest Magdalen frag-ment—5.0 cm × 5.5 cm (1^{15}/$_{16}$ in. × 2^{1}/$_{8}$ in.) compared to 4.1 cm × 1.3 cm (1^{5}/$_{8}$ in. × ^{1}/$_{2}$ in.)—more than a third, all of it with text, would be irretrievably destroyed.

In fact, only scrolls or papyri with large enough margins or edges that are completely free of writing can be used for radiocarbon dating, which, it should be stressed, does not date the handwriting, but the material—the papyrus, the leather, or other medium. Thus, several

Dead Sea Scrolls were radiocarbon-dated in 1991, and the result came as no surprise to the experts. The date was identical with that previously arrived at by papyrologists, using their traditional methods of comparative paleography.[66] Bearing this conclusion in mind, we shall investigate the date of the Magdalen Papyrus paleographically in Chapter 5. But first we turn our attention to the enigmatic figure who sent these ancient fragments to Oxford for safekeeping—the Reverend Charles Bousfield Huleatt.

4

THE DISCOVERY OF A
LIFETIME

EVERY ONE OF US IS A MAGDALEN MAN—THE POOREST, THE LEAST CLEVER, THE LEAST CONSPICUOUS . . . WE ARE EITHER WORTHY OF IT, OR WE ARE NOT WORTHY OF IT. ITS NAME, ITS FAME IS IN OUR HANDS: WE CANNOT DISOWN IT.

—LECTURE GIVEN BY T. H. WARREN TO MAGDALEN UNDERGRADUATES (JUNE 1885)

WHAT FURTHER DISCOVERIES OF THE LOST DOCUMENTS OF EARLY CHRISTIANITY STILL AWAIT US IN EGYPT IT IS IMPOSSIBLE TO SAY.

—A. H. SAYCE (1896)

IT IS FAR MORE THE SECOND-HAND FALLACIES OF STRAUSS AND RENAN THAT I HAVE TO COMBAT IN REALITY THAN ANY ROMAN DOCTRINES.

—CHARLES B. HULEATT, UNDATED LETTER

The Reverend Charles B. Huleatt,
Victorian Missionary and Scholar

The name Charles Bousfield Huleatt (1863–1908) means little today in Luxor. At the entrance of the hotel where he was Anglican chaplain for a decade of winters is a striking commemorative plaque to this forgotten man of faith and letters. It reads: IN LOVING MEMORY OF THE REV. CHARLES BOUSFIELD HULEATT, M.A. CHAPLAIN AT LUXOR 1893–1901: WHO PERISHED IN THE EARTHQUAKE AT HIS POST OF DUTY AS CHAPLAIN AT MESSINA 1908. WELL DONE GOOD AND FAITHFUL SERVANT, ENTER THOU INTO THE JOY OF THY LORD. MATT.XXV.21

For the amateur scholar who found the earliest known fragment of the Gospel according to St. Matthew, there could scarcely be a more apt scriptural tribute. Yet it has small significance to the locals who sit on the verandah of the Luxor Hotel these days sipping tea and puffing expansively on pipes as the impossible heat of the summer afternoon slowly releases its stranglehold. To them, the brass plaque is little more than an attractive hieroglyph in a foreign tongue, rather than a stately record of a man who made a remarkable discovery. The earnest Oxford graduate who came to their land a century ago and sent home something extraordinary has left behind no folk memory. Who was this man and what brought him to Egypt to spread the Word and, perhaps, to seek truth? The most the traveler who asks about Huleatt can expect is an indulgent smile and another glass of fierce Egyptian wine. That this should be so is a melancholy irony symbolic of the chaplain's life, its frustrations and the recognition he was denied.

Opened for the winter of 1877–78, the Luxor Hotel was for many years one of Egypt's most important institutions, a crossroads of scholars, soldiers and wealthy expatriates wintering on the Nile. It was probably the travel entrepreneur Thomas Cook's finest achievement, rivaled in prestige only by the neighboring Winter Palace Hotel. Though its rooms do not look over the river, the hotel is but a stone's throw from Luxor Temple, the awe-inspiring monument built by Amenophis III and other scions of the Eighteenth Dynasty to the greater glory of the god Amon. According to legend, Jesus and the Virgin visited the temple during the Holy Family's Egyptian exile, by which stage its buildings were already a monument to the ancient past, its hieroglyphs meaningless to Nazarene eyes.

The grounds of the temple are an unparalleled museum to the religious history of a species, bearing traces of Roman, Christian and Muslim worship. Each era has left its mark and its mysteries, aside from less reverential curiosities such as the large inscription carved by the poet Arthur Rimbaud into the ancient stone of the south end's transverse hall. Turning to the north, one gazes down the avenue of sphinxes which once led all the way to the yet more spectacular temple of Karnak. The powerful impression which this majesty must have made upon the Victorian mind is clear from this account left by one traveler in 1898:

> When the boat pulls up at Luxor the landing-stage appeared to be a colossal temple. Really this is across the road, but, even so, it was wonder enough. Arcades of huge pillars, some complete, some half

broken down, some sprawling in hideous dislocation—they loomed grey and motionless and solemn in face of the ancient river and the flaming sunset . . . As we went to bed almost under them they seemed to be rebuking squalid, modern Egypt—rebuking modernity altogether, that was so small and fretting, while they remained so great and unsurprised.[1]

For a decade, this extraordinary place was the setting of Charles Huleatt's life and missionary work. Even today, a century later, the Luxor Hotel still seems like a traveler's annex to the temple, a place where those who are drawn to Egypt's past gather to see the ruins of Thebes, Homer's "city with a hundred gates." It was natural—perhaps even de rigueur—that Howard Carter and Lord Carnarvon should announce the discovery of Tutankhamun's tomb in November 1922 from the Luxor Hotel. Their portraits still hang in its gloomy lobby, tribute to the legends which quickly arose around their names and achievements. They are not forgotten.

The same cannot be said of Charles Huleatt. As humble as it seems in comparison to the young pharaoh's funerary treasures, the Magdalen Papyrus, with its handful of verses from the Gospel according to St. Matthew, has far more to tell us about the origins of our culture, and the belief system which has dominated it for centuries, than all of Tutankhamun's gold. Yet Huleatt has been granted none of the celebrity which fell so easily to Carter and Carnarvon. Indeed, his fate has been quite the opposite. The college to whom he entrusted the papyrus in 1901 treated it with comparative indifference at the time. Its arrival at Magdalen stirred no scholarly debate or excited speculation; only since Carsten Thiede's redating in 1994 has the papyrus become the center of collegiate attention. And if the young chaplain had a scholarly inkling of what he held in the palm of his hand, he was denied the chance to pursue his intuition. Seven years after he sent the fragments to Magdalen, he was swept away by an act of God which all but eradicated his name from history. Huleatt never saw the papyrus again, and his name was forgotten.

The redating has, of course, made his life and beliefs matters of great interest for historian and theologian alike. Yet the fates have conspired against those who would reclaim his memory; the sources are fragmentary, thanks to an uncanny series of accidents. He, his wife and four children were all lost in the earthquake which destroyed the Sicilian port of Messina on December 28, 1908; so, too, were all his private papers, save a bundle of personal letters retrieved from the rubble by his close friend William Collins, Bishop of Gibraltar. Two years later, the mud-brick Anglican church on the grounds of Luxor Hotel was washed away by flood, along with its tombstones. Two trunks full of Huleatt family records disappeared some years ago. At the time of this writing, the English missionary archive at All Saints Cathedral in Cairo remained closed—a matter of regret for all researchers into the connections be-tween Victorian religion and Egyptology. To go in search of Charles Huleatt is like tracing the fugitive steps of a shadow. Yet his story—the story of a devoted Evangelical with an inquisitive intellect, who chanced upon the earliest Gospel text in the world—is integral to the history of the papyrus. Without his scholarship, the fragments might never have left Egypt; without his filial devotion to Oxford, they would never have reached Magdalen, there to remain for almost a century before they would be accurately dated. Fugitive as it is, Huleatt's is a shadow that must be chased.

From Boyhood to Magdalen

Charles Bousfield Huleatt was born on October 19, 1863, in the Parson-age, Potters Bar, Hertfordshire,[2] second son and third child of the Reverend Hugh Huleatt (1822–98) and his wife, Cornelia. The Huleatt family—whose name is a variant of Hewlett rather than anything more exotic—had its roots in Ireland and observed strong traditions of service in Church and Army. Hugh Huleatt, a formidable patriarch who fa-thered eleven children, honored both traditions as a chaplain to the armed forces between 1854 and 1879 (a role which, by coincidence, Carsten Thiede plays today) and served with distinction in the Crimea and China. In 1859, Padre Huleatt returned to England, where he mar-ried Cornelia Sophia Bousfield, daughter of the extremely wealthy Charles Pritchett Bousfield, who was to be a powerful force in the life of his eponymous grandson.

In spite of his father's robust example, Charles Huleatt suffered from poor health throughout his life and was evidently a sickly child. The 1871 census describes the seven-year-old boy—almost certainly with exaggeration—as "blind." However poor Charles's eyesight was at the time, he was sufficiently able-bodied to enroll at St. Paul's School on December 1, 1873. By this time, Padre Huleatt had moved from St. George's Church in the Royal Artillery Barracks in Woolwich to the chaplaincy at the Royal Military Asylum, Chelsea. St. Paul's was an entirely predictable choice for a well-to-do London family of means with high expectations for their frail son.

It was Charles's great fortune that this should be so, for at St. Paul's he was to forge one of the most important friendships of his life. In December 1876, William Gunion Rutherford arrived at the school as a classics master, fresh from Balliol, which, under Benjamin Jowett, had become Oxford's most intellectually formidable college.[3] Rutherford's undergraduate career had been one of enormous promise and he was rapidly to make his name as a classical scholar, initially with the ground-breaking First Greek Grammar (1878) and then, three years later, with The New Phrynichus, one of the greatest works in English on Attic form.

Rutherford is best known for his later role as headmaster of another great English public school, Westminster College. But it was in these formative years at St. Paul's that he befriended and became an inspiration to the young Charles Huleatt, whom The Oxford Magazine later described as "one of his favourite pupils."[4] It was Rutherford who awoke Huleatt's precocious interest in textual criticism—a passion which always surpassed his dedication to his formal studies at university.

Indeed, their interests continued to coincide after both master and pupil left St. Paul's. During the 1890s, Rutherford followed closely the emergence of new papyrus evidence from Egypt and in the last years of his life addressed himself assiduously to the text of the New Testament. He believed that the Greek used by its authors was radically different from the classical Greek he knew so well. In the preface to his 1906 translation of St. Paul's Epistle to the Romans, Rutherford wrote of this distinctive biblical language:

> With every generation it changed, departing more and more widely from literary grace and logical precision, ceasing in time to be the cherished language of a race that of all races has best loved

accuracy of thought and limpidity of expression, and becoming by degrees a tolerant speech whereby many races, all differing greatly in habits of mind and in national circumstances, sought for a time to eschew the curse of Babel.[5]

As we shall see in Chapter 6, Huleatt's erstwhile mentor might easily have been describing the multicultural Greek in which the Magdalen Papyrus was written. And though there is no evidence that Rutherford knew of his former pupil's find in Egypt, it is intriguing that their academic concerns remained so similar. The fact that *The Oxford Magazine* thought their association worth underlining in Huleatt's brief obituary suggests that his revered teacher may well have assumed the role of muse in later life.

Huleatt excelled sufficiently at St. Paul's to win an exhibition to read classics at Magdalen College, Oxford. Having achieved this distinction at a relatively youthful age, he stayed on an extra year at school before taking up his university place in 1882, flush with an additional Pauline scholarship worth £50 for four years.

For a Victorian gentleman of Huleatt's background and academic promise to read classics at Oxford was almost a rite of passage. The school of litterae humaniores was not only regarded as the most intellectually prestigious path for a young English gentleman to pursue; it was also thought to be ideal cerebral preparation for those who were to take up posts, clerical and lay, in the British Empire. The history of the Greek city states and Roman Empire were considered parables of instruction for the elite charged with the government of Britain's dominions and territories; the classical model of the *vita activa* was held up to Oxford's young scholars for emulation in the glittering careers that lay ahead of them. In 1873, Jowett wrote to Florence Nightingale that "I should like to govern the world through my pupils." This was more than a donnish quip; to many of his contemporaries, it sometimes seemed that Jowett's influence did indeed stretch the length and breadth of the British Empire.[6]

The talented young classicist from St. Paul's spent four undergraduate years in a university where it was natural to seek dignified occupation abroad in the service of God and Empire. To take up a chaplaincy in Egypt, as he was to do not long after leaving Oxford, was to pursue an honorable calling rather than to submit to second-rate exile. More surprising, perhaps, is that Huleatt performed so modestly in Oxford's examinations. In 1884, he gained a respectable second class degree in Classical Moderations. Two years later, he was awarded only third class honors in Litterae Humaniores. This may well have been a disappointment to Huleatt, who took his B.A. in 1888 and M.A. four years later. Yet the importance of examinations to the Oxford system at this stage in the university's history is easily exaggerated. Since the Royal Commission of 1850–52 and the Oxford Reform Act of 1854, the clerical and nepotistic character of the university had certainly been addressed by committed reformers such as Jowett, who had vigorously encouraged hard work in their undergraduates. Nonetheless, the old habits died hard. Tom Brown, Thomas Hughes's fictional character, was bemused by the lack of academic pressure:

> First and foremost, it's an awfully idle place; at any rate for us freshmen. Fancy now. I am in twelve lectures a week of an hour each—Greek Testament, first book of Herodotus, second Aeneid, and first book of Euclid! There's a treat! Two hours a day; all over by twelve, or one at the latest.[7]

It was still said of Oxford that "every freshman brings to it a little knowledge and no graduate takes any away." Charles Huleatt probably performed as he did in university examinations because the pressure to do otherwise was still so relatively modest. More important to his long-term intellectual development and his later role in the story of the St. Matthew papyrus was his continued amateur interest in textual scholarship—an interest he seems to have pursued quite independently of the formal studies on offer at Magdalen. His achievements in this field were such that in 1885 *The Journal of Philology* published an article by him proposing a series of textual emendations to Catullus and Propertius. That an undergraduate should have his work published in a learned journal was remarkable in itself. Still more impressive was the fact that Huleatt's suggestions seem to have been favorably received by his elders. In 1909, *The Oxford Magazine* described the Propertius emendations as "highly ingenious" and noted that they had been accepted by "several subsequent editors." There is no reason to think that Huleatt had the application or inclination to be a professional academic. But his under-graduate flair in this field adds luster to the theory that his interest in the papyrus which he found in Upper Egypt years later was more than that of the antiquarian hobbyist.

Why did Huleatt send the fragments back to Magdalen in 1901? Of all the questions posed by the papyrus, this is perhaps the easiest to answer.

Founded in the fifteenth century, Magdalen is one of the most cap-tivatingly beautiful of the colleges of England's two ancient universities, blessed with a deer park, the imposing New Buildings behind cloisters, and a tower which is to many the architectural epitome of Oxford. Those who are undergraduates there never forget their youthful idyll in its quads and gardens. In 1901, the historian J. R. Green recalled the haunting experience of May Morning, when Magdalen's choristers usher in the summer at dawn, a rite which Huleatt must first have experienced in 1883. It is a recollection worth quoting at length:

> We used to spring out of bed, and gather in the grey of dawn on the top of the College tower, where choristers and singing men were already grouped in their surplices. Beneath us, all wrapped in the dim mists of a spring morning, lay the city, the silent reaches of Cherwell, the great commons of Cowley marsh and Bullingdon now covered with houses, but then a desolate waste. There was a long hush of waiting just before five, and then the first bright point of sunlight gleamed out over the horizon; below, at the base of the tower, a mist of discordant noises from the tin horns of the town boys greeted its appearance, and above, in the stillness, rose the soft pathetic air of the hymn *Te Deum Patrem Colimus*.[8]

Such were the collegiate rituals which would have nurtured Huleatt's lifelong attachment to Magdalen. Indeed, he was fortunate to be a student at the college during one of its high seasons. Edward Gibbon had famously condemned his fourteen months at Magdalen as "the most idle and unprofitable of my whole life." But by the 1880s, when the young Pauline arrived to read classics as one of about a hundred undergradu-ates, the college was in the full bloom of institutional renaissance. Build-ing on the foundations laid by President Martin Joseph Routh—whose

St. Matthew, from an eleventh-century illuminated manuscript of
the Gospels of St. Matthew and St. Mark (MS. Douce 292, fol. 6v).
(The Bodleian Library, Oxford)

Charles Bousfield Huleatt (1863–1908) — missionary, scholar, Magdalen man. The discoverer of the now famous Magdalen Papyrus once told his wife, "I have failed in everything." *(By kind permission of the Intercontinental Church Society and Guildhall Library, Corporation of London; from Guildhall Library MS. 15726/9)*

Charles B. Huleatt (seated on far right of middle row), along with the Wycliffe Hall class of 1887. Wycliffe Principal, the Reverend Canon Robert Girdlestone (with full beard, standing second from right in back row), told Huleatt, "There is one remedy and one only for this evil state of things, namely the *Gospel*." *(Reproduced by kind permission of Wycliffe Hall, Oxford)*

The Luxor Hotel: Thomas Cook's finest monument and Charles Huleatt's home away from home for a decade of winters: "a place of delights" for British expatriates. *(Matthew d'Ancona)*

The Nile River, the heart of Egypt, the basis of its burgeoning tourist industry, and the key to Thomas Cook's business empire. While taking tea in the impressive library on Archibald Henry Sayce's sizable houseboat, Huleatt would have had a view like this. *(Matthew d'Ancona)*

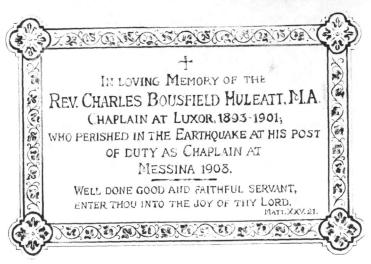

The little-noticed plaque to the chaplain's memory at the Luxor Hotel, funded by an appeal in *The Times* launched by Huleatt's mentor, the distinguished Egyptologist Archibald Henry Sayce. *(Matthew d'Ancona)*

Luxor Temple, the ancient monument a stone's throw from Huleatt's lodgings, was said to have been visited by Jesus and the Virgin Mary. The chaplain was fascinated by these "relics of heathendom."
(Matthew d'Ancona)

Carsten Peter Thiede and Christine Ferdinand, Fellow Librarian
of Magdalen College, Oxford, at the epifluorescent confocal laser
scanning microscope developed by Georg Masuch and Thiede for
the in-depth and three-dimensional analysis of ancient papyri.
(Carsten Peter Thiede)

The beautiful and enchanting campus of Magdalen College,
Oxford. "Its name, its future is in your hands," Huleatt was told
by Herbert Warren, its long-serving President.
*(Used by kind permission of the President and Fellows of Magdalen
College, Oxford)*

The Old Library at Magdalen College, where the Magdalen Papyrus
lay mostly unnoticed in a display case for nearly a century.
*(Used by kind permission of the President and Fellows
of Magdalen College, Oxford)*

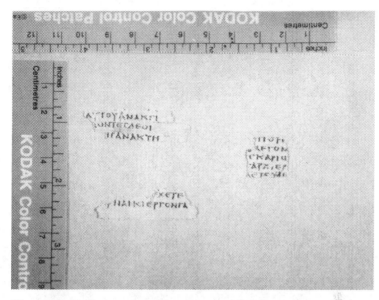

The Magdalen Papyrus, verso.
(6408/1, copyright photograph Magdalen College, Oxford)

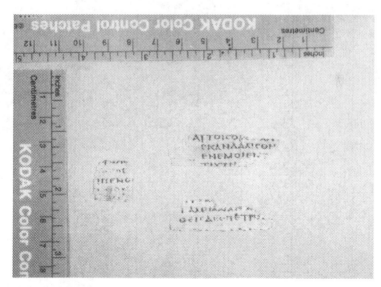

The Magdalen Papyrus, recto.
(6408/2, copyright photograph Magdalen College, Oxford)

Qumran manuscript fragment 7Q5,
identified as lines from St. Mark 6:52–53.
(Courtesy of the Israel Antiquities Authority)

wig curlers, incidentally, have been casually displayed near the papyrus in Magdalen's Old Library for most of this century—his successor, Frederic Bulley, and the classics tutor Herbert Warren were driving the college to the forefront of Oxford life.[9]

Warren, like William Rutherford, was a product of Jowett's Balliol, where he had been a spectacularly successful classics undergraduate. From 1878 to 1885, he was a tutor at Magdalen, importing Jowett's strong belief that undergraduate teaching should be at the heart of college life. Warren succeeded Bulley as President in 1885 at the remarkably early age of thirty-two and held the office until 1928. In those forty-three years, the character of the modern Magdalen was shaped, as Warren raised academic standards, increased the numbers of its undergraduates and—perhaps above all—defined its esprit de corps.

In 1932, Warren's friend and biographer Laurie Magnus described him as "the second Founder of Magdalen," a worthy successor to Bishop William Waynflete, and noted "his unforgotten method of making 'Magdalen men' out of sometimes reluctant material; of making the conception of a Magdalen man real and vital for life, as, by common consent, it had not been so made before his time."[10] There can be no doubt that Charles Huleatt was one such Magdalen man. That Warren liked and admired him is clear from a letter he wrote while Vice-Chancellor of Oxford University—a letter which appeared in *The Times* on May 25, 1909. "He was my pupil here," wrote Warren. "I had a very genuine regard for him. He was no common scholar; indeed he had a genius for textual criticism and kept up his interest in scholarship, both sacred and secular, in a way that not many do."

What sense of collective identity and institutional loyalty would Huleatt have taken from Magdalen when he left in 1886? He would never forget the deer park, the lawn in the cloisters, the afternoons wandering down Addison's Walk. But there was more to it than that. The year before Huleatt left the golden stones of Magdalen, on June 7, Warren gave a speech to the undergraduates of the college which does much to define the sense of mission with which they would have left Oxford.[11] Addressing the subject of "College Unity" on the last Sunday afternoon of the summer term, he took as his text St. Paul's Letter to the Ephesians: "I beseech you that ye walk worthy of the vocation wherein you are called."

Warren's speech was a hymn to duty, active living and a college ethos that celebrated the brilliant oarsman as well as the brilliant scholar. He singled out those "leaders among us" who were leaving the college. He urged each of the fortunate few before him to make something exceptional of himself:

> It is not a question of each one of us being conspicuous, each one of us doing much, each one of us being a leader, distinguished from the rest; we cannot all be that. But we can, we must, all be something, and it is enough if that something is on the side of right.[12]

Above all, he charged the undergraduates before him to remember that they were Magdalen men, citizens for life of a collegiate republic which he explicitly compared to Athens:

> Every one of us is a Magdalen man—the poorest, the least clever, the least conspicuous . . . We are either worthy of it, or we are not worthy of it. Its name, its fame is in our hands: we cannot disown it . . . you go carrying the name of this place with you everywhere.[13]

It was an injunction that Charles Huleatt would not forget. He would one day send the college an exceptional and sacred gift. He would try to be as worthy of his vocation as St. Paul and Herbert Warren would wish. But first he must find where it lay.

Man with a Mission

What can we know of Charles Huleatt? He was married twice, first to Edith Bury in 1892 and then to Caroline Wylie in 1900. His first wife died in labor in 1897, giving birth to a daughter, Edith Irene, who survived. Charles had three more children with Caroline: Charles Percy, born in 1901; Gwyneth Cornelia Charlotte, born in 1903; and Rhoda Muriel, born in 1904.

From the wreckage of their home in Messina, William Collins, Bishop of Gibraltar, retrieved a small bundle of letters, mostly from Caroline, which shed a little light upon her husband's nature.[14] They had first been engaged after he left Oxford, breaking off the betrothal in 1891. But Caroline seems never to have fallen out of love with her "beloved knight," her "Sir Galahad," and continued to write to him—often from St. Petersburg, where her family were in business.

The letters suggest that Charles was sometimes abrupt with her, intolerant of disagreement. "I know that in essentials we think alike & you will forgive me if I cannot always think the same as you in minor matters," she wrote on one occasion, "for you know that I w[oul]d never try to teach our little one, or any other child God may give us, anything that was not what you thought and wished."

In their long correspondence, Caroline endlessly reassured "Charlie dear" of her love and trust, but referred in a letter in January 1900 to the times when he had been "so outwardly cold." It is clear, too, that memory of Edith often came between them. "I think you will know that I can feel nothing but love for her," she wrote, "& if I write as if I forgot this, I do not for one minute forget it in my heart."

His demands upon his second wife were great. He told her that he "had failed in everything." He scolded her for proposing he take up an "easy post" in England and sending him a book entitled Rest. There are frequent references to his poor health and even to his "trying exile." But Caroline found reward in the fact that he treated her as a thinking person, quoted Ruskin to her in letters and turned to her "for intelligent intercourse on subjects of interest."

Charles Huleatt was a difficult, driven man whose yearnings could, it seems, be satisfied only by pious service to the Lord. If Magdalen College gave him an institutional home, the Evangelical movement provided him with a spiritual cause which was to shape his life. He was a man for whom the Word of God was the alpha and omega of faith, an implacable enemy of the High Church tendency, of the cult of priesthood and of the taste of nineteenth-century Anglicans for ritual. He believed in the literal truth of Scripture. If he ever suspected the true antiquity of the St. Matthew papyrus, this suspicion would merely have strengthened the deepest foundations of his faith. For an Evangelical of Huleatt's severity, the claim that the Gospels were written by contemporaries of Jesus was fundamental; it was not a matter for idle scholarly speculation. Every sentence in the Gospels was divinely authorized.

This aspect of Huleatt's character and beliefs is clear from those scattered remarks on doctrine and ecclesiastical matters made by him which have survived. While Anglican chaplain at Messina, he wrote to a friend deploring "the second-hand fallacies of Renan and Strauss," which, he claimed, exercised an even more pernicious influence upon the educated than "any Roman doctrine."[15] Huleatt's choice of heretic was appropriate to his times.

In 1835, David Friedrich Strauss (1808–74), a tutor at Tübingen University, had argued in *The Life of Jesus* that the discrepancies between the Gospels showed that they could not have been written by eyewitnesses and that the miracle stories were simply myths invented by much later writers. Thus, for instance, the account of the Transfiguration in the New Testament was regarded by Strauss as simply a mythical means of likening Jesus to Moses or—more obscurely—Socrates in Plato's *Symposium*. It was impossible, therefore, to write a meaningful life of Jesus. Strauss compared the sayings of Jesus to a broken necklace of pearls which "have been worked away from their original position and like rolling pebbles have been deposited in places to which they do not properly belong."

Seven decades later, in *The Quest of the Historical Jesus,* Albert Schweitzer would write that "[i]n order to understand Strauss one must love him. He was not the greatest, and not the deepest of theologians, but he was the most absolutely sincere." Strauss considered himself a true believer confronting the reality of faith and its relationship to Scripture. Yet to most of his contemporaries his work was at best outrageously iconoclastic and at worst pure blasphemy. Several attempts were made to ban the book, which was vilified in the press by writers often ignorant of his work. For his audacity, Strauss was expelled from his university and later became a humble schoolteacher.[16]

In his own *Life of Jesus* (1863), the French Catholic Ernest Renan (1823–92) drew a sharp distinction between the Jesus of history and the Christ of faith. He denied that any evidence for miracles acceptable to a historian had ever been produced. The life of Jesus was a purely human story of a man who more or less stumbled into martyrdom:

Did he remember the clear brooks of Galilee at which he might have slaked his thirst—the vine and the fig-tree beneath which he might have rested—the maidens who would perhaps have been willing to love him? Did he regret his too exalted nature? Did he, a martyr to his own greatness, weep that he had not remained the simple carpenter of Nazareth? We do not know![17]

These ideas proved influential as well as shocking. In the first three months of the book's publication, eight printings were required. George Eliot wrote of Renan's achievement: "We can never have a satisfactory basis for the history of the man Jesus, but that negation does not affect the Idea of the Christ in its historical influence or its great symbolic meanings."[18] Schweitzer dedicated an entire chapter of *The Quest* to Renan, celebrating his ability to make readers see "blue skies, seas of waving corn, distant mountains, gleaming lilies, in a landscape with the Lake of Gennesaret for its centre, and to hear with him in the whispering of the reeds the eternal melody of the Sermon on the Mount."[19]

This was the intellectual backdrop against which Charles Huleatt ministered and wrote. To a man of his unswerving belief in the Word, the campaign to drive an intellectual wedge between faith and history was to be opposed by all means available. Nor, it seems, was he afraid of the controversy which strong Evangelicalism tended to stir in the more skeptical age of Renan and Strauss. In a letter to *The Anglican Church Magazine* in 1904, for instance, he championed an openly sectarian approach to parish organization in the Church of England. "Is it not time to face the truth officially," he wrote, "and admit in our theory of organization, what we all admit in practice, that the Church of England contains two sets of Christians, with views as divergent as the politics of Liberals and Conservatives?" He contrasted the individual church where "the teacher bids his hearers to try his teaching only by the Word of God" with another where "they are expressly warned against opposing their own private judgment to the voice of the Church."

Better, he argued, that believers offended by the particular traditions upheld by their priests be able to transfer to another parish rather than slide into "Dissent or indifference."[20] Huleatt's plan was ostensibly offered in the spirit of friendship; but it was offered at all only because he believed some of the differences in question to be utterly irreconcilable. The subtext of his letter was the pang of conscience the true Evangelical felt in a congregation which did not share his values. Nor was Huleatt afraid of the fury which such views could provoke. Two years later, in the same publication, he prompted an angry exchange of letters with an outraged reader, writing under the pseudonym "An Anglican," who was appalled by Huleatt's description of the Virgin Mary as "a dead woman."

Huleatt replied disingenuously that "Anglican" 's objection was "quite unintelligible." But the polemical nature of the doctrinal point he (Huleatt) was trying to make was clear enough: "I intended to signify that Mary is removed by God from the possibility of intervening in our aid." In other words, Huleatt was sufficiently antagonized by the contrary belief in the Roman Catholic Church (as he observed it in Messina) to use language blunt enough to offend many of his fellow Anglicans.[21]

Uncompromising Evangelicalism was the core of Huleatt's adult identity. This was partly a dynastic characteristic. His wealthy maternal grandfather, Charles Bousfield, was a bounteous contributor to missionary organizations and was to fund Huleatt's theological studies as a candidate for the priesthood. The records of the Colonial and Continental Church Society for 1899 reveal that Bousfield—whom *The Times* later described as "a wealthy, and in his later years, somewhat eccentric philanthropist"[22]—had contributed more than £10,000 to their work, a fabulous sum in those days.[23] Eight years later, Huleatt himself, writing from Sicily, reminded the society that the late Bousfield's "abstemious self-denial" had paid for the Sailors' Rest at Messina. Huleatt family legend has it that £250,000 of bonds were found in his desk when he died.[24]

Though more often associated with Clapham and Cambridge, the Evangelical tradition was also a significant force at Oxford;[25] its Evangelicals formed, in the view of their historian, "not merely a party, but a school of thought."[26] Between 1807 and 1871, forty-five identifiable Evangelicals were elected to Oxford fellowships and tutorships, while twenty served the office of Select Preacher before the university in the same period. In 1877, the foundation of Wycliffe Hall, sister hall to Ridley Hall at Cambridge, gave Oxford a theological institution designed specifically for the ordination of young Evangelicals to the priesthood. Upon leaving Magdalen in 1886, Huleatt enrolled at Wycliffe and was a student there until 1888.

That he did so is a measure of his commitment to his beliefs. In its early years, Wycliffe Hall had great difficulty reaching its full complement; only ten students appear in the 1887 photograph, Huleatt among them. At Oxford, the new hall was regarded with a degree of suspicion; most colleges preferred graduates seeking ordination to do so at the diocesan theological schools or by remaining at their old university colleges. It was particularly unusual to spend two years at Wycliffe, as Huleatt did, although this may have been a reflection of affluence as much as commitment.

What would Huleatt have learned there? Wycliffe, named after Oxford's greatest biblical scholar, was founded as part of an Evangelical offensive to counteract the spread of rationalism, ritualism and High Church practices in the Church of England.[27] The teaching, organized by its principal, Robert Girdlestone, was intended to be practical rather than narrowly scholastic and to provide candidates for the priesthood with a command of Scripture, the techniques of preaching and other aspects of pastoral work. In essence, it served as an Evangelical seminary.

There were fixed times for morning and evening prayer, for lectures and for meals, and students were expected to act as Sunday school teachers or play a similar role in the life of local congregations. Typically, a week's schedule might include Monday, Wednesday and Friday lectures on subjects such as the Epistle to the Romans, textual interpretation, the names of God in the Bible and sermon preparation. On Tuesday, Thursday and Saturday, lectures might be given on "The Pentateuch; its Authenticity and Contents, (Historical, Legislative, Theological)." In the evenings, open discussions would be held on a broad range of subjects such as "Personal dealings with the careless and the anxious," "Reformatory work among London lads" and "Illustrations of Scripture from Josephus." More important than the detail of these classes, however, was the spiritual backbone of the place. In an 1878 prospectus for Wycliffe Hall, Girdlestone warned of the expectations that would be made of a candidate for ordination:

[T]here is *one thing* about which he ought to be firm and clear in his belief and teaching. Knowing as he does that beneath the civilized surface of society there lurks worldliness, sensuality, superstition, and atheism,—and feeling as he must the plague of his own heart, and his constant proneness to depart from the Living God, he ought to be absolutely certain that there is one remedy and one only for this evil state of things, namely *the Gospel* . . . Other doctrines must be held in their due proportion, but we are bound to keep the Gospel of CHRIST in the fore-front at all hazards.[28]

This might be a text for Charles Huleatt's later life and the Evangelicalism that would propel him until his death. Wycliffe Hall lacked the venerable grandeur and social confidence of Magdalen; Girdlestone was certainly much less of an Oxford grandee than Warren. Yet Huleatt's spell at this theological college was surely decisive in setting him on a path that led first to the papyrus and then to an untimely death.

To Luxor

For a high-minded Oxford classicist to seek patriotic employment overseas was, as we have seen, natural enough; all the more so for a young Evangelical with a strong sense of vocation. There were frequent missionary breakfasts at the university at which hundreds would gather to see off those who had chosen the evangelist's life.[29] Societies such as the Oxford Mission to Calcutta, founded at Christ Church in 1880, acted as a focus for such enterprises, while prospective missionaries like Huleatt could look for inspiration to the legends of great Oxford evangelists such as Henry Watson Fox (d. 1848), a Wadham man who had made his life's work in India, and Thomas French (d. 1891), Fellow of University College and Bishop of Lahore.[30]

This aspect of Oxonian romanticism was inextricably linked with the mythology of the Empire. As the Warden of Keble College, the Reverend W. Lock, put it in 1907: "The British Empire is itself an expression of the Christianity which the Church has to guard, and Christians have now not only to teach that the powers that be are ordained of God, but see to it that they act as powers so ordained."[31]

No organization better epitomized the sacred bond between God and Empire than the Colonial and Continental Church Society (C&CCS), to which Huleatt was to devote the rest of his life.[32] Founded in 1851 by the amalgamation of the Colonial Church Society and the Newfoundland School Society, the purpose of the C&CCS was to provide Evangelical clergymen, schoolteachers and missionaries for the territories of the Empire and Commonwealth and for British residents in other parts of the world. Its purpose was to minister to Greater Britain abroad; its doctrinal requirements were simple and conservative. A recruitment questionnaire drawn up in 1842 asked the candidate's views on "the sufficiency of the Holy Scriptures as the rule of Faith." Huleatt's response would have been clear enough.

After Wycliffe Hall, Huleatt was finally ordained in 1888 in Hereford Cathedral and joined the ministry as a curate at St. Mary's, Swansea, and then at St. Mark's Church, Broadwater Down, Sussex. Among the papers retrieved from the rubble at Messina in 1908 was a letter of recommendation written sixteen years previously by J. H. Townsend, Vicar of St. Mark's, who described Huleatt as "thoroughly loyal, reliable & hardworking. He has won the esteem of all in the parish in the short time that he has been here. The working men like him and the young men and lads have quite gathered round him. He is a good preacher & in preaching and visiting tries to reach the spirits of men and not only their understanding."

Huleatt, in other words, might have settled down to a productive and successful life as an English parish priest. Yet his sights were set elsewhere by this time. He spent the winter of 1890–91 as English chaplain at Luxor, an appointment he was to take up every winter from 1893 to 1901. His enthusiasm for the task was evident from the start, in a report he sent back to the C&CCS from Luxor Hotel.[33]

"Any detailed report of the winter's work would have to consist chiefly of a record of the kindness of all with whom I was brought in contact," he wrote. The presence of a resident winter chaplain in Luxor had, he said, become well known among travelers on the Nile, "so that in very many cases they shape their plans accordingly, and arrange to be at Luxor for Sunday, both on the voyage up and when coming down." Huleatt described the congregations as "very satisfactory,

though apt to fluctuate,'' and recalled that ''in one instance a gentleman, though in haste to reach Cairo, sacrificed two days' sight-seeing
in order to avail himself of the ministrations provided by the Colonial
and Continental Church Society.'' The congregation had even held a
successful Christmas service, with four or five carols sung, and the new
chaplain was also able to report the arrival of a communion table, the
gift of two lady worshippers.

What had led Huleatt to Upper Egypt? Once again, family connections had played a part. In July 1891, John Mason Cook, son of Thomas
Cook, wrote to the society seeking further information about the young
chaplain before he made a more formal appointment. ''The arrangement
he made with Mr. Huleatt was quite an exceptional one, he being the
son of an old personal friend of his . . . before a chaplain is appointed
he would like to know something of the clergyman it is proposed to
send.''[34] Evidently, Cook was soon given the reassurances he sought
and made the appointment a regular one.

This was a defining moment in Huleatt's life. In the summers to
come, he would hold temporary chaplaincies in Varese and Bad
Schwalbach, and would intermittently return to England to see his family. But Luxor unquestionably became his home and the center of his
activities. Doubtless the dry heat of the winter was appealing to someone who was so often in poor health. The Thomas Cook program did its
best to make the Luxor Hotel sound a blessed sanctuary for the invalid,
quoting a ''medical gentleman'' to that effect: ''Here the sick man finds
a friendly region where he can breathe the fresh out-door life-giving air,
and bask in the reviving rays of a generous Egyptian sun. Here he
discards the respirator; here he has no need of the stifling stove-heated
indoor refuge.''[35]

Egypt's fragile Christian inheritance seems also to have been part of
the attraction to Huleatt's missionary soul. ''It is much to be hoped that
the work of aiding the torpid Coptic Church to reform itself and to
revive Egyptian Christianity may soon be set about with greater vigour,''
he wrote to the society. ''It is much to be prayed and worked for that
Egyptian Christianity may once more dominate the land and be a power
for good, instead of remaining an obstacle to missionary enterprise, a
reproach to the name of Christ, and so singular a specimen of an effete
and fossilized church.''[36] The Cook family, famous for their upright

Evangelicalism, would have endorsed such sentiments. Huleatt certainly admired the "real Christianity" of his patron.

To be chaplain at the Luxor Hotel and thus a significant figure within the Thomas Cook organization was also to be part of an empire within an Empire. Since the nationalist uprising of 1882 and the British occupation of Egypt, Lord Cromer had been its Consul General and effective ruler. Yet many considered that true power lay with the Cook family, which, by transforming Egypt's tourist industry and infrastructure, achieved complete control over the Nile steamers and established an unofficial dynastic cult.[37] It was said that the Sphinx had broken its silence to congratulate Cook Pasha on his success, while at Aswan, there was a hieroglyphic inscription to the "king of Upper and Lower Egypt, John, son of the sun, Cook and Son, Lords of Egypt, Pharaoh of the boats of the north and south."

The Cook organization was considered by the natives to be far more accessible and trustworthy than the Cromer regime. Indeed, its assistance was often needed by the British administration, not least during Gordon's relief expedition, when Cook transported eighteen thousand troops more than five hundred miles. In 1889, *Vanity Fair* wrote of him that the "Sovereign becomes more and more potent as we get further up the Nile and here at Luxor, where a special hotel has arisen under the light of his countenance, he figures quite as a modern Amon-Ra."

Thus Huleatt—no stranger to grand institutions—had found himself part of a splendid court as well as chaplain in a humble mud-brick church which lacked electric lighting until 1898. The guests to whom he ministered were affluent travelers, some of whom would be staying in the hotel for their health or cruising slowly down the Nile on steamer or dahabeah. Once an unwelcoming village of mud huts, described by Florence Nightingale in 1849 as "fearful," Luxor had become a winter playground. Beside Huleatt's plaque is a brass portrait of Albert Ferdinand Pagnon, who, as Cook's agent, made the Luxor Hotel a luxurious sanatorium for the wealthy, a civilized oasis of palms and acacias with a billiard room, a tennis court, gardens, a smoking room and even a hairdresser's salon. Many of the guests were consumptives searching for respite from their condition in the dry air of Upper Egypt; others were unabashed pleasure-seekers. In 1892, the journalist Charles A. Cooper wrote gushingly of its charms in *The Scotsman:*

> Days at Luxor were delightful, and nights in the Luxor Hotel
> dreamless . . . Everything was clean and fresh and pleasant. The
> scent of mimosa flowers floated in at the window and open door.
> The sound of chirruping birds met your ear. The air seemed to be
> golden with the sunlight by day, and silvern with the moonlight at
> night. Tall palm-trees shaded you from the mid-day sun . . .
> Truly, the Luxor Hotel was for me a place of delights.[38]

Life at the hotel was cosmopolitan rather than secluded. In 1898, there
were reckoned to be fifty thousand visitors in Egypt; Cairo was even
referred to in the press as "a suburb of London," a caricature which
might as easily have been applied to Luxor. Huleatt would never have
wanted for like-minded company.

The Cook empire was also avowedly paternalist in spirit, a spirit in
which the young chaplain instinctively shared. It was traditional for
Europeans to give medical assistance to the natives wherever possible
and the Luxor Hotel's resident had made his services informally available
to sick villagers during the 1880s. In 1887, John Cook began collecting
donations for a native hospital, which was opened with great ceremony
by the Khedive of Egypt, Tewfik Pasha, in January 1891.

Huleatt was evidently impressed by the Khedive's speech declaring
the hospital open, in which he "made a striking comparison between the
colossal ruins left in the neighbourhood by the ambitious monarchs of
pagan days and the less pretentious building which he hoped would
remain for many long years to bear witness to the goodness of heart (he
might have said also the real Christianity) of Mr Cook and the English
speaking travellers on the Nile."[39] The chaplain was to remain closely
involved with the hospital, which by 1898 was seeing thirty-two thousand cases a year. Such, indeed, was his reputation there that the Luxor
Hospital Committee lobbied to have a ward endowed in his name after
his death.[40] The hospital still stands, a few minutes walk from the hotel,
but the chaplain's name is not remembered there today.

The Discovery of the St. Matthew Papyrus

That Charles Huleatt led a worthy life at Luxor is not in doubt. Yet the chaplaincy was not only an opportunity for Huleatt to serve God and his fellow man. To be in Egypt in these years was to be at the center of an extraordinary scholarly reconquest of the past. Napoleon's nine-volume *Description of Egypt*, published between 1809 and 1822, had reawakened the outside world to the majesty of Egyptian antiquity and heralded a century of groundbreaking Egyptology. In 1822, Jean-François Champollion had provided scholars with the key to the door by deciphering the ancient hieroglyphs which covered the walls of Egypt's monuments. In his wake followed a generation of brilliant archaeologists led by Auguste Mariette, founder of the Egyptian Antiquities Service, and Gaston Maspero, his successor. Luxor Temple, the pyramids at Giza, the Serapeum at Memphis and the tombs of Deir al-Bahri—all were excavated and investigated by men who were often left breathless by the pace of their own discoveries.

When Huleatt arrived in Egypt in 1890, major excavations had been under way at Luxor Temple for five years and for considerably longer at Karnak. In one report to his society, the chaplain wrote that the latter monument was "said to be the greatest ruin in the world" and noted with Evangelical approval that the temple confirmed "by the record on its walls the Bible account of Shishak's invasion of Judah." He thought Luxor Temple "scarcely less noble" and was fascinated by the "traces left of the time when Christians had consecrated these relics of heathendom to the service of their and our Lord and Master."[41]

But it was not only monuments that were being reclaimed from the earth and studied in the Near East. A wealth of manuscript evidence was also emerging, much of it early Christian in origin. In May 1844, the German linguist Konstantin von Tischendorf had found the Codex Sinaiticus at the Monastery of St. Catherine on the slopes of Mount Sinai (near the southern tip of the Sinai Peninsula), a fourth-century text of the Old and New Testaments which he instantly realized was "the most precious Biblical treasure in existence—a document whose age and importance exceeded that of all the manuscripts which I had ever examined during twenty years' study of the subject."[42]

This codex was written on vellum and would have needed the skin of 360 sheep and goats. Far more humble were the countless fragments of papyrus coming to light, naturally preserved for centuries by the dry Egyptian climate. The natives considered the papyrus plant sacred, claiming that its stem resembled a pyramid in cross section and that its stalks looked like the rays of the sun. For visiting scholars, however, the ancient papyri were precious as historical sources. As we have seen, Pliny the Elder believed that civilization depended on papyrus scrolls, "at the most for its life, and certainly for its memory." As a result, the script on papyri covered everything from the sayings of Jesus to laundry lists and receipts. Some were very long, such as the Prisse Papyrus (c. 2000 B.C.), which the French Egyptologist Achille Prisse d'Avennes had bought from a man from Gourna and presented as a gift to his motherland. Most, in contrast, were very small, tiny fragments of the past surviving to be puzzled over by posterity.[43]

Their survival was, of course, completely arbitrary. In the 1770s, for instance, papyri found at Giza were burned by natives because they liked the smell it created. But those that did survive were generating intense scholarly interest by the time Huleatt took up his post in Egypt. In 1877, Byzantine archives had been unearthed in the Fayyûm, while the great English Egyptologist Flinders Petrie had made major papyrus discoveries at Hawara. In 1895, crucially, the Egypt Exploration Fund decided to include the Graeco-Roman period in the scope of its research and funded one of Petrie's assistants, Bernard Grenfell, to search for further papyrus evidence.

In the years that followed, Grenfell's partnership with his Oxford friend Arthur Hunt yielded some of the most spectacular finds in the history of papyrology, notably at the former Hellenistic settlement of Oxyrynchus, 120 miles south of Cairo. Trawling through the town rubbish dumps, they discovered verses of Sappho and part of a lost play by Sophocles. One day, as he sorted through the scraps, Hunt's eye was caught by the word *karphos,* Greek for "small dry stalk" or "twig," a word which occurs six times in the Greek Bible and is part of a saying attributed to Jesus. The fragment, which included seven sayings (*logia*), was quickly identified as a noncanonical Gospel text, about a century older than the Codex Sinaiticus discovered by Tischendorf. Of this historic find, Grenfell remarked: ''I wouldn't have taken any one else's word, but Hunt does know his Bible.''[44]

Hunt was shortly to play an incidental but crucial role in the life of Charles Huleatt. There is no evidence that the two men knew each other. The regrettably poor sources for the Luxor chaplain's life have nothing to say about his reaction to these sensational discoveries. Yet it is inconceivable that he was not aware of and intrigued by them. This much can be guessed from the fact that one of his closest friends at Luxor was Archibald Henry Sayce (1845–1933), the distinguished Egyptologist and philologist.

Sayce had been a rising star in the Oxford firmament, a Fellow of The Queen's College by the age of twenty-five and a recognized authority on ancient inscriptions by thirty. In 1890, however, ill health and the curiosity of an intellectual pilgrim drove him to resign his Oxford post and make for Egypt, where he spent many winters in his large Nile boat, the *Istar,* which had a crew of nineteen and a library of two thousand volumes. In Egypt and England, he worked closely with Petrie on Greek papyri, an experience he describes in his memoirs as a private Renaissance of humanistic rediscovery and interpretation.[45] This autobiography records many visits to Luxor and at least two detours in the summer to Varese to see Huleatt. For his part, the chaplain later described Sayce as ''an old friend'' who had given him ''an entirely free hand'' to reprint his books and disseminate them among the English-speaking flock at Messina. It was to Sayce that Warren would write after Huleatt's death, remembering him with fondness, and Sayce who launched an appeal in *The Times* to fund the brass tablet to his memory at the Luxor Hotel.

In this scholar's presence, Huleatt would have experienced a boundless and infectious enthusiasm for the possibilities of papyrology. ''Countless manuscripts of priceless value have already perished,'' Sayce wrote in 1896. ''But the soil of Egypt is archaeologically almost inexhaustible, and the land of the Septuagint, of the Christian school of Alexandria, and of the passionate theology of a later epoch cannot fail to yield up other documents that will throw a flood of light on the early history of our faith.''[46] It is intriguing to speculate what Sayce might have made of the papyrus fragments which Huleatt sent to his old college five years later, and what advice he would have given to his younger friend as they took tea together in the library of his Nile boat. Sadly, the Sayce papers, now in the Bodleian Library, Oxford, include no correspondence between the two on this or any other subject. But it is reasonable to speculate that Huleatt would have maintained an amateur's interest in the emerging science of papyrology, if only to keep up with his scholarly friend.

At some stage during his time in Egypt, Charles Bousfield Huleatt came upon three scraps of papyrus which he considered very important. Before taking up his next post, in Messina, he arranged for his mother to send them to Magdalen, which she did by recorded delivery in October 1901, together with some rough notes by her son (now lost). Two months later, Huleatt himself wrote to the college librarian, H. A. Wilson, to check that the package had arrived and remarked regretfully en passant upon the recent robbery of mummies and papyri from one of the tombs at Luxor. This is the only record left to us of Huleatt's discovery and bequest of the Magdalen Papyrus—now the most widely discussed fragment of the New Testament in the world.

Where might he have come upon it? The market in such treasures was prodigious and still underregulated, in spite of the efforts of the Antiquities Service to prevent the unauthorized sale of discoveries. Writing in 1895, the author Henry Stanley was scandalized by the contempt in which such regulations were held in Luxor and by the trade in mummies and other antiquities, many of them fake. ''Oh certainly Thebes is the place to buy souvenirs,'' he wrote, recalling that one man had bought ''three men's heads, one woman's head, one child's head, six hands large and small, twelve feet, one plump infant's foot, one foot minus a toe, two ears, one part of a well-preserved face, two ibis mummies, one dog mummy.''[47]

Such grotesque and ghoulish purchases would never have been to Huleatt's taste, of course. But Stanley's example illustrates the easy availability of antiquities, authentic or otherwise. The *antika* shops and bazaars of Egypt were full of illicitly acquired goods, and scholars were frequently approached with papyri—those in Coptic and hieroglyphic script generally supposed by the natives to be more valuable than those in Greek. Sayce's memoirs make clear how liquid this market actually was.[48] Even a man as conscientious as Huleatt might not always have

been able to distinguish between a sale which was fully legitimate and
one which was not, especially if the papyrus was a gift from one of his
many admirers and acquaintances among the guests at the Luxor Hotel.

His overriding instinct was evidently to send the papyrus somewhere
where it would be safe. This it would certainly be at Magdalen. His alma
mater would indeed keep the fragments secure, safer than they would
ever be in a land of grave robbers, *antika* dealers and tourists. But the
college's reaction when presented with the papyrus was that of the
relaxed antiquarian rather than the fascinated scholar. Huleatt's letter of
December 1901 to the librarian reveals that the college had not even
acknowledged its receipt of the fragments in October. Arthur Hunt, a
Senior Demy at Magdalen from 1896 to 1900, before his election to a
fellowship at Lincoln, was asked to estimate the fragments' date, following Huleatt's own tentative suggestion that they might be third century.
Hunt, it seems, thought this too early and suggested that "they may be
assigned with more probability to the fourth century."[49]

The fragments were laid in a display cabinet in the Old Library, a
magnificent but inaccessible room up a steep staircase in the college
cloisters, which directly adjoin the President's lodgings. Gibbon used to
labor over his books there and Magdalen Fellows still use the library as a
quiet workplace away from the busier parts of college. It is Magdalen's
inner sanctum—although the papyrus was scarcely treated as its holiest
of holies. Instead, it lay among other college memorabilia—the corrected typescript of *Lady Windermere's Fan,* a portrait of Henrietta Maria—exciting little attention among the members of the college.

Arthur Hunt's verdict effectively snuffed out the debate on the fragments' age until after the Second World War. He found a scholarly
niche at Lincoln, while Grenfell returned to The Queen's College,
which has remained a stronghold of papyrology throughout the twentieth
century. In 1953, Colin Roberts redated the Magdalen papyrus to the
later second century and established its relationship to two scraps at the
Fundación San Lucas Evangelista, Barcelona.[50] That judgment was to
stand until Carsten Thiede's redating, more than forty years later. By
this stage, few Fellows of Magdalen even knew of the existence of the
papyrus.

Tragedy in Messina

The final chapter of Charles Huleatt's life—the postscript to his discovery of the papyrus—was one of personal fulfillment ending in unexpected tragedy. The chaplaincy at Messina in Sicily was perhaps one of the least desirable posts offered by the Colonial and Continental Church Society. Forty miles from Mount Etna, and facing Reggio di Calabria, Messina was one of the Mediterranean's busiest ports, a noisy, violent town in which crime, disease and disorder were part of everyday life. In 1895, the British Consul described it as "one of the worst that sailors can visit." Yet Huleatt seems to have taken to his new pastoral task with relish. The spiritual poverty of the place ignited his missionary instinct as never before.

His dispatches to the society became more frequent and more animated. In 1902, he reported "the prevalence not only of gross immorality but of spiritualism, which has become a sort of worship of evil spirits . . . there are families with English names such as Barrett and Hopkins whose members are unable to speak English."[51] The focus of his work was the Sailors' Rest and the Anglican church on the ground floor of a large warehouse building, described by the Bishop of Gibraltar as "the heart of the colony" of 130 people of English descent.[52] Huleatt's work was certainly more trying than his routine had been at Luxor. On one occasion, the chaplain was presented in his drawing room with a woman threatening to commit suicide unless he resolved a marital dispute with her husband.[53] On another, he found himself ministering in the hospital to a sailor who had been viciously attacked by a Sicilian. Yet such trials were outweighed by the small spiritual triumphs of his work—not least, persuading men of the sea to attend his services, teaching the English children of the colony the rudiments of Bible stories or baptizing a boy of fourteen whose drunken father had forgotten to arrange the sacrament when he was a baby. Huleatt also became independently involved in the conversion of Roman Catholics at Reggio di Calabria to the Church of England, providing a small congregation there with subsidy as well as moral support.

One of the many consolations of the hard work at Messina was friend-

ship with William Collins (1867–1911), the Bishop with responsibility
for European chaplaincies such as Huleatt's. (His successor, John Hind,
is responsible for Carsten Thiede's chaplaincy in Germany today.) Like
the chaplain, Collins suffered from delicate health and was a scholar; by
the age of twenty-six, he was a professor of ecclesiastical history. As
Bishop of Gibraltar, he was a tireless itinerant and came to know Huleatt
well, remembering him later as "an indefatigable worker, large-hearted
and tolerant, with a very true pastoral instinct."[54] Collins passed
through Messina on December 20, 1908, preached at the church and
was hoping to return before the end of the year. Eight days later, the
town was obliterated, left in ruins by a powerful earthquake, and thousands of Messinesi perished with it.[55]

The Bishop was in Malta when the earthquake struck and returned at
once on board the HMS *Minerva*. The scene of devastation—of biblical
proportions—that greeted him early on the morning of December 30
was one he would never forget:

> Whole streets were so filled up with almost impassable masses of
> *debris* that it was often difficult to recognise parts of the city which
> one had formerly known well. It was a veritable city of the dead
> . . . The survivors wandered aimlessly to and fro, with horror in
> their eyes, suffering agonies from thirst or hunger, and wearing
> anything they could lay their hands on.[56]

One survivor compared the horror to Dante's *Inferno*. Grimly, Collins
made his way to the ruins of the church, where he found Huleatt's robes
and the Christmas carol books lying open. The tall house on Via Tor-
rente Trapani where the chaplain lived in a household of nine had col-
lapsed. There were conflicting stories about the fate of the inhabitants.
On January 1, 1909, *The Times* reported that the Huleatt family had been
saved but had to correct itself five days later:

> The rescuers dug with frantic energy, being certain that Mr
> Huleatt, with his wife and four children, were under the ruins.
> The groans apparently proceeded from one person only. The diffi-
> culties encountered were very great, and in the evening another
> shock of earthquake rendered the work still more dangerous, for

the tottering walls around threatened to collapse. Finally, Mr Huleatt and one child were found in bed, crushed but recognizable, death having been instantaneous.

On January 12, Collins buried Percy Huleatt and Mrs. Kirby, an English lady who lived with the Huleatts. On February 3, Charles's and Caroline's bodies were laid to rest at Taormina. It was an ordeal from which the ailing Bishop never properly recovered, finding solace only in faith. "To those who see aright," he wrote ruefully, "sudden death loses its terrors, and fellowship in pain is gain."[57]

The grief expressed for Charles Bousfield Huleatt was widespread and sincere. The C&CCS reported that "the personal tributes to our departed friend have been numerous and have come from unexpected quarters." Sayce and the Cook family launched an appeal in *The Times* to fund a brass tablet to the chaplain's memory (the one at the Luxor Hotel). *The Oxford Magazine* remembered him as "a genuine scholar and a most amiable and devoted man."[58] In time, the whole family was commemorated by a plaque in St. Mary's Church, Shalford, headed FAITHFUL UNTO DEATH.

Thus ended a life of scholarly and clerical pilgrimage, a quest for knowledge and decency which had led Huleatt thousands of miles from home. By some, he might be judged a mediocrity who had lived his life in the shadow of his patrons: Rutherford, Warren, Cook, Sayce and Collins. Yet in his quiet but determined fashion, he had crusaded to save souls and to spread the Word. And, along the way, had he but known it, he had chanced upon a treasure far more precious to an Evangelical than a Holy Grail or a Crown of Thorns—a treasure that would one day prove how ancient the New Testament Scriptures truly are and cast doubt on the "second-hand fallacies" of Renan and Strauss. But that day had yet to come. For Charles Huleatt and the papyrus he found, decades of obscurity beckoned.

5

REDATING THE
MAGDALEN PAPYRUS

IF ACCEPTED, THIS DATE WOULD REVOLUTIONIZE OUR UNDERSTANDING OF
THE ORIGIN OF THE GOSPELS AND JUST ABOUT EVERY OTHER ASPECT OF EAR-
LIEST CHRISTIANITY.

—GRAHAM STANTON, *GOSPEL TRUTH?* (1995)

IT IS CLEAR THAT A PAPYROLOGICAL NEMESIS AWAITS THOSE WHO, WITHOUT
GOOD REASON, THROW AWAY EXPLICIT ANCIENT TESTIMONY.

—E. G. TURNER, *GREEK PAPYRI. AN INTRODUCTION* (1968)

Where Do We Begin?

"It would be a very brave man who would deny that such a text, or any
text, might be susceptible to further improvement": a wise insight by
the famous papyrologist Herbert C. Youtie. Unfortunately, perhaps, this
sage observation was published in a somewhat specialist collection of
lectures, and even specialists cannot read everything.[1] Thus, even
though papyrologists must be "very brave men" (and women), from
time to time—as we have seen in the preceding chapters—the "further
improvement" of existing texts and editions is not always a challenge
they relish. There are new papyri, unknown documents, desperately
waiting to be identified and published —several thousand in the Berlin
collection alone: more than enough for the next generation or two of
papyrologists. There are few incentives, therefore, to examine thoroughly a text published more than fifty years ago. In the case of the
Magdalen Papyrus of St. Matthew's Gospel, the reasons were obvious
enough.

There are now some one hundred New Testament papyri at museums
and libraries all over the world. Some were found and published last
century, others only a few years ago; others are still awaiting the day

when a scholar will have the time to publish them; and there are even some fragments which may or may not be part of the New Testament: small scraps, whose nature is hotly disputed among scholars. The oldest among these papyri are the very first remnants of the text of the Gospels, of St. Paul's letters and, indeed, of any of the twenty-seven writings collected in the New Testament. Some would say that they are the most valuable literary treasure of Christendom and, as such, a priceless part of mankind's heritage. In that light, every single New Testament papyrus deserves the most careful scrutiny. It demands the painstaking application of the papyrologist's and historian's tools. Nor is the art of the papyrologist static. New insights, improved analytical techniques and the latest generation of microscopes have ensured constant progress in the field. Hence it is always fair to ask: Does the work done fifty or one hundred years ago stand up today?

When the Reverend Charles Huleatt acquired these three fragments in Luxor and sent them to his old college, he knew that they contained phrases from St. Matthew's Gospel. He even had a vague idea of their date, but was content to leave a more scholarly assessment to the specialists back at Oxford. As we have seen, two of the greatest papyrologists of the time were Oxford men (both mentioned in Chapter 4). One of them, Arthur Hunt, was a member of Huleatt's former College, Magdalen; the other one, Bernard Grenfell, was a Fellow of The Queen's College, a couple of hundred yards along "the High" (Street). In 1898, as we saw in the preceding chapter, they had begun their joint work of editing the Oxyrhynchus Papyri: Greek, Latin and Coptic texts found—by them and by others—at the town of Oxyrhynchus in Upper Egypt. So vast was the number of papyri that even today, almost a hundred years later, not all of them have been published.

The discovery of those texts, their sheer number and variety, had unforeseeable consequences for the science of papyrology. For the first time, a cache of papyri had been discovered which included not one or two, but thousands of letters, documents, contracts, applications, poems, dramas and New Testaments texts. Here, at last, was a treasure trove of writings which could be compared to each other, dated and analyzed back and forth. The finds at Oxyrhynchus also covered several centuries and bore witness to a continuous culture from Hellenistic times, when the town was a Greek colony, to its later Roman status as a provincial capital and, finally, a Christian bishopric. Slowly, patterns of analysis appeared to emerge, which soon became a framework of scholarly yardsticks and categories. Grenfell and Hunt depended on a system of fixed coordinates to match the evidence—faced by hundreds, even thousands, of fragments, basic criteria were a means of survival. It was impossible to reinvent the wheel every time a new, unexpected papyrus with potentially mold-breaking characteristics turned up. One of these safety-net criteria was applied to the dating of codex fragments.

In classical antiquity, the scroll was the common format. It had text on the inner side only (with very few exceptions, one of which is mentioned in the New Testament: Revelation 5.1); rolled up, the scroll protected the writing inside. The length of a scroll was decided by the customer: sheet after sheet of papyrus, parchment or leather was attached to the next in the same way until the required length was reached. With appropriate practice, the finished product was easy to handle—and it was pleasant to look at. Even today, scrolls are used for valuable documents, contracts and certificates because of their traditional appeal. A codex, on the other hand, whatever its practical advantages, was a comparatively untidy affair. Sheets of papyrus were folded once, twice or more often to yield the required size—a process still used in modern book production. Although this was economical in that both sides of a "page" could be used for writing, it meant that the scribes had to use both surfaces, front (or recto, in technical terminology) and back (verso), rather than just the smooth, stylus-friendly inner surface of the scroll. This could cause problems for the scribe. When the papyrus fiber went "the wrong way," vertically rather than horizontally, letters could become irregular and less elegant, and ink would tend to flake off later. For a long time, until the second half of the first century, no one was interested in "inventing" the codex, although—as we saw in Chapter 3—precursors such as booklets of three, four or five wax tablets held together by leather strings were in general circulation.

In fact, at the end of the nineteenth century, when the Magdalen Papyrus came to light, and for much of the twentieth century, scholars were convinced that the codex had been invented and introduced by Christians, and systematically disseminated from scribal centers under the benevolent eye of the imperial authorities. When could this have happened? During the persecution-free lull after Decius, in the second half of the third century perhaps, and then, of course, with renewed vigor and encouragement under the first Christian emperor, Constantine, in the wake of the toleration Edict of Milan in A.D. 313. On this basis, there was no reason to assume that the codex preceded the later third century. The implications for dating were clear enough. It could be taken for granted that the possible date was the late third or early fourth century.

Yet this approach failed to differentiate between fact and presumption. There was no factual basis for assuming that the codex was a late Christian invention—we discussed this in Chapter 3. Texts and manuscripts can be dated in several ways. One of them is reliable information about related historical events. If archaeologists, in the year 3096, discovered a document referring to the Berlin Wall as a barrier between East and West, they would know immediately that this document could not have been written before A.D. 1961, the year in which the Wall was built. Nor could it have been written after A.D. 1989, the year in which the Wall was pulled down, heralding German reunification. It sounds simple, but it is essential. Sometimes, there is only one such date, as at the archaeological sites of Pompeii and Herculaneum: they were destroyed by an eruption of the Vesuvius volcano in A.D. 79. The tablets and papyri found there by archaeologists must, by definition, predate that year. Conversely, any fragment of a gospel must be later than A.D. 30, which is the year of the last events recorded in them. Anyone conversant with Latin literature would know that a similar date of reference existed for the codex: epigrams by the Roman poet Martial, who died in A.D. 102.

Martial, born in Spain, spent most of his active life in Rome. His poems, fifteen books in all, have survived the vagaries of time; most of them are short, trenchant satires, mercilessly attacking the decadence of Roman society. But Martial, like his fellow satirist Juvenal, often used very accurate, reliable sociological observations as a foil to his witticisms. One can learn more about Roman society of the late first and early second centuries from his writings than from many a learned study. One of Martial's quirkier pursuits was his attempt to encourage what we would call paperback editions of some of the classics: Homer, Virgil, Cicero, Livy, Ovid and others. In one of his poems, Epigram I.2, he praises the enterprise in the eloquent terminology of a professional public relations manager:

> If you want to take my books with you, wherever you go,
>> So that they may accompany you on long journeys,
>> Go and buy those small-size paperback editions.
>> Others fill your bookshelves, but mine are handy.
>> However, do not be ignorant and do not look in vain
>> All over Rome. I tell you where to go and find them:
>> Go straight to Secundus who once served under the learned
>>> Lucensis.
>> You will find him behind the Temple of Pax, at the
>>> Palladian market.

This epigram belongs to Martial's middle period, A.D. 84–86. The Latin words used to describe those paperbacks clearly refer to the codex, the book format with folded pages and text on both sides of the sheet. In other words, even before the first actual codex or codex fragment was rediscovered by archaeologists, there existed clear evidence for the existence of the codex in the eighties of the first century—New Testament times, in other words. Was Martial aware of Christian precursors? Needless to say, such a conclusion would be sheer speculation. But in view of Martial's testimony, it was always wrong to assume that codex fragments should be dated by definition to the late third or early fourth century. Yet this is precisely what happened, and even Bernard Grenfell and Arthur Hunt fell into their own trap. In 1898, they published a Latin codex fragment on vellum, found at Oxyrhynchus.[2] It is a fascinating text containing parts of a lost *History of the Macedonian Wars*. Their analysis of the handwriting led them to a very early date indeed: first century A.D., perhaps even before A.D. 79, the year of the eruption of Vesuvius—precisely the period of Martial's epigrams. However, they proceeded to assign it to the late third or even to the fourth century. Why? Simply *because* it was a vellum *codex*.

Scholarly prejudice can be an intellectual prison. When the Spanish papyrologist José O'Callaghan suggested in 1972 that there was a fragment of St. Mark's Gospel among the Dead Sea Scrolls, many critics rejected the identification out of hand because they "knew" that this Gospel could never have reached the Essene community at Qumran and Cave 7, where it was found. Today, we know much more about the Qumran community, as well as the origins of the scrolls and the Hebrew, Aramaic and Greek fragments, than we did in the 1970s. Even Jewish scholars like Shemaryahu Talmon, with no Christian axe to grind, have argued that the discovery of a Gospel fragment at Qumran is by no means a logical impossibility. It took us more than twenty years to reach this stage, and there are still Christian New Testament scholars who cannot come to terms with the idea of Christian texts at Qumran. In other words, the misassumptions made by Grenfell and Hunt are anything but relics of a bygone age. We now know that Hunt made a mistake when he looked at the Magdalen Papyrus codex in 1901 and decreed that it must be dated to the third, but "with more probability to the fourth century."[3] And yet, the methodology behind this error is still with us. Indeed, it has implications beyond the world of scholarship. As the famous "Seventeenth Devotion" of John Donne warns us, the intellectual issues which academics address must be seen in the broadest possible context: "No man is an island, entire of itself; every man is a piece of the continent, a part of the main." Texts, literary documents, belong to the continent of our shared heritage. We are responsible for their safekeeping in every sense of the word. Nothing undermines this inherited duty more gravely than the complacent assumption that conclusions reached by scholars in the past should not be challenged. Again, this point is best illustrated by an example.

When Carsten Thiede suggested that the Magdalen Papyrus and its two sister fragments in Barcelona should be dated to the first century A.D., toward A.D. 70 or even earlier, three principal lines of criticism emerged. First, it was argued that there was no Gospel according to St. Matthew at such an early date and that no such date could therefore be assigned to a papyrus fragment of it. Second, it was claimed that the author had overlooked the monograph on biblical uncials by the Italian scholar Guglielmo Cavallo, who states that this particular style was late, not early. Third, it was suggested that Thiede had based his redating on comparative material from areas of the Roman Empire which bore no relation to the origins of the Magdalen Papyrus. Other equally erroneous arguments followed. For example, since Charles Huleatt had bought the papyrus at Luxor in Egypt, it was alleged that it must be of Egyptian origin. If, as some claim to "know," there were no Christian scribal centers in first-century Egypt, the papyrus could not have been written in the first century.

These criticisms are ultimately self-defeating. Take the last objection, for instance. It is like saying that someone who bought a bottle of Chianti in London could not have done so in 1996, as there were no Italian vineyards and wineries in southern Britain at that time. This would be nonsense, since anyone can buy a Chianti in any number of shops in London. There may not be Italian vineyards in southern Britain, but there are wineries in Britain; and, as is the case all over Europe, many Italian wines are bottled outside their country of origin. It is the individual wine that has to be considered. Likewise, in papyrological terms, it is simply not possible to assert that a papyrus bought at Luxor must have been written at Luxor (or even in Egypt, for that matter). It could have come from practically anywhere in the Roman Empire (and beyond), imported, used, stored, forgotten or thrown away, redis- covered, and sold almost two thousand years later.

And what about those wineries or rather, scribal centers? Many En- glishmen are oblivious to wine producing and vineyards in their home country. Does that mean that they do not exist? Yet there the vineyards are, yielding some excellent crops and very palatable whites—in the Thames Valley, in Kent, in Norfolk and elsewhere. The only reason to assume that there were no Christian scribal centers in first-century Egypt is a lack of knowledge and sources to prove their existence. How would we know about such a center? It might be mentioned in litera- ture, by people who had seen it or used it. Alternatively, the evidence might be the existence of a document coming from such a scribal center.

We do know that there were first-century Christians in Egypt, in Alexandria for example. Alexandria was one of the focal points of Medi- terranean Judaism. In fact, one of the synagogues was so huge that the corporate "Amen" had to be signaled by flags. Increasingly, Jews in this city became Greek speakers—so much so, that by the third century B.C., their Hebrew was so deficient that the Bible had to be translated into Greek for them. This practical purpose lay behind the production of the Greek Old Testament, the so-called Septuagint, which soon spread all over the Roman Empire. With the advent of the New Testament, people even in Palestine often preferred to quote from the Greek translation rather than from the Hebrew original. Many of the Old Testament quotations in New Testament texts are taken from the Septuagint. Even the synagogal community of Alexandrian Jews in Jerusalem—mentioned in Acts 6:9—was Greek-speaking; their Bible would have been the Greek Septuagint.

But Alexandria was more than just a center of translators and scribes. Highly elaborate philosophical works were written here, such as the Book of Wisdom, which we still have in the Apocrypha to the Old Testament. And Philo, one of the greatest Jewish theologians and philosophers, an exact contemporary of the first Christian generation who lived from 15 B.C. to A.D. 50, was an Alexandrian; his works, written exclusively in Greek, combined Greek philosophy and cosmology with Jewish piety and influenced many Christian thinkers. Indeed, we already encounter one of these Christians in the pages of the New Testament: Apollos, the brilliant preacher and missionary, who is described as ''an eloquent man, well versed in the scriptures'' (Acts 18:24) and who later continued St. Paul's work in Corinth (Acts 18:27–19:1), was a Jew from Alexandria. Tradition has it that St. Mark lived in Alexandria for a long time, and that his Gospel, written in Rome, was received particularly warmly in this Egyptian cultural center, and was copied and distributed to other places of Christian worship. In the second century, one of the most eminent Christian authors was Clement of Alexandria. Born at Athens, he studied and taught in Alexandria—a shift of location which indicates the renown and cultural importance of the Egyptian city.

Against such a background, the argument that Christians could not have written, copied and distributed papyrus documents in first-century Egypt is quite implausible. They could, and they did. Thus, to rule out a first-century date for that papyrus of St. Matthew's Gospel because there allegedly were no Christian scribal centers in first-century Egypt is wishful thinking rather than sound scholarship. And even if no such centers existed, that would be insufficient grounds to reject an early date. The papyrus could have come from Rome, or Corinth, or any other place where real people lived in a real world.

This is a central observation which helps us to do justice to dates, periods and whole cultural environments. We are speaking of real, imaginable historical situations and of real people. Copying and distributing letters, books, gospels was not an abstract exercise; it took place in the context of a specific social world. St. Luke, for example, made excellent use of the system. He dedicated both his Gospel and its sequel, the Acts of the Apostles, to a high-ranking Roman civil servant, "His Excellency" Theophilus (Luke 1:3; Acts 1:1). In those times, dedicating a book to a person obliged him or her to pay for the copying and the distribution of the work. Thus, an impoverished poet would look for a wealthy patron, and if the poems were innovative or flattering enough, the customary system would be set in motion. In St. Luke's case, Theophilus himself was apparently eager to obtain the book—and the author provided him with an in-depth account so that he might "know the truth concerning the things of which you have been informed." A Roman of Theophilus's stature had easy access to the scriptoriums of the imperial administration, to individual scribes whom he could employ and, most important, to the so-called *tabellarii,* the efficient postmen of the Empire. Everyone could send mail even to distant destinations, using an irregular but efficient network of couriers. But it was the privilege of the nobility and of those in public service to use the imperial mail, which managed to cover vast distances in the shortest possible time. Both systems were capable of remarkable feats. Corinth (Greece) to Puteoli (Italy) in five days was normal, Rome to Alexandria in three days was possible under favorable weather conditions. Thessaloniki (northeastern Greece) to Ascalon (Palestine) in twelve days seems to have been routine, and there are other, similar examples. These achievements surpass even today's postal services. Who could hope to get a letter posted in Rome to Alexandria in three days, or even from Ascalon to modern Thessaloniki in twelve?

The outstanding efficiency of communication techniques in New Testament times must be seen as an integral part of our investigation of dates, contacts and mutual influence. Nothing happened in a social vacuum. Here, too, our understanding of first-century life continues to evolve. Until quite recently, for example, scholars assumed that the Dead Sea Scrolls were written and stored by an exclusivist Jewish sect of antiestablishment fundamentalists, the Essenes. These people had supposedly rejected the liberalism of the Jerusalem Temple and retreated to a sort of monastery in the Judaean desert, living an austere, highly disciplined life. By-products of this community were hundreds of scrolls with Old Testament texts, intricate commentaries and their own distinctive theology, which they then stored in caves. Somehow, Essene teaching then reached the early Christians, via John the Baptist perhaps, and all sorts of Qumranic elements finally found their way into Christian faith and liturgical practice. This romantic image, still current in many textbooks, has had to give way to a much more realistic and complex assessment. There is still a lunatic fringe of Qumran publications—books which claim that Jesus was crucified at Qumran and buried alive in Cave 7, or that the Dead Sea Scrolls contain coded information about St. Paul as a Roman secret agent and James the Just as Teacher of Righteousness, or that Qumran itself was a fortress manned by heavily armed zealots. Nonetheless, more respectable work has revealed much about Qumran, its inhabitants, their caves and their relationship to their social world.

The people at Qumran participated in the uncomplicated, rapid exchange of information available at the time. They imported scrolls, from Jerusalem, perhaps from Damascus and even from Rome: in Cave 7, a jar was found which carried the Hebrew inscription ROMA twice on its neck, indicating the origin of its contents. Only quite recently, in 1995, inscribed jar fragments were found on Masada, Herod's palace and fortress overlooking the Dead Sea, which was conquered by the Romans in A.D. 73. Those jars did not contain scrolls—they were wine jugs. Herod the Great had ordered his favorite wine from Italy, the renowned Falernian vintages from Campagna perhaps. And the sender dutifully indicated in Latin—a language obviously understood by the people at Masada—who the sender was and where the wine was to go. Those sherds are our only contemporary documents mentioning Herod's name in Latin. Doubtless these imports reflect the privilege of the upper classes, but they also say much about contemporary communications. Even up there, on a mountain fortress in the desert, overlooking the lifeless Dead Sea, a buyer could get vintage wine straight from his favorite vineyard in Italy, within a couple of weeks.

Wherever one looks, one is confronted by evidence of this first-century "internet." Should it surprise us, then, that Christian papyri were found at Qumran, or that the first thing a Roman officer did after the capture of Masada was to leave behind a papyrus sheet with the earliest extant quotation from Virgil?[4] Should it surprise us to find that there are, among hundreds of Hebrew and Aramaic texts rediscovered at Qumran, twenty-five Greek documents—six in Cave 4, nineteen in Cave 7—part and parcel of a multilingual society? Or, indeed, should it surprise us to realize that the nationalist defenders of Masada, in their last stand against the Roman Tenth Legion, were at home as much in Greek as in their traditional languages, Hebrew and Aramaic? These papyri, potsherds with Greek inscriptions and the Greek letter of Abascantos sent to his friend Judas at the oasis of Ein Gedi are all witnesses to the ease and fluency with which a basically alien tongue—and Greek was, after all, the cultural language of the Roman oppressors—could be integrated into everyday life. If we take those jars sent to Herod from Rome into account, then even Latin, the official language of the West, was anything but Greek to the inhabitants of Palestine.

St. Matthew's Gospel and its earliest surviving papyrus fragments must be considered in this context. It is important to realize that the social arrangements and the technology of the first century permitted extremely fast connections between people and an equally fast development of texts. Let us assume, as most scholars would do, that this gospel was written somewhere, such as Antioch, in the Syrian province of the Roman Empire. Antioch, modern Antakya in southeastern Turkey, is situated about 500 km (310 mi.) north of Jerusalem. Christians, as well as non-Christians, were regular travelers on the road between these cities. It was, so to speak, a routine journey, for private citizens as much as for merchants or postal services. A gospel—or any other book— written in Antioch and meant to be read in Jerusalem could easily have reached its destination within a week. Sent to Rome, or to Alexandria, the parcel would have gone by sea mail whenever possible. Even allowing for detours, it would have been in the hands of the local community before very long. In other words, where a gospel originally came from had little effect upon the time it took to reach its user. A papyrus of St. Matthew in Luxor? It could have been arranged a few weeks after the composition of St. Matthew's original. A scroll of St. Mark's Gospel at Qumran, sent from Rome? Wait a fortnight and it would be there, either via Jerusalem or straight from the port of Yafo or Caesarea Maritima, where the ship from Rome would have berthed.

Considered in such terms, this feasibility study sheds some of the trappings of the technical language which tends to confuse the average person. The first Christian communities took these speedy communications for granted. St. Paul, for example, tells the recipients of his Letter to the Colossians: "After this letter has been read among you, send it on to be read in the church of the Laodiceans, and get the letter from Laodicea for you to read yourselves" (Colossians 4:16). Did they have to convene a committee to find out how this could be done? Of course not; they knew exactly how to copy the letter—for they would have wanted to keep the original. And they knew how to send the copy on to Laodicea, by messenger or through the postal services, with a covering letter telling the Laodiceans to send their own missive. There is also an intriguing snippet of information preserved by Eusebius of Caesarea, the famous church historian, librarian and Bishop of Caesarea Maritima, who lived c. A.D. 260–340. He quotes a source from Rome, where St. Mark's Gospel was written after the departure of St. Peter from the city.[5] "And they [the Romans] say," Eusebius tells us, "that the Apostle, knowing by the revelation of the spirit to him what had been done, was pleased at their zeal and ratified the scripture for study in the churches."[6] Again, this arrangement would not have posed any logistical problems. Copies of this short gospel, dozens perhaps or more, could be produced even by amateur scribes, quickly and efficiently, and dispatched to the "churches," north, west, east or south, from Rome to Corinth, Jerusalem or Alexandria, and so on, where local scribes would copy the copies and pass them on in turn.

Applying the Tools of the Trade

Having seen how documents could be copied and carried in a short time to destinations throughout the Roman Empire, we can turn our attention to the key question of the comparative material which can be used for the dating (or indeed redating) of a manuscript like the Magdalen Papyrus. We should first consider the basic prerequisites for the papyrologist facing such a question. Confronted with a manuscript of unknown date, one describes its handwriting—its paleographic traits—and the manifold characteristics which distinguish the writer, like fingerprints: general appearance; typology of lines, such as average length, height, punctuation marks and so forth; individual, typical letters, their formation and the way they are linked (ligatures) or strictly separated. Following this procedure, one achieves a fairly comprehensive analysis of the script. The next step is fraught with danger, for now one has to compare the script to that of other papyri. We look for resemblances, for near or complete identity—in short, we apply the methods of comparative paleography to find a yardstick with which to suggest a plausible date. In doing so, however, we face two perils.

The first danger lies in the choice and quantity of comparable material to be used. In 1994, Carsten Thiede argued that manuscripts from three different places—from Qumran, from the Nahal Hever and from Herculaneum—would suggest a date during the second half of the first century for the Magdalen Papyrus, which came from a fourth place, Luxor. The point is that the latest possible archaeological date for anything found at Qumran is A.D. 68, and A.D. 79 for Herculaneum. He was immediately accused of making the false assumption that "all scribes of the Jewish diaspora wrote in the same script."[7] If put in such general terms, they probably did not. Taking into consideration the ease and speed of communication, exchange and textual development, Thiede would have confirmed the memorable statement by Peter Parsons of Oxford University, one of the key figures in international papyrology. Parsons, a master of the old school and hence not easily persuaded of new ideas and paradigms, was asked back in 1991 to date the inscription preserved on a vase discovered in Italy, at a site called Mola di Monte Gelato. He wrote:

> Palaeographers debate whether different areas practised different sorts of script. For documentary hands there is indeed some evidence of local peculiarities . . . For literary hands, the evidence itself . . . is minimal. The Monte Gelato text adds interestingly to that evidence, and speaks for uniformity: I can see nothing in the script that would be surprising in Greco-Egyptian manuscripts of the same period.[8]

Thus, the obvious conclusion was to look not only for comparative material from central Italy but also for "parallels from the other side of the Mediterranean."[9] These are precisely the methods Carsten Thiede used in redating the Magdalen Papyrus.

The second danger in choosing material for comparison lies in the fact that every good papyrologist knows hundreds if not thousands of papyri to which he, she or others have assigned dates. They are neatly categorized—one such category being the biblical uncial, already mentioned. And the papyrologist often yields to the temptation to open a scholarly drawer and place a new manuscript alongside others of a category which more or less seems to match, without wondering—from time to time, at least—if the category itself is correctly dated.

Applied to the Magdalen Papyrus, the category biblical uncial sounds good. No one doubts that the papyrus is biblical, and the letters on the fragment are of the type which is indeed uncial, that is, they are capital letters with certain forms of curvatures, inclinations and so on. Thus, those critics who drew attention to the biblical uncial and to Guglielmo Cavallo's standard textbook on this style[10] appeared to have a point. But the redating had not ignored Cavallo or the biblical uncial; it had been carried out in the spirit of objective analysis. The weakness of previous estimates was clear: certain key assumptions had persisted out of respect for tradition rather than because they were logically defensible.[11] The question was: What really *is* the closest possible approximation—is it the demonstrable result of applied comparison or the most attractive and familiar category?

When the British papyrologist Colin H. Roberts published the first edition of the Magdalen Papyrus in 1953, he knew of course that others had looked at it before, and he was aware of two unofficial datings: the one suggested by the Reverend Charles B. Huleatt, a date somewhere in the third century, and the oral assessment given to Magdalen College by its Fellow Arthur Hunt in 1901 and quoted in the librarian's report of that year. H. A. Wilson, the librarian, cited Hunt's tentative agreement with Huleatt, and the addition: "They may be assigned with more probability to the fourth century." This was, as we have seen, based on the faulty principle that manuscripts written in codex form could not be earlier than the third, preferably the fourth, century. As we saw in Chapter 3, this principle had already led to intellectual error in 1898, in Hunt and Grenfell's edition of the first-century *History of the Macedonian Wars,* to which they had assigned a late date, against their own better instincts, simply because it was a codex. Colin Roberts had freed himself from those shackles, and by looking at papyri that really were from the late third or early fourth century, he soon realized that the Magdalen Papyrus was considerably older.

His reasons were comparative, gleaned from an evaluation of general characteristics and individual letters in other papyri from the Berlin and Oxyrhynchus collections. A good example of this procedure can be found in his statement that "in the Magdalen fragments the minute *omikron* and the flat *omega,* common in third century hands, are absent."[12] Though his method helped to correct the error of Hunt, it suffered from the familiar problem of relativism. The papyri used by Roberts for comparison are neither precisely dated nor datable. Where it is possible to estimate a probable period, as in the case of the Oxyrhynchus Papyrus 661 (from the *Iambi* of Callimachus), one ends up with a late second-century date. Yet the manuscript is visibly later in its style than the Magdalen Papyrus.

With the late-second-century date proposed by Roberts, the papyrus had however gained a new significance. It now became the oldest known papyrus of St. Matthew's Gospel. But it never made the news, as Roberts himself had published the oldest known papyrus fragment of St. John's Gospel in 1935, dating it to the first quarter of the second century. Ever since, the St. John papyrus 𝔓52 (or John Rylands Greek 457, after the inventory number of its home, the John Rylands University Library, Manchester) has been considered by far the oldest surviving New Testament manuscript. Even Roberts's redating of the Magdalen Papyrus did not come remotely close to this. Three years later, in 1956, the status quo seemed to be confirmed by the Spanish papyrologist Ramón Roca-Puig, who published two further papyrus fragments from St. Matthew's Gospel at the Fundació Sant Lluc Evangelista. Roberts recognized them as fragments of the same codex to which the three Oxford fragments had once belonged; he wrote a "Complementary Note" to Roca-Puig's second edition, giving his undisputed reasons.[13] Both men agreed that the five fragments belonged to the late second century. The two most popular editions of the Greek New Testament followed Roberts and Roca-Puig almost entirely: "About 200" is the date given in the Greek New Testament of the United Bible Societies, and "ca. 200" is the date in the *Novum Testamentum Graece,* the so-called Nestle-Aland.

Thiede's re-edition of the Magdalen Papyrus was not primarily concerned with dates and redatings. He was interested in an improved edition of the Greek text of the fragments; only the Oxford scraps, in contrast to their Barcelona counterparts, were in need of such improvement. Thus, the Barcelona papyrus $\mathfrak{P}^{67}$ (or P. Barc. inv. 1) is hardly ever mentioned in the new edition. But since no one could possibly doubt the common origins of the five fragments in these two distant collections, any claim regarding the Oxford pieces would equally apply to the fragments at Barcelona. And since a discussion of the date is a natural part of any textual edition, the question had to be asked: Was Roberts right? Was he too daring, or not courageous enough, in his reversal of Hunt's previous, extremely late dating? Is there anything in our improved techniques, or in the growing number of papyri available for comparison, that would contribute to confirmation or correction of the date as it stood?

Perhaps the most fascinating group of new manuscripts from antiquity are the Dead Sea Scrolls. Discovered between 1947 and 1955, the scrolls and fragments from the Qumran Caves have been subjected to almost countless investigations, in a number of cases even to radiocarbon dating. But until Thiede's redating study, the Greek fragments among them had not been used for comparative purposes in dating other Greek literature, even though their latest possible date was certain: A.D. 68, the year when the settlement of Qumran and the caves were abandoned, immediately before the arrival of the Tenth Roman Legion "Fretensis."[14] The Qumran texts thus fulfilled one of the conditions of comparative paleography: they were datable, and therefore an ideal starting point for a reassessment of the date of the Magdalen Papyrus.

Being datable is not a particularly rare quality in a papyrus manuscript—all one needs are certain indications either from the archaeology of the place where the text was found or from a clue in the text itself. For example, in the same way as Qumran finds must precede the year A.D. 68, or texts found at Herculaneum and Pompeii must precede the year of the eruption of Mount Vesuvius, A.D. 79, a reference to the reign of emperor Domitian would date a papyrus to the period A.D. 81–96. Such a papyrus, the P. London 2078, a private letter, had been used by Colin Roberts in his search for the earliest end of the range in his dating of the St. John papyrus $\mathfrak{P}^{52}$. Compared to the archaeological dates of Qumran or the Vesuvius sites, it has an added advantage: although the date is not precise to the year, it provides both ends of the spectrum, the earliest and the latest possible year. Thus, we would call such a papyrus "datable" rather than "dated." Sometimes, archaeology and datability come together. At Pompeii, archaeologists discovered the house of the banker L. Caecilius Iucundus, containing an archive of tablets with his bills and accounts. They cover the period from A.D. 15 to 62.

Dated documents—that is, manuscripts with precise information about the year and, ideally, even the month and day—are rarer. Literary texts, novels, poems, plays and historical writings hardly ever include such evidence. In fact, the earliest Greek New Testament manuscript with a date is the minuscule number 461 at St. Petersburg, a Gospel codex of A.D. 835. The earliest dated manuscript of any biblical text is a Syriac Peshitta translation of Genesis and Exodus on vellum, dated to the year 775 of the Greek era, which is A.D. 463/64 in modern chronology. But even for the first century, nonbiblical dated manuscripts do exist and can be used comparatively.

How then do we proceed? There is the starting point, the date previously assigned to our Magdalen Papyrus, "late second century." It was a date arrived at by excluding all criteria which could—theoretically—be mustered in favor of a later date. A run through third- and first-century texts, just to make sure, confirms Roberts and Roca-Puig: whatever their earliest possible date, these fragments of St. Matthew's Gospel cannot be later than the late second century. So what about the second century itself? There are indeed a number of similarities in second-century hands, but they are tenuous and remote. Such manuscripts are better said to belong to the very late, "decadent" remnants of a style flourishing a century before. More important, those second-century manuscripts which look most comparable at first sight are themselves only indirectly dated; they are papyri with no related archaeological or internal chronological information. Such a state of affairs could lead one to accept a kind of stalemate, and to agree with the unproblematic, uncontroversial dating of Roberts. The stimulus to go on, however, came from Colin Roberts himself, albeit indirectly.

As we discuss in Chapter 6, one of the peculiar elements of the Magdalen Papyrus is the occurrence of so-called *nomina sacra* ("holy names")—abbreviations of the Greek words for "Lord" (*kyrios*) and "Jesus" (*iesous*). They became very popular in early Christianity, soon extending to other words like "God" (*theos*), "[Holy] Ghost" (*pneuma*) and many further terms related to the Holy Trinity. Usually, the first and the last letter would be used, *KS* for *kyrios, IS* for *iesous* and so forth, similar to our modern, if less holy "Mr." for "Mister" and "Dr." for "Doctor." The almost immediate and general acceptance of this new system of abbreviations was probably a conscious attempt to emulate the Jewish custom of abbreviating the name of God. It was a momentous decision, for—as we shall see—it implied a theological position about the nature and role of Jesus. Colin Roberts, for one, was convinced as early as 1979 that such a far-reaching system could not have been the spontaneous decision of an individual scribe. "The system was too complex for the ordinary scribe to operate without rules or an authoritative examplar," he wrote.[15] He suggested that the system was developed and introduced by one of the two early Christian communities which possessed such an authority, the Church at Jerusalem or the Church at Antioch, where the followers of Jesus were called Christians for the first time (Acts 11:26). Roberts tends to prefer Jerusalem because of its traditional authority—after all, it was the community of St. Peter and St. James. And of necessity he then opts for a date before A.D. 70, when the city and its Temple were destroyed. In fact, as the Christians left Jerusalem at the beginning of the Jewish revolt against the Romans, in A.D. 66,[16] this is the more probable "final date" for any directives from Jerusalem. However, there are reasons other than Roberts's incentive to investigate potentially early dates for such a papyrus—it is, after all, a *codex* fragment. And the origins of the codex, as the Italian papyrologist Italo Gallo reminds us, have been pushed back, by papyrologists, to the first century A.D., "not later than 70 A.D."[17] Whatever problems many theologians and New Testament scholars may have with the idea of such an early provenance of a codex papyrus from St. Matthew's Gospel, for technical, methodological reasons, the papyrologist has no choice but to address it. He is obliged to look into first-century comparative material when examining papyri that are codex fragments with *nomina sacra*.

This takes us back to Qumran, for, as we saw, the Dead Sea Scrolls from the Qumran Caves provide us with Greek texts which may be even older than the first century B.C., but which cannot be later than A.D. 68. Can they help us with a first marker? Following the rule of "general appearance," we scrutinize the six sizable texts found in Qumran Cave 4: fragments from four leather and from two papyrus scrolls.[18] And indeed, one of the leather scrolls and one of the papyri look promising enough to warrant closer investigation: both preserve passages from Leviticus (their official catalogue names are 4QLXXLev[a] and pap4QLXXLeviticus[b]). The papyrus consists of no fewer than ninety-five fragments, is written in a far from uniform script, as Peter Parsons noted when he commented on its date on behalf of the editors,[19] but could be dated to the mid-first century A.D. The general appearance does present similarities to the Magdalen Papyrus, especially on the more uniform fragments 24 and 25 (Leviticus 5:8–10); but it is, more particularly, some individual letters which are close to the Magdalen script, particularly the *alpha, beta, gamma, epsilon* and *omikron*. An interesting starting point but, on its own, not quite enough for a reliable dating reference.

Apart from the Leviticus papyrus, however, there is the leather manuscript from the same Old Testament book. And here the proximity in overall appearance and individual letters is indeed remarkable. Peter Parsons provides drawings of letters from the Qumran fragment, so as to highlight their characteristics. And although he must have been unaware of it, which makes the result even more objective, his drawings underline the likeness of the Qumran text and that of the Magdalen Papyrus still further. If anything, the Qumran leather manuscript is more archaic, as though it belongs to a slightly earlier period of the same style. More regularly than in the Magdalen Papyrus and its Barcelona counterpart, for example, letters touch or nearly touch each other. But even in the three small Magdalen fragments, we find this phenomenon (which was almost completely abandoned in second- and third-century Bible manuscripts) surprisingly often: between *epsilon* and *tau* (fragment 2, verso, line 2), between *upsilon* and *tau* (fragment 1, recto, line 4, and verso, line 2), between *nu* and *tau* (fragment 1, recto, line 3, and verso, line 3), between *alpha* and *iota* (fragment 2, recto, line 2) and between *nu* and *alpha* (fragment 2, verso, line 3).

ET	rather than	E T
YT	rather than	Y T
NT	rather than	N T
AI	rather than	A I
NA	rather than	N A

It may not be one of the most obvious characteristics of the Magdalen Papyrus, but it exists and must be noted.

And yet another similarity between the Oxford and Barcelona fragments of St. Matthew's Gospel on the one hand and the Leviticus leather text on the other is noteworthy. Unlike typical examples of the second-, third- or fourth-century biblical uncials, the letters on the two papyri are drawn in an even manner—the horizontal and vertical strokes are equally "thick." The leather scroll from Qumran Cave 4 shares this hallmark of an early style which predates the so-called biblical uncial.

Peter Parsons suggests a date in the late first century B.C. for the leather scroll, which would make it some fifty years or so older than the papyrus scroll of Leviticus found nearby. This makes sense, even though it is a dating based on indirect assumptions, as the Qumran leather Leviticus itself is not dated but merely datable, providing only the latest possible date. It makes sense because in the context of a Gospel papyrus, the earliest possible date that could be considered is the year of the last events accounted in the Gospels: the Crucifixion, Resurrection and Ascension of Jesus, which most scholars would place in A.D. 30.[20] To put it in different terms, the leather fragment 4QLXXLev[a] from Qumran Cave 4 provides us with a useful example of a Greek hand which indicates a mid-first-century date for the Magdalen Papyrus.

Staying with the Dead Sea Scrolls, our investigation takes us to Cave 7, just underneath Cave 4, overlooking the Wadi Qumran. Here, eighteen Greek papyrus fragments were discovered in 1955, as well as one reversed imprint of a Greek papyrus on hardened soil.[21] The importance of the texts from this cave was discussed in Chapter 3. At this juncture, we want to look only at their style of handwriting. It comes as no surprise that there is a range of different styles, but we do indeed find similar kinds of handwriting—in fragment 7Q6[1], for example, and, to a lesser degree, in fragments 7Q1 and 7Q2. But these two caves are not the only ones to harbor Greek finds among the Dead Sea Scrolls. We also have, for example, the Nahal Hever south of Qumran, where a sensational discovery came to light in August 1952. Unexpectedly, Bedouins found a cave with a Greek scroll of the Minor Prophets. In later years, Israeli archaeologists discovered the so-called Cave of Horrors and found nine further fragments of the same scroll. Two different scribes with their distinctive approaches had been employed to write this scroll. While scribe A comes closest to the Magdalen Papyrus, in general appearance as much as in individual letters, scribe B also offers a number of similarities, particularly and interestingly in those letters (*eta* and *mu*) which are less similar in the handwriting of scribe A. From time to time, both scribes use characteristics of the so-called *Zierstil* (decorated style) or *Häkchenstil* (hooked style), ornaments with added little dots and hooks, or elongations which were popular in the first centuries B.C. and A.D. Much less frequently, they also occur in the Magdalen Papyrus, for example in the letters *alpha, gamma, delta* and *lambda*. Scribe B furthermore brings to mind a style which has been named Herculanean, as most examples of it were discovered during the excavation of Herculaneum. Outside Herculaneum, Qumran fragment 7Q6[1] is another, albeit tiny, example of the same type. As we already know, texts from Herculaneum must predate A.D. 79. Quite without reference to this site, the Nahal Hever scroll of the Minor Prophets was indeed dated to the mid-first century A.D.[22]

Summing up the circumstantial evidence from the Dead Sea Scrolls, we can be satisfied that these Greek texts, dated to the mid-first century A.D. and earlier decades, are closer to the fragments of St. Matthew's Gospel than alternative second- or third-century papyri. This is sufficiently compelling to suggest a first-century date, a date toward A.D. 70 or earlier, for these Matthean fragments. And it is all the more thought-provoking because the Greek comparative material from Qumran has not been used before to date other Greek handwritings. Seeing the Dead Sea Scrolls in this context is a vital part of the debate. Again and again, we realize how much even the Dead Sea communities who collected these scrolls played an active part in a Greek-speaking world, which included such distant places as Rome, Herculaneum, Alexandria and Luxor.

And we must not overlook another Dead Sea site—Masada. Here, many people who had fled from Qumran just in time found refuge until the fortress was in turn overrun by the Romans in A.D. 73/74. For whatever reason, they took some of the Qumran scrolls with them to Masada, the *Sabbath Songs* for example, and they, like the other inhabitants, continued to live multilingually. Among the many Hebrew and Aramaic texts, quite a few Greek documents were found, including letters and notes with information on water or food supply and distribution. And, as so often in antiquity, potsherds, the so-called *ostraca,* were also used for all sorts of writing purposes, to record whole poems or for the briefest of communications. Among the Greek Masada *ostraca,* there are several examples which look familiar to us in our quest: they resemble the style of the Magdalen Papyrus. An astonishingly close match is the fragmentary *ostracon* no. 784, with the personal names of Lea and Amm[ias]. For obvious historical and archaeological reasons, this potsherd must be earlier than A.D. 73/74.[23]

Critics of such comparative work—particularly those who are inexperienced in paleography and are therefore prone to risk hasty judgments[24]—continue to argue that reference material from the Dead Sea Scrolls is not enough when considering a papyrus from Upper Egypt. However, we have exposed the weakness of this argument. Both the Greek Dead Sea Scrolls and the papyrus of St. Matthew could have come from practically anywhere in the Roman Empire, and theoretically even from the same place; looking for examples, a city like Alexandria, where both Jews and Christians were actively writing and copying, would be a likely candidate. Nonetheless, it is still useful to scrutinize Greek papyri which were, like the Magdalen Papyrus, found or acquired in Egypt. This is the next step in our quest for the evidence.

As we saw in Chapters 3 and 4, Egypt is the major source of all Greek manuscripts that have survived from antiquity, with Oxyrhynchus, some 400 km (c. 249 mi.) north of Luxor on the Upper Nile, the most famous site. First-century papyri are common enough at Oxyrhynchus, and by perusing the published finds, one soon comes across a striking manuscript—the oldest known papyrus of a work by the Greek comedian Aristophanes (c. 448–c. 380 B.C.), *Equites* (*The Knights*). It is written in a careful round hand, with medium to small letters, and is distinctly bilinear (that is, the letters are kept between two imagined lines), with the exception of the two letters with extensions: *phi* and *psi*. A technical description of this manuscript matches the Magdalen Papyrus as much as its general appearance and individual letters; in the Magdalen Papyrus, the two "exceptional" letters that do not keep within the lines, as it were, are *rho* and *tau*. The date assigned to this unique Aristophanes papyrus is "late first century B.C. or early first century A.D." And it does look, in many respects, like an older sister to the fragments from St. Matthew's Gospel.

The Qumran texts are safely datable, at one end of the spectrum. But neither the leather scroll of the Minor Prophets nor this Aristophanes papyrus is dated or datable; their dates had to be ascertained by comparative methods. Thus, we encounter one of the inherent dangers of the dating process. By depending exclusively on such manuscripts, one could find oneself in a fragile building of loose data only kept upright because the pieces of evidence happen to be leaning against each other—much as in a house of cards. In the words of the famous British theologian Austin Farrer, commenting not on papyri but on the dating of New Testament writings: "The datings of all these books are like a line of tipsy revellers walking home arm-in-arm; each is kept in position by the others and none is firmly grounded. The whole series can lurch five years this way or that, and still not collide with a solid obstacle."[25] And similarly, relying on the range of dates associated with a particular style, be it called biblical uncial, decorated or some other name, is like a straitjacket which prevents us from looking at individual cases on their merits. Any attempt at "precision dating," difficult as it is and will always remain, obviously depends on one's readiness to keep an open mind and to be prepared for an exception to, rather than a confirmation of, the rule. The great Cambridge Latinist and poet A. E. Housman summed this up in a comment on textual criticism which also applies to these areas of paleography:

> Textual criticism is . . . not susceptible of hard-and-fast rules. It would be much easier if it were; and that is why people try to pretend that it is, or at least behave as if they thought so. Of course you can have hard-and-fast rules if you like, but then you will have false rules, and they will lead you wrong; because their simplicity will render them inapplicable to problems which are not simple, but complicated by the play of personality. A textual critic engaged upon his business is not at all like Newton investigating the motions

of the planets; he is much more like a dog hunting for fleas. If a dog hunted for fleas on mathematical principles, basing his researches on statistics of area and population, he would never catch a flea except by accident. They require to be treated as individuals; and every problem which presents itself to the textual critic must be regarded as possibly unique.[26]

What we need therefore, at this point, is a precisely dated and possibly unique manuscript which corroborates the results reached so far. And such a manuscript, a dated papyrus resembling the Magdalen Papyrus almost like a twin—in general appearance and in the shape and formation of individual letters—does indeed exist. By appropriate coincidence, it comes from Oxyrhynchus, and was published in the second volume of the Oxyrhynchus Papyri in 1899. Two years before the Magdalen Papyrus reached Oxford, the one dated papyrus that helps us to pinpoint its date was edited by Bernard Grenfell and Arthur Hunt for the Egypt Exploration Fund in London.[27] This papyrus is a fascinating document in its own right: it is a letter written by (or on behalf of) the Egyptian farmer Harmiysis to the civil servant Papiskos and his colleagues at Oxyrhynchus. He tells the appropriate authorities, in remarkably clear, careful uncial handwriting, that he had twelve lambs some time ago and now wants to add seven new lambs to that number. At Oxyrhynchus, three officials signed the letter with their attestations, in their own distinctive, hurried cursive styles. All four, the farmer and the three officials, date the document. Harmiysis, in the common, florid style of the time, has this to say: "I declared, in the present 12th year of Nero Klaudios Kaisar Sebastos Germanikos the Autokrator, at the abovementioned [town of] Phthochis, that I have twelve lambs from my stock of animals." Translated into modern chronology, this twelfth year of Nero's reign is the period A.D. 65/66. The three officials, in their attestations, are slightly more bureaucratic and confirm the seven new lambs with the date "In the year 12 of Nero the Lord, Epeiph 30"—which is, according to our calendar, July 24, 66. Thus we have a precise date and, into the bargain, a reference to Nero as "Lord"—*kyrios* in Greek—which is of course the title of God in the Old Testament and of God and Jesus in the New. This formal imperial address—and formal it must have been, since the three civil servants used it three times—was anathema to both Jews and Christians. Any reader of the Magdalen Papyrus can understand the implications by looking at the recto of fragment 3 (Matthew 26:22–23), where "Lord" (*kyrios*) is used by the disciples in addressing Jesus, and where it is abbreviated as a "holy name," a *nomen sacrum*.

In a nutshell, then, our tour of indirectly dated, datable and precisely dated papyri from the period suggested by Colin Roberts and Italo Gallo has reached a conclusive result. The comparable material yields a date of c. A.D. 66, with a distinct tendency toward an even slightly earlier date. Conversely, there is no equally conclusive, comparable material from later periods. Thus, the usual paleographic "margin of error" would allow for earlier, but not for later, dates: the fragments at Oxford and at Barcelona belong to a particular type of uncial writing that flourished in the mid-first century A.D., with precursors at the beginning of the century. Since the text on the fragments belongs to a complete gospel, as we saw in Chapter 3, rather than a separate, earlier collection of Jesus' sayings or Passion Stories, we also know that the manuscript cannot predate the year A.D. 30. In other words, and as we noticed in the comparison with the Qumran leather scroll and the Aristophanes papyrus, the St. Matthew fragments represent the last phase of this type of handwriting.

Remaining Challenges

The Oxford and Barcelona fragments come from a codex. As we saw in Chapter 3, the Christian codex presupposes the Christian scroll. St. Matthew's original—the lost "first scroll," so to speak—necessarily precedes the approximate date of c. A.D. 66 by a number of years. Small wonder that this claim is unpopular with those New Testament scholars who are convinced that St. Matthew's Gospel is a very late community creation, artfully describing Jesus as miracle worker, theological thinker and prophet according to the liturgical need of the eighties of the first century. To other scholars and many ordinary Christians who have always been convinced that the Gospels consist of trustworthy eyewitness material from apostolic times, the result has come as no surprise. The papyrologist can only offer his findings without joining the fray. Papyrological analysis, the editing and dating of ancient manuscripts, must be conducted free from theological and doctrinal agendas. But it is of course quite legitimate to point out where the consequences of papyrology and paleography affect other disciplines. The worldwide sensation caused by the redating of the Magdalen Papyrus reflected its impact on a broad range of orthodoxies about the early Church, the historic Jesus and the origins of the Gospels. In our final chapter, we examine this impact.

The quest does not end at this point. Let us ask two simple questions. If two papyri of St. Matthew's Gospel, one of St. Luke and—following the datings suggested by Herbert Hunger and Young-Kyu Kim—one papyrus codex each of St. John and of the Pauline Epistles can be redated to the first and early second centuries, respectively, should we not persevere and continue our investigation into other papyri as well? Since, as we have seen, the biblical uncial category has been mislabeled, should we not look afresh at our scholarly assumptions and establish whether there are other early papyri which may be much older than has hitherto been assumed? There are plenty of candidates.

To remain with St. Matthew's Gospel, there is the $\mathfrak{P}^{77}$ from Oxyrhynchus (P. Oxy. 2683), a small papyrus codex fragment preserving St. Matthew 23:30–39. Its editors, among them John Rea and Peter Parsons, dated it to the late second or early third century; Philip W. Comfort suggested c. A.D. 150.[28] It is decidedly later than the Magdalen Papyrus, less carefully written but clearly in the same category as, say, the St. John papyrus at Manchester, the $\mathfrak{P}^{52}$, or Gr.P. 457, which has been dated to the first quarter of the second century but could be still older, as we saw. Another example from the same gospel—in fact no. 1 in the list of all New Testament papyri—is $\mathfrak{P}^1$, or P. Oxy. 2, now at the University of Pennsylvania in Philadelphia, which includes St. Matthew 1:1–9, 12 and 14–20. It is a magnificent example of a precise, almost elaborate hand, and the third-century date commonly ascribed to it is definitely much too late. One could not place it in the same early period as the Magdalen and Barcelona fragments, or even the Paris St. Luke, but it is not much later.[29]

Other papyrus fragments from other gospels also strongly suggest earlier dates. Take the $\mathfrak{P}^5$, or P. Oxy. 208, with passages from St. John, chapters 1, 16 and 20, now at the British Library, London. Its common

date, "third century," is as widely accepted as it is deceptive and late.[30]
Let us look at the 𝔓[69], or P. Oxy. 2383, at the Ashmolean Museum,
Oxford, with St. Luke 22:41, 45–48 and 58–61. Freed from the preoc-
cupation with "biblical uncial," who could *now* conceivably date it as
late as the third century—as it is at the moment? When Edgar Lobel,
Colin Roberts and others first edited it in 1957,[31] they were limited by
the scholarly orthodoxy of their time, which enabled Roberts to see that
Arthur Hunt's fourth-century dating was wrong, but which also prevented him from probing deeper—as he was eventually to do with his
work on the origins of the codex. A thorough reassessment of the 𝔓[69]
might well show its closeness to the Lukan papyrus at the Bibliothèque
Nationale, Paris, with its new, early-second-century or even late-first-
century date.

And we could go on. There is the 𝔓[70], or P. Oxy. 2384, with parts at
the Ashmolean Museum, Oxford, and others at the Papyrological Institute G. Vitelli in Florence. Fragments from St. Matthew, chapters 2, 3,
11, 12 and 24. Third century? Only if tradition holds sway over new
thinking. However, one recent edition of a New Testament papyrus has
risked a comparatively early date. T. C. Skeat dated the papyrus codex
fragment 𝔓[90], or P. Oxy. 3523, with St. John 18:36–19:7, now at the
Ashmolean Museum, Oxford, to the (late) second century.[32] He was
attacked for his courage, but he is right, if perhaps a little too cautious.
A mid- to early-second-century date appears to be more likely, given the
new range of comparative options we have been discussing. Skeat, at any
rate, has shown that progress is possible even within the traditional
paradigm, of which he is undoubtedly one of the great and undisputed
proponents. He may be less courageous in other areas, but here, for
once, he has given us another good reason to pursue this process of
paleographic reevaluation. One thing is certain: if the 𝔓[90] belongs to the
second century, as Skeat maintains, the decidedly older paleographic
characteristics of the Magdalen Papyrus put its considerably earlier date
beyond reasonable doubt.

These are only a few examples of what has already been done to
redate New Testament origins, and of what still needs to be done. The
worldwide sensation arising out of the redating of the St. Matthew
papyrus at Magdalen College, Oxford, is not an end in itself but merely
a beginning.

6

SCRIBES AND CHRISTIANITY

WHAT HAPPY APPLICATION, WHAT PRAISEWORTHY INDUSTRY, TO PREACH TO
MEN BY MEANS OF THE HAND, TO UNTIE THE TONGUE BY MEANS OF THE
FINGERS, TO BRING QUIET SALVATION TO MORTALS, AND TO FIGHT THE
DEVIL'S INSIDIOUS WILES WITH PEN AND INK! FOR EVERY WORD OF THE LORD
WRITTEN BY THE SCRIBE IS A WOUND INFLICTED ON SATAN. AND SO, THOUGH
SEATED IN ONE SPOT, THE SCRIBE TRAVERSES DIVERSE LANDS THROUGH THE
DISSEMINATION OF WHAT HE HAS WRITTEN.

—CASSIODORUS, *INSTITUTIONES* (C. A.D. 536)

DESPITE A WIDELY HELD OPINION TO THE CONTRARY, CLASSICAL STUDIES
MAKE RAPID ADVANCES.

—L. D. REYNOLDS AND N. G. WILSON, *SCRIBES AND SCHOLARS: A GUIDE TO THE
TRANSMISSION OF GREEK AND LATIN LITERATURE* (1991)

WHAT CAN WE know about the men and women who first used
the Magdalen Papyrus more than nineteen hundred years ago? How
educated and skilled were they? And what do these tiny fragments tell us
about the doctrinal development of early Christianity? As we have seen
in Chapter 5, and as has been demonstrated time and again by archaeologists, historians and historically trained New Testament scholars, Jewish society in first-century Palestine was trilingual. Hebrew (the language of the synagogue and Temple), Aramaic (the traditional everyday
language) and Greek (the cultural language of the eastern Mediterranean
countries ever since the Greeks had conquered them) were accessible to
everyone, in spoken and literary language. Some, particularly those who
were dealing with the Roman administration, would have acquired a
working knowledge of Latin. That the Romans also used Latin in Palestine, in spite of their own fluency in Greek, is obvious from the Latin
Pontius Pilate Inscription found at Caesarea Maritima, the only extant

inscription mentioning the name of Pilate. It is part of Pilate's dedication of a *Tiberieum,* a building in honor of Emperor Tiberius. It is also obvious from St. John 19:20, where the inscription which Pontius Pilate had fixed to the cross of Jesus is described: "This notice was read by many of the Jews, because the place where Jesus was crucified was near the city, and the writing was in Hebrew, Latin and Greek."

A Multilingual Society

Needless to say, not everyone was equally gifted. Even an otherwise intelligent man like the Jewish historian Flavius Josephus admitted that he found it difficult to attain fluency in Greek and to get rid of his accent (although some of this self-critique may be a so-called *captatio benevolentiae,* the popular rhetorical attempt to elicit a flattering reply). Even the New Testament is full of instances where an acute awareness of Greek language and Greek (or Hellenistic) culture shines through. Bethsaida, the town where Simon, later to be called Peter, and his brother Andrew grew up, belonged to the realm of the tetrarch Philippus, who had done much to Hellenize the area. Personal names are indicative of the popularity of these measures: Andrew, for example, is a thoroughly Greek name, and even Simon is bicultural. In literature, the name Simon first occurs in the lines of a Greek play, not a Hebrew text—in Aristophanes' comedy *The Clouds,* verse 351, written in 423 B.C. A third disciple, Philip, also from Bethsaida (St. John 1:44), is also Greek-named. This site, discovered by the Benedictine monk and archaeologist Bargil Pixner, was recently described by the American theologian Elizabeth McNamer as, from a Christian point of view, "the most important town after Jerusalem."[1] Among the discoveries at Bethsaida: a fisherman's house with anchors, fishing hooks and a needle for mending nets. A wine cellar was found, an oven and two basalt slabs on top of each other, used for grinding grain. McNamer explained what happened after this discovery: "One of my students tried to push the upper stone and she couldn't. Then I had two of them push it. And of course, Jesus said, "Two women will be grinding" (St. Matthew 24:41), and it does take two to do this."

Jesus himself was brought up in Nazareth, only 6 km (3³/₄ mi.) or one and a half hours' walking distance from Sepphoris, which was just being rebuilt as the capital of Galilee during his youth. Some scholars maintain that Jesus and his father, Joseph, both builders by profession, actively participated in the construction of Sepphoris. (The Greek word *tecton* in St. Matthew 13:55 does not mean "carpenter," as most Bibles mistranslate it, but "builder"—we can still recognize the word in our modern "architect," the "archi-tecton," or arch-builder, as it were.) Sepphoris, again, was a profoundly Hellenized place. Contemporary inscriptions demonstrate as much, as does the magnificent theater, which was built while Jesus was a young man. Even in Palestine, plays were performed exclusively in Greek, for a Greek-speaking population; the theater of Sepphoris was capable of seating five thousand spectators in a town of twenty-five thousand inhabitants. Given this ratio, we can surmise that a certain mastery of Greek, sufficient at least to understand Greek plays, must have been widespread beneath the upper echelons of first-century Jewish society in Galilee, the home county of Jesus and his disciples.

What about the stories told in the New Testament itself? No one would seriously doubt that Jesus' native language was Aramaic and that he knew how to read Hebrew. We find evidence of the latter in St. Luke 4:16–30, where he unrolls a scroll of Isaiah, reads from it and interprets the text. But at least one direct piece of evidence and a number of indirect ones show that he was also able to speak Greek. To begin with, there is the incident of his meeting with the Syro-Phoenician woman in "the territory of Tyre" (St. Mark 7:24–30). St. Mark, slightly more interested in linguistic subtleties than the other Gospel authors—from time to time he uses Latin, Greek and Aramaic technical terms, always with translation—offers an illuminating snippet of information in 7:26. The Greek text, *He de gyne en Hellenís,* means "And the woman was Greek-speaking."[2] Thus, St. Mark informs us, almost in passing, that her ensuing conversation with Jesus was conducted in Greek. A similar usage appears in St. Mark 12:13–17, the incident of Jesus and the Pharisees debating the tribute to Caesar. The German archaeologist and New Testament scholar Benedikt Schwank demonstrated some time ago that this conversation must have been conducted in Greek.[3] Between 37 B.C. and A.D. 67, not a single coin with a Hebrew or Aramaic inscription was allowed into or minted in Palestine. The text on the coins was

Greek, and occasionally—if the money had come via Lyons in France, for example—in Latin. However, in this scene, everything depends on the text on the coin, right up to Jesus' punch line, which, in any case, cannot be translated into equally effective Aramaic: "Give to Caesar what belongs to Caesar, and to God what belongs to God." Indeed, such a coin, with a portrait of the emperor Tiberius, was anathema to orthodox Jews—while the portrait itself violated the second commandment, the inscription also included the title of the Caesar as the son of the DIVUS AUGUSTUS, the God (or the deified) Augustus. This was blasphemy, fully understood as such by all those who handled such coins, which made Jesus' conclusion all the more telling, of course. And it was fully understood only because it was in Greek.

Incidentally, in the same incident, Jesus uses a term borrowed from the language of the Greek theater. He calls the Pharisees "hypocrites"—indirectly, in the words of St. Mark 12:15: *hypókrisis* ("hypocrisy"); and directly, in form of an address, in the parallel text, of St. Matthew 22:18, where Jesus accuses them: *"hypokritai!"* ("You hypocrites!"). The Greek word means "actors"—and hence people who pretend, who act a role. We may speculate that Jesus derived this word, rarely used in its figurative sense before his time, from his experience as a theatergoer at Sepphoris. Other, indirect examples of situations where he might have used Greek have been examined: the interrogation by Pilate and the scene in the garden, after the Resurrection, where the risen Christ meets Mary Magdalene (St. John 20:11–28). Apparently, the conversation between the two took place in Greek, a language not inappropriate for a discussion with the gardener (for whom Mary mistook Jesus), until he addresses her by her name. Only then does she turn round to face him, and to say in Aramaic, *"Rabbuni"* ("Master"): a sudden, conscious change of idiom. St. John's delightfully precise depiction of this dramatic scene could well contain sociological information about the use of languages in first-century Palestine. But this may be open to question. A clear example which tells us much about the nuances of the multilingual society to which the first Christians quite naturally belonged occurs in the Acts of the Apostles.

St. Paul, himself a well-educated Jew of Pharisaic origins, capable of quoting Greek authors whenever he saw fit (Aratus in Acts 17:28, Menander in 1 Corinthians 15:33, Epimenides in Titus 1:12, to name but three), had a life-changing experience on his way to Damascus—one of the decisive events described in Acts. In that blinding "light from heaven," he encountered Jesus and was converted. St. Luke considered this Damascus Road event so pivotal that he told it three times, at important turning points in his book. The first version is his own (Acts 9:1–9), a straightforward narrative told at a chronologically suitable moment. The second version is St. Paul's; in Acts 22:5–11, he addresses the Jews of Jerusalem, having just been given protective custody by the Romans. The background of this story is fascinating in its own right. Arrested by the Romans, he surprises the officers—who had mistaken him for an Egyptian—by addressing them in Greek ("You speak Greek, then?" [Acts 21:38]), and then gets permission to speak to the Jews, which he does in Aramaic. They react in an equally pleased if slightly surprised way ("When they realized he was speaking in Aramaic, the silence was even greater than before" [Acts 22:2]). His version of the Damascus experience is geared toward a Jewish audience; its idiom and the explanations he uses flow from their common starting point, "the Law of our ancestors" (Acts 22:3).

In Acts 26:12–20, St. Paul tells the story a second time. The scene is a court appearance before the authorities at Caesarea Maritima. Once more, he is in Roman custody. King Herod Agrippa II and the recently arrived Roman procurator, Festus, interrogate him. Both men had been brought up within the Roman educational system; they were conversant in the literature, philosophy and, naturally enough, languages of the Empire. So as a well-educated Roman citizen, St. Paul speaks to them in Greek. But he also adapts his story to the specific "target group" interests of his audience, making no allusions to "the Law of our ancestors." Here, and only here, St. Paul adds a saying of Jesus himself, with important implications:

"Saul, Saul, why are you persecuting me? It is hard for you to kick against the goad" (Acts 26:14). The Greek text must have sounded quite familiar to them: *"sklerón soi pròs kéntra laktízein"*—almost a quote, but in any case an unmistakable allusion to one of the most popular cycles of Greek tragedy, the Oresteian trilogy by Aeschylus, which is still frequently performed today. In the first of the three tragedies, *Agamemnon,* Aegisthus speaks to the Chorus and says (vv. 1623–24): "Does not this sight bid you reflect? Then do not kick / Against the goad, lest you should strike out [against it], and be hurt." Jesus, as Paul points out, said this in Aramaic (which makes it the only known reference to the translation of a quote from a Greek play into Aramaic), while he, Paul, of course quotes it in Greek to Festus and Agrippa, who had no Aramaic.

The central part of this passage, the kicking against the goad ("*pròs kéntra me láktize*"), occurs again in a less recognizable context elsewhere in Aeschylus, in his tragedy *Prometheus* (v. 325). It was also used, in a similar form although in a completely different context, by a third great Greek playwright, Euripides, in his *Bacchae* (v. 795). Even a Latin comedian, Terentius, made use of it, in his play *Phormio* (vv. 77–78): "The saying came to my mind: For what stupidity it is if you kick against the goad" ("*Nam quae inscitia est? Advorsum stimulum calces*"). In short, therefore, these words on the lips of Jesus must have rung a bell. The context of *Agamemnon* (v. 1624) was particularly incisive. But whichever play Agrippa and Festus thought of first, they would have recognized a shared frame of reference. Above all, they could not have escaped the notion that Jesus of Nazareth, the crucified Galilean, was familiar with such idioms, and that his apostle Paul could quote him in Greek with ease. Jesus, St. Paul and the first Christians were anything but uneducated. If the situation demanded it, they would speak eloquently and in more than one language. Christianity was there for everyone; it was meant to be accessible to the Jewish masses at the Temple of Jerusalem, to a Hellenized Jewish king and to a Roman procurator. This, at any rate, is the message we get from St. Paul's two versions of his Damascus experience. Agrippa's response in Acts 26:27 somehow summarizes the potential effectiveness of this strategy: "A little more, and your arguments would make a Christian of me."[4]

Scribal Techniques

We have seen how the nationalistic defenders on Masada, in their last stand against the Romans, thought nothing of communicating in Greek among themselves, how Greek documents had reached even the orthodox community at Qumran, how St. Luke used the services of a high-ranking Roman to get his Gospel copied and distributed, and how St.

Paul's circle of friends was accustomed to notebooks with a Latin name, the *membranae*. Another widespread custom, common among Greeks and Romans, was also employed by Christian authors and their scribes: the system of using secretaries or *amanuenses,* trusted helpers who were well versed in literary techniques and scribal methods. Some of them are mentioned by name in the New Testament, others have remained anonymous. In a broad sense, St. Luke refers to them at the beginning of his Gospel: "Seeing that many others have undertaken to draw up accounts of the events that have reached their fulfillment among us, as these were handed down to us by those who from the outset were eyewitnesses and ministers of the word . . ." (St. Luke 1:1–2). Note the importance St. Luke attributes to the eyewitnesses behind the written records (including those preceding his own); and the "ministers of the word" are, in Greek, the *hyperetai,* the "helpers." In New Testament times, the word was often used to denote helpers, attendants or servants in the synagogues, or attendants of kings and magistrates. But here, it clearly refers to those who helped spread the good news, the gospel, of Jesus in writing. The Greek term recurs, interestingly enough, in the sequel to St. Luke's Gospel, Acts 13:5. The New Testament scholar R. O. P. Taylor was the first to notice that John Mark, traditionally identified as the author of the oldest Gospel, is called a *hyperetes* as a member of the missionary team organized jointly by Paul and Barnabas in about A.D. 46, but not as helper of either of these two. He is merely styled "the" *hyperetes,* as though this was intended to be his title or qualification. Could this refer to the information that by then he had already composed his Gospel, or at least a first version of it, that he was a true "servant of the word"?[5]

Less obliquely, highly qualified assistants are mentioned elsewhere in the New Testament, and two striking examples are provided by 1 Peter 5:12 and Romans 16:22.[6] "I write these few words to you through Silvanus, who is a trustworthy brother, to encourage you and attest that this is the true grace of God. Stand firm in it!" (1 Peter 5:12); and St. Paul's letter to the Romans 16:12 reads: "I, Tertius, the writer of this letter, greet you in the Lord" (*Ego Tértios ho grápsas ten epistolen*). On the strength of the latter remark, the American New Testament scholar Gary Burge entitled a recent article on Tertius "The Real Writer of Romans."[7] Men like Silvanus (or Silas, as he is also called) and Tertius were more than mere scribes. No one would have doubted, in those days, that St. Paul was the real author of Romans (see 1:1), or that St. Peter was the author of his first letter (1:1); but the role of the secretaries could, at times, be very important. We may assume, with many scholars, that the rather polished Greek of 1 Peter—compared to the rough and gritty, Hebraic style of 2 Peter—was entirely due to Silvanus, an experienced secretary who had already proved his worth in 1 and 2 Thessalonians. And in Romans, Tertius was more than just a mindless pen pusher.

St. Paul must have appreciated his influence on the finished product; how else could he have allowed him to get away with such a proud remark—"I, Tertius, who wrote this letter"? Secretaries often composed entire letters on the basis of mere notes, or they completed them out of separate draft paragraphs, and so forth. Yet the authority of the person whose thoughts or teachings had to be conveyed was never in doubt. Modern-day political speech writers and the ghost writers who work with some novelists and autobiographers play a broadly similar role. St. Paul, in any case, well understood the need to provide a guarantee of authenticity at the end of a completed text. There were those who would doubt—as they doubt today—that he really was the author, given the obvious and natural differences in style and vocabulary between some of his letters. At the very end, he occasionally added his personal signature: "This greeting is in my own hand—Paul" (1 Corinthians 16:21); "Look how big the letters are, now that I am writing to you in my own hand" (Galatians 6:11); "I add this greeting in my own hand—Paul" (Colossians 4:18); "This greeting is in my own handwriting; all genuine letters of mine bear the same signature—Paul" (2 Thessalonians 3:17); "Here is my signature—Paul" (Philemon 19).

Paul's secretary Tertius may also have had another qualification not uncommon among Christian professionals working in this part of the Graeco-Roman world: he may have been a shorthand writer, or, to use the technical term, a *tachygraphos*.[8] Shorthand writing was a virtually compulsory skill for a trained scribe. One of the reasons why Tertius, otherwise unmentioned among the members of St. Paul's circle, was chosen for his singular and praiseworthy role could easily have been his ability to record and edit the apostle's somewhat longish oral communications. An example of St. Paul's verbosity is Acts 20:7–9: "Paul was due to leave the next day, and he preached a sermon that went on till the middle of the night . . . and as Paul went on and on, a young man called Eutychus who was sitting on the window sill grew drowsy and was overcome by sleep and fell to the ground three floors below.'' Among the disciples of Jesus, Levi-Matthew, the former customs official at one of the most important land-and-sea borders in Galilee, would have had a working knowledge of *tachygraphy*. Naturally enough, scholars have suggested that he was quite capable of taking down the long Sermon on the Mount verbatim, much as Tertius would have been ready to take down St. Paul's utterances. Needless to say, the idea of an authentic Sermon on the Mount is annoying to those New Testament critics who are convinced that St. Matthew never wrote his Gospel, and that the Sermon is a late concoction of the early Christian community, a piecemeal collection of scattered sayings rather than the summary of a real sermon by a real Jesus. But it is essential to approach the historical evidence without bias.[9]

Shorthand writing in New Testament times is bracketed, so to speak, by a biblical reference in the third century B.C. and by a leather manuscript of the early second century A.D. The Greek translation of the Hebrew Bible, the so-called Septuagint of the third century B.C., is (occasionally at any rate) a free rendering of the Hebrew text. It takes into account what Greek-speaking readers would understand and, as far as certain expressions are concerned, what they would expect in the terms of their own culture. Modern translations of the Bible do the same thing. In Psalm 45:2, the "expert scribe" (New Jerusalem Bible, Revised English Bible), the "skillful writer" (New International Version), the "ready writer" (King James Version—v. 1) is an *oxygráphos*, a synonym for the tachygráphos, the shorthand writer.[10] The translator of this verse from Hebrew into Greek knew what he was doing when he chose this Greek technical term for the Hebrew *sofer macher;* in Ezra 7:6, he preferred *grammatéus tachys* to describe the qualifications of Ezra— hence *tachygraphy*. ("Expert scribe," the Revised English Bible once again translates, and the King James Version again offers its "ready scribe.") The technical term *oxygráphos* must have been common enough among Greek-speaking Jews; otherwise, its use in a translation, the primary purpose of which was to be an easily understandable version of the Hebrew original, would have been pointless.

Then there is the text on leather, found in a cave in the Wadi Mur-raba'at near the Dead Sea, with the inventory and plate number 164.[11] It has never been properly analyzed since the first editors recognized that it was in Greek shorthand (without being able to decipher it), and it is in desperate need of restoration.[12] Because of the archaeological context of its discovery, it must be dated to the early second century A.D. at the very latest. And it is probably a *Christian* text. Whatever successful deciphering may yield one day, there is, clearly visible in the middle of the larger of the two fragments, a so-called *Chi-Rho,* the monogram of Christ, consisting of the first two letters of his name in Greek (*christos*), *chi* and *rho.* These are joined into one symbol by placing the *rho,* which looks like an English *P,* on top of the *chi,* which looks like an English ☧.[13] Jewish and Christian Greek shorthand writing, in other words, was a normal, everyday element of the social world in which the New Testament came into being.

This setting of Greek education and knowledge of shorthand helps us to understand the role the Magdalen Papyrus played within its social world, one in which unembellished Greek was spoken and written by ordinary people as well as by the more affluent classes and the intelligent-sia. It was written by scribes for whom Greek shorthand was a familiar skill—a skill, indeed, which the apostle Matthew himself may have used. But what do these tiny fragments tell us about the beliefs of these early Christians? Here, we have one more literary element to investigate—a conscious, purposeful and strategic innovation of this period known as the "holy names," or *nomina sacra.* New as it was, this element reflected possibilities available to people who used words, letters, signs and sym-bols in more than one of the languages which we have just encountered.

Shorthand for "Holy Names"

We encountered the "holy names" in Chapters 3 and 5 as a striking feature of the Magdalen Papyrus. There are two fragmentary but visible examples, one of them on fragment 3, recto, line 2 (*KE* for *kyrie* ["Lord!"] in St. Matthew 26:22), and the other one on fragment 1, recto, line 1 (*IS* for *iesous* ["Jesus"] in St. Matthew 26:31). Fragmentary as they are, the horizontal line above the abbreviations is lost, although it must have been there, as we can gather from later, completely visible examples. And there is a third instance, which can be reconstructed from the stichometry of the line: on fragment 2, verso, line 1 (*IS* for *iesous* ["Jesus"] in St. Matthew 26:10). Even before the redating of the Magdalen Papyrus to the mid-first century, and without knowledge of the redating of other papyri mentioned at the end of Chapter 3, the first two cases were cited as the earliest examples of these "holy names."[14] The reason for this is clear. The famous $\mathfrak{P}^{52}$ of St. John 18:31–33/37–38, traditionally dated c. A.D. 120 and commonly quoted as the earliest known New Testament papyrus until recently, has no visible *nomen sacrum;* because of the reconstructed length of the once complete lines, it is nonetheless plausible that *iesou, iesoun* and *iesous* were abbreviated *IU, IN* and *IS* in recto line 2 (St. John 18:32), recto line 5 (St. John 18:33) and recto line 7 (St. John 18:34).

The same speculative identification of "holy names" applies to the sister codex of the Magdalen Papyrus, the Barcelona fragments, which we discussed in Chapter 3. Visible "holy name" abbreviations do occur in the nearly complete codex $\mathfrak{P}^{66}$ of St. John's Gospel, commonly dated to c. A.D. 200, but probably some seventy-five years older,[15] and also in a controversial early Christian text of unknown origins, the so-called Papyrus Egerton 2 at the British Library, London, which has been dated to c. A.D. 110–30.[16] The Egerton Papyrus—a combination of Gospel material and free-floating traditions and sayings not included in the Gospels (remember St. John 21:25: "There was much else that Jesus did; if it were written down in detail, I do not suppose the world itself would hold all the books that would be written")—is particularly important. It confirms the widespread, commonplace use of these abbreviations in early Christianity, even beyond the range of texts which were to receive "authorized," canonical status.

Why are these "holy names" so important for our understanding of the origins of the New Testament? First, they are clearly no accident. Even the oldest manuscripts demonstrate their regularity. There was a system behind them from the very beginning. On the whole, abbreviating certain words was more common in classical manuscripts than it is in modern typescripts: we encountered an example in the Magdalen Papyrus, fragment 3, verso (St. Matthew 26:14), where "twelve," *dodeka* in Greek, is abbreviated ιβ. The Greeks and the Romans had a precise system for the abbreviation of numerals, and the Latin one has remained with us to this day; C. H. Roberts's way of indicating chapter 26 of St. Matthew's Gospel (in his first edition) as "xxvi" serves as a pertinent reminder, not least because here it is dictated by tradition rather than practicality: after all, "26" would have been somewhat shorter than "xxvi." But both are of course shorter than the full English "twenty-six" and the Latin *sex et viginti* or *viginti sex*. Numbers apart, popular personal names or titles, names of months and established terms could occasionally be abbreviated, in manuscripts as much as in inscriptions.[17] Thus, the idea of using well-known abbreviated forms and inventing new ones can hardly have seemed revolutionary to the first Christian scribes and secretaries, well trained as they were in the scribal techniques of their time. But what they then did was quite unprecedented, and it has puzzled commentators ever since.

They introduced a system of abbreviations or contractions of names and words associated with Jesus, God and the Holy Spirit, beginning with these very words. "Jesus" (*iesous*) became "JS" (*IS* = *iota* + *sigma* in Greek). (Like all other "holy names," this went through all Greek forms of declination, as we saw earlier in the example from $\mathfrak{P}^{66}$). "God" (*theos*) became "GD" (*THS* = *theta* + *sigma* in Greek). And the "[Holy] Spirit" (*pneuma*) became "SPT" (*PNA* = *pi* + *nu* + *alpha* in Greek). Associated words acquired their sacred status through such abbreviations. "Lord" (*kyrios*), for example, could be applied to persons far removed from the Holy Trinity. Nero was called *kyrios*, as we saw in Chapter 5. But the moment this word was written *KS*, it became a divine name, referring to the biblical Lord. The Magdalen Papyrus provides us with the first example—*kyrie* ("Lord!") in St. Matthew 26:22 is spelled *KE*.

It was the German scholar Ludwig Traube who invented the term "holy names" (*nomina sacra*) for this new category.[18] He established that there were possibly fifteen words which would be entitled to the status of a *nomen sacrum*. Not all of them were abbreviated all the time, but when they were, the following system applied: five of them were contracted by using the first and last letter only (*theos*, "God"; *iesous*, "Jesus"; *christos*, "Christ"; *kyrios*, "Lord"; *hyios*, "Son"—needless to say, the latter word was only abbreviated when it referred to the Son of God). The other ten could be abbreviated by using either the first two and the last, or the first and the last two letters: *pneuma*, "Spirit"; *david*,

"David"—in his capacity as the royal ancestor of Jesus; *stauros*, "cross"; *sohtehr*, "Savior"; *pater*, "father," referring to the father of Jesus; *meter*, "mother," referring to the mother of Jesus; *anthropos*, "Man," as in "Son of Man" and similar references to Jesus; *israehl*, "Israel"; *ierousalem*, "Jerusalem"; *ouranos*, "Heaven", as in, e.g., "the Kingdom of Heaven."

Those "holy names" reflected a theological position. The scribes imported the Graeco-Roman and Jewish custom of abbreviations into the written records of Christianity not for idle reasons, or just to save space on a sheet of papyrus, but to make a point. Since the Magdalen Papyrus is our earliest surviving example of this custom in Christian literature, we may be sure that this was happening before A.D. 70. But we must still ask: When, why, and to what avail?

The "when" question could of course be eliminated by contenting oneself with saying "before A.D. 70"—after all, this would be early enough. But let us remember that the Magdalen Papyrus is a *codex*, and that we established, in Chapters 3 and 5, that the Christian *scroll* preceded the Christian codex. We also already know that the Qumran scroll papyrus 7Q5 with St. Mark 6:52–53 does not contain any word which could have been abbreviated as a *nomen sacrum*. But what about other 7Q fragments? The ongoing debate about the contents of Cave 7 and the Markan papyrus 7Q5 tends to overshadow the fact that there is a papyrus scroll fragment from this cave (7Q4) which was identified by José O'Callaghan as 1 Timothy 3:16–4:3. This claim has proved resilient in the face of criticism, muted as that has been.[19] Indeed, even scholars who remained skeptical as to the identification of 7Q5 were convinced by the identification of 7Q4 as verses from 1 Timothy.[20] For trained papyrologists, the fact that the first of the two fragments of papyrus 7Q4 is preserved with its right margin—which means that we know precisely how the lines ended—is of course extremely useful. Coming from Qumran Cave 7, this papyrus scroll fragment profits from the same archaeological end date as all the other Qumran manuscripts: it was deposited in A.D. 68 at the latest and, by definition, it must have been written before that date. And paleographically, it also belongs to the same period as papyrus 7Q5, discussed in Chapter 3. As it happens, 7Q4 appears to preserve two instances of a word that would qualify as a *nomen sacrum*, but it is not abbreviated.

From the technical introduction to the procedure in Chapter 3, we know that we have to look at the stichometry first. We note that in line 2 of the larger of the two fragments, this counting of letters per line, as applied by José O'Callaghan in his edition,[21] appears to rule out an abbreviated *pneuma* ("Spirit") in 1 Timothy 4:1 ("The Spirit has explicitly said that . . ."). The gap, or *spatium*, preceding 4:1 already has a reconstructed length of nine letters, which is by no means extraordinary; but with an abbreviated *pneuma* (*PNA*), it would be twelve letters—not impossible, yet unlikely. An apparently helpful second example in line 4 turns out to be the exact opposite, the exception that proves the rule: it is true that we read *pneu* at the end of this line, but this syllable belongs to a word to be completed in line 5, *pneumasin*. And here, the text speaks of the "deceitful spirits and doctrines that come from the devil" (1 Timothy 4:1). These spirits are anything but "holy names," of course, and they would therefore never have been abbreviated. So we turn to fragment 2 of papyrus 7Q4, a tiny scrap of two lines with remnants of ink in line 1 and just three clearly legible letters in line 2: *omikron/theta/epsilon*. If O'Callaghan's readjustment of fragments 1 and 2 is correct, then this is 1 Timothy 4:3 "(. . . foods which) God (created . . .)." The two first letters of "God," *theta* and *epsilon*, could thus be conclusive proof that this is not an example of a *nomen sacrum*—for as we saw above, as a "holy name," "God" would consist of the first and *last* letter, "Gd," or in Greek, *theta* + *sigma*.

Unfortunately perhaps, even with the safe identification of 7Q4 as 1 Timothy 3:16–4:3, we must accept that the evidence for or against "holy names" is not absolutely airtight either way. The identification rests on the larger fragment, while the smaller, unattached one, which looks as though it might settle the question, could—hypothetically, at least—belong to another, later passage of 1 Timothy where this combination of letters might occur. However, there is no such passage which combines these letters and fits the stichometry, other than 4:3. Thus, we may risk a tentative conclusion, based on the cumulative evidence of the only extant New Testament *scroll* fragment which includes words qualifying for the status of *nomina sacra*. At the earliest stage of the textual tradition, the stage of the scroll, the "holy name" abbreviations had not yet been introduced. It looks as though this happened at the same time that the scrolls were copied onto the new format, the codex, possibly beginning with the dramatic watershed year of A.D. 62, which we examined in Chapter 3. The Magdalen Papyrus, with its three "holy names," would thus be a "first" in yet another respect. Are there any "theological" or sociological reasons why the change from scroll to codex might have coincided with the introduction of *nomina sacra?*

Most first-century Jews, and non-Jews for that matter, read the Jewish Bible—that is, what Christians call the Old Testament—in Greek rather than Hebrew. In these Jewish scriptures, the name of God was considered to be so holy that it was taboo to pronounce it; and in writing, God's name was abbreviated. In Hebrew manuscripts, this usage was almost undetectable because classical Hebrew was written without vowel signs (or points), whether or not the word was sacred or profane, holy or not. God's name was spelled *YHWH*—the so-called tetragrammaton. Since no one was supposed to know which vowels had to be added between the consonants to make the divine name intelligible, other words were usually substituted when such a text was read out aloud: *Adonai* ("Lord"), for example. Scholars now believe that the correct, voweled pronunciation of *YHWH* should be *Yah-weh*. But playing around with other vowels, and inserting the Hebrew vowels from *Adonai,* readers came up with all sorts of combinations, and in particular with one pronunciation that has had a lasting influence on history: *Je-ho-va.* With the first Greek manuscripts of the Old Testament, *YHWH* acquired the visible form of an abbreviation—initially, because the Hebrew consonants were inserted into the Greek text wherever "God" appeared. This custom was continued into the Middle Ages and it had its variations, which made the abbreviating nature of the exercise even more obvious—such as writing only the first letter of the Hebrew word *yod,* doubling it to look like a twinfold *z* and drawing a horizontal bar through the middle of both letters. A find from Qumran dating from the period just before the "birth" of the first Christian texts documents the use of Greek rather than Hebrew letters to abbreviate God's unpronounceable name.

In a fragmentary Greek papyrus scroll discovered in Cave 4—Pap4QLXXLev[b], with parts of Leviticus—"God" is written neither with the full Greek word *theos* nor with the Greek translation of *Adonai, kyrios* ("Lord"), but with the Greek vowels alone (!) *iota/alpha/omega,* to sound something like *Ya-oh* or *Ya-ho.*[22] In brief, by the time the first

Christians wrote their own Greek manuscripts rather than copying Old Testament texts, they were already accustomed to the concept of contracting the name and title of God. We do not know if *kyrios* was already contracted at this earliest stage, the period of the scrolls. It could have been abbreviated in Greek consonants (*KS*) or with the Hebrew tetragrammaton or with the Greek vowels *IAO*. But we have no direct Christian manuscript evidence of this word dating from this period. However, if the identification and reconstruction of 7Q4 as 1 Timothy 3:16–4:3 is any indication of standard practice, the word "God" itself, *theos,* was apparently not abbreviated, nor was another extant *nomen sacrum, pneuma* "[Holy] Spirit." Let us suppose, then, that the first (Jewish)-Christian scribes initially did what they had always done as Jews, resisting the temptation—if temptation it was—to break with the traditional practice. Suddenly, however, all of this changed.

Almost at a stroke, at the beginning of the second phase of transmission, the phase of the codex, "holy names" were being abbreviated in Christian papyri. As we saw in Chapter 3, this was also the period when Jews and Christians were becoming estranged, beginning with the killing of St. James, the Lord's brother, in A.D. 62. This was the moment for the scribes to make a statement—a statement of faith. It was no longer necessary to show diplomatic or missionary consideration for Jewish sensitivities. Christian documents could begin to assert unequivocally the divinity of Jesus. It was a final step, from oral preaching via the more cautious scroll documents to the boldly unambiguous handwritten signs in the oldest codex and its successors: *Jesus the Christ is Lord and God.*

"In other words," the American New Testament scholar and Egyptologist Schuyler Brown comments, "the four nouns which are universally accorded special treatment in the early papyri of the New Testament are not simply *nomina sacra* but rather *nomina divina.*"[23] The written words *theos* ("God"), *kyrios* ("Lord"), *iesous* ("Jesus") and *christos* ("Christ") thus became the verbal core of early Christian self-awareness and self-definition. The Magdalen Papyrus, containing two of them, *kyrios* and *iesous,* and probably others on the pages now missing from our codex, provides vital evidence that this was indeed the case. Its sister papyrus in Barcelona does not preserve any visible "holy" (or "divine") "names," as we saw in Chapter 3. But the Paris papyrus of St. Luke's Gospel, the P. Suppl. Gr. 1120/5 at the Bibliothèque Nationale, the date of which we briefly discussed in Chapter 3, is not only related to the Magdalen Papyrus, as its younger sister, so to speak—it also confirms the usage revealed in the Oxford fragments and provides us with further examples of *nomina sacra: theta* + *sigma* and *theta* + *upsilon* for *theos/theou* (St. Luke 1:68, 3:38, 4:34, 6:4.12), *chi* + *sigma* for *christos* (St. Luke 3:15) and *PNA* for *pneuma* (St. Luke 3:22; *pneumatos* = *PNOS* in 1:67; *pneumati* = *PNI* in 1:80).[24]

Colin Roberts was the first papyrologist to realize that such a momentous development could not have been the isolated invention and decision of a single scribe. It was simply too far-reaching for that, and was picked up and copied too soon by other scribes to have been the unauthorized caprice of an inconsequential local scribe. Indeed, as Roberts stated as early as 1979, "the system was too complex for the ordinary scribe to operate without rules or an authoritative exemplar."[25] Once again we are back in the decisive period in which things changed radically for the Christians, particularly in the "mother church" at Jerusalem. Consequently, Roberts suggested that the *nomina sacra* were first introduced by the Jerusalem community before its dispersion—or rather its voluntary escape—prior to the Jewish revolt against the Romans, which began in A.D. 66. As we have seen, it looks as though he was right. We may endorse his conclusion—the conclusion not of a theologian but, remarkably, of a papyrologist: the "holy names" were "the embryonic Creed of the first Church."[26]

This embryonic Creed soon became even better established. One of the oldest extant papyri of Acts, the early-third- or late-second-century 𝔭[29] (= P. Oxy. 1597) at the Bodleian Library, Oxford, includes a remarkable feature. Small as this fragment is, with parts of Acts 26:7–8 and 26:20, it preserves two instances of a *nomen sacrum*. On each occasion it is the word "God," *theos,* which is abbreviated: once on the front, the recto, in line 5, *theos* becomes *theta* + *sigma.* And again on the back, the verso, line 4, *theon* is turned into *theta* + *nu.* There is nothing exceptional about this. But the first letter, the *theta,* does not resemble this Greek letter at all. It is not, as it should be, a nicely rounded or oval circle with a horizontal stroke in the middle, but a triangle with a horizontal bar. A mistake? Probably not, since the same form occurs on both sides of the papyrus. Was it a Roman scribe, thinking in Latin—

Deus instead of *theos,* and writing a Greek *D,* the delta, which does indeed look like a triangle, instead of the circle? Equally unlikely, judging from what we know about scribal habits and margins of error. So what then is it? In all probability, this particular scribe was making a doctrinal statement. He used the triangle for the initial letter of the "holy name" of God because it was the trinitarian symbol.[27]

Reading and writing, understanding the words, the signs and symbols, was not simply a pursuit of the elite and their employees. It was common for one person to read a text aloud, and for others to listen to him, not because of illiteracy but because copies were scarce. The experience of our own time, where virtually everyone who wants a Bible has his or her own copy, reflects a very recent development in the reading of Scripture. The Benedictines, for example, continue the ancient tradition: at mealtimes, one from their midst will read from a chosen text while the others listen silently. Obviously, the monk selected for this task—and it will be a different one every fortnight or so—has to get accustomed to the style of the author, to idiosyncrasies of the print, simply to avoid making mistakes. Equally, an ancient reader, whether reading aloud to others or to himself, had to learn and to practice how to do it. He or she had to understand the system of the "holy names," for example, which was made easier by a horizontal bar above the abbreviated word. Likewise, the reader had to alter the level of his voice for a chapter ending, which again was facilitated by a horizontal bar underneath the beginning of the line (the *paragraphus,* followed by a gap at the exact place) or, as is the case in the Magdalen and Barcelona papyri, by one letter projecting into the margin of the following line. There are many examples of such notes for guidance, none of which required years of education to be understood. Indeed, the sheer number of New Testament references to people reading or reciting tells us a good deal about the literary skills and worship practices of the first Christians.

Jesus himself sets an example in St. Luke 4:16–19, where he unrolls a scroll of Isaiah and reads chapter 61:1–2. Interestingly, this is a text where the tetragrammaton for the "holy name" of God would have occurred in fact twice: "The Spirit of YHWH is on me, for he has annointed me" and ". . . to proclaim a year of favor from YHWH."

As in many surviving Hebrew manuscripts, these four letters may well have been singled out by their ancient, paleo-Hebrew script. And Jesus assumes that those who listen to him have read the Torah and the Prophets themselves: "Have you not *read* what David did?" he asks the Pharisees (St. Matthew 12:3); "Or again, have you not read in the Law?" (12:5); and many more times throughout the Gospel. Then there is St. John 19:20, the comment on the notice affixed to the cross of Jesus: "This notice *was read* by many Jews."

The Ethiopian "Chancellor of the Exchequer," or chief treasurer, happily returning from a trip to Jerusalem is seen "reading the prophet Isaiah" (Acts 8:28). And he is reading aloud; when Philip, the missionary apostle, meets him near Gaza—"he *heard* him reading"—he asks him, "Do you understand what you are reading?" The negative response of the Ethiopian was no indictment of his literacy: it reflected his need to have the text and its implications explained to him: "How could I, unless I have someone to guide me?" The Isaiah scroll in the hands of the chief treasurer from a land that did not even belong to the Roman Empire was probably in Greek, not in Hebrew. But no matter—both he and the Galilean Philip were at ease reading and discussing Isaiah in a common language.

There are other examples. "The party left and went down to Antioch, where they summoned the whole community and delivered the letter. The community *read it* [i.e., not merely "listened to it"] and were delighted with the encouragement it gave them" (Acts 15:30–31). Or 2 Corinthians 1:13: "In our writing, there is nothing that you cannot read clearly and understand." Indeed, "blessed is anyone who reads the words of this prophecy" (Revelation 1:3). St. Paul's preaching was double-checked against the old documents by reading them carefully: "Every day they [the Jews at Beroea] studied the scriptures to check whether it was true" (Acts 17:11). Logically, St. Paul could have used those everyday events even in a metaphorical sense: "You yourselves are our letter, written in our hearts, that everyone can read and understand, and it is plain that you are a letter from Christ, entrusted in our care, written not with ink but with the Spirit of the living God, not on stone tablets but on the tablets of human hearts" (2 Corinthians 3:2–3).

The ability to write is treated as a perfectly commonplace skill throughout the New Testament. Even Jesus himself, otherwise content with preaching and teaching, once wrote (and the Greek text is quite specific—he was not just doodling): "Jesus bent down and started writing on the ground with his finger . . . then he bent down and continued writing on the ground" (St. John 8:6–8).[28] In St. Luke 1:63 Zechariah, the temporarily mute father of John, the Baptist-to-be, asks for a writing tablet and writes "His name is John." One also thinks of the postscript to St. John's Gospel: "This disciple is the one who vouches for these things and has written them down" (St. John 21:24).[29] There is John, commanded by "a voice sounding like a trumpet" to write, with his own stylus, ink and scroll, the seven letters to the churches of Asia (Revelation 1:9–13). We have already noted the possibility that St. Matthew was a shorthand writer, and we have seen how St. Paul authenticated some of his letters by writing final words of greeting and his name in his own hand. In other words, even without professional scribes and secretaries like Tertius and Silvanus, and without the help of the Roman copying and distribution network provided by Theophilus, members of the inner circle of disciples and apostles were competent enough to read and write, to contribute to the preservation, copying and spreading of the good news in its literary form. It is no great leap to acknowledge that the early community of Jerusalem, and perhaps of Antioch as well, developed and authorized the change from scroll to codex and the introduction of the "holy names" no later than the sixties of the first century. They had all the literary skills and media that they would have needed to take such a momentous doctrinal step.

The Acts of Peter

At the end of this chapter, we offer entertainment—a story from an early Christian novel. Towards A.D. 180, an unknown author, probably living in Rome, wrote what we would today call a historical novel about St. Peter. Only parts of it have survived, some of them in Greek, others in a Latin translation. We read about St. Peter's stay in Rome, his miracles, his controversy with Simon the Magician, his sermons, his encounter with Christ on the Appian Road, the Via Appia, and finally his death. Scenes from this novel have become familiar to many through another, more recent novel, Henryk Sienkiewicz's Nobel Prize–winning *Quo Vadis?*, and the film which it inspired, starring Peter Ustinov as Emperor Nero. They owe their title and some of their plot to this second-century *Acts of Peter:* in 35:6, St. Peter is fleeing from Rome, persuaded by the Church in the city, to escape certain death. Outside the city walls, on the Via Appia, the Lord appears to him. *"Kyrie, pou hóde?"* ("Lord, where are you going"), St. Peter asks him, or, in Latin: *"Domine, quo vadis?"* And the Lord replies: "I am going to Rome, to be crucified once more." The apostle gets the message. He immediately returns to the city, to face martyrdom himself.[30]

A little church can be seen on the spot where this is supposed to have happened, and inside, the imprint of Jesus' feet is preserved—an interesting challenge to comparatists, perhaps, since there is also an imprint of his feet in the Chapel of the Ascension on the Mount of Olives in Jerusalem. Has anyone ever dared to compare sizes? Such visual traces seem to have appealed to people in less "enlightened" times—the scene from the same *Acts of Peter* where the apostle fervently (and successfully) prays for the downfall of his opponent, Simon the Magician, is immortalized by the imprint of his knees on a stone which can be seen affixed to a wall in the Church of Santa Francesca Romana near the Roman Forum—the site where the events are supposed to have happened.

The *Acts of Peter* does not mention such visual evidence. It is content with spinning the yarn, and it is indeed an entertaining mixture of suspense, amusement and devotion. We can easily envisage second-century readers following with bated breath the culmination of the contest between Simon and St. Peter, laughing at the conclusion (in an exercise of one-upmanship, Simon tries to prove that he can fly, takes off, falls down and breaks his leg) and being left in a pensive mood about St. Peter's encounter with the Lord and its consequences. As with modern novels, the exuberant inventiveness of the author must have had a basis in verifiable memory and fact. Hard information runs like a thread through the *Acts of Peter:* the fact that St. Peter was in Rome, the fact that he was crucified in the city, places and place-names, and so forth. It is the historian's task to distinguish between fact and fiction. One such scene, where recent research has made the factual background increasingly clear, occurs in the novel's twentieth chapter.

St. Peter visits the house of a Roman senator, Marcellus.[31] In a separate room of the house, a service is taking place: a scenario confirmed by archaeology, which has revealed that in the first three centuries, Christian assembly places were mostly rooms in private houses; separate buildings were not allowed. The apostle opens the door and realizes that the lesson—the Gospel—is being read (*"videt evangelium legi"*). He enters the room, takes the scroll from the person appointed as reader, rolls it up and begins his own sermon (*"involvens eum dixit . . ."*). He explains to the assembled congregation how the "Holy Scripture of our Lord" should be proclaimed (*"qualiter debeat Sancta Scriptura Domini nostri pronuntiari"*). And—an interesting detail—he refers to the authority behind this Scripture in the plural: "what we have written in His grace" (*"quae gratia ipsius quod coepimus scripsimus"*). He explicitly employs the passage that was being read when he entered the room: the story of the Transfiguration of Jesus (St. Mark 9:2–13; 2 Peter 1:16–19).

These are the historical details contained in this passage: St. Peter was in Rome; oral tradition took precedence over literary tradition when the former was available, but literary tradition—a complete gospel—existed while St. Peter was still alive; it existed, during his lifetime, in the form of a scroll (even in A.D. 180, when the codex had long since replaced the scroll, its use was obviously still commonly recalled, as is clear from the murals of the Domitilla Catacombs of about the same time); the apostle was the authority behind the Gospel of St. Mark ("We . . ."). And we may even find traces of an indirect reference to St. Peter's second letter: the plural "we" ("what we have written") could be understood as an allusion to the one incident mentioned both in the gospel and in this letter—the event of the Transfiguration.[32]

Leaving this last aspect aside, the *Acts of Peter* offers us a number of reliable details which only recent studies in archaeology, history and papyrology have been able to confirm. People at the end of the second century still knew what we are only just beginning to rediscover. Much has been hidden under layers of embellishment, just as papyri may be hidden underneath the rubble of a dump in Egypt, the lava of Vesuvius or the sand and debris of a Qumran cave. These imaginative layers can be and have been removed. But that is not the end of the task. To see the papyrus, and manuscripts like it, for what they truly are, one must clear away a different kind of smokescreen: the smokescreen of cultural suppositions and scholarly assumptions which have gravely affected biblical scholarship throughout this century. It is to this subject that we now turn in our concluding chapter.

7

FRAGMENTS OF THE TRUTH?
THE MAGDALEN PAPYRUS
IN OUR TIMES

THEN ONE OF THE TWELVE, THE MAN CALLED JUDAS ISCARIOT, WENT TO THE
CHIEF PRIESTS AND SAID, "WHAT WILL YOU GIVE ME TO BETRAY HIM TO
YOU?"

—MATTHEW 26:14–15

WE SHALL NOT CEASE FROM EXPLORATION
AND THE END OF ALL OUR EXPLORING
WILL BE TO ARRIVE WHERE WE STARTED
AND KNOW THE PLACE FOR THE FIRST TIME.
—T. S. ELIOT, "LITTLE GIDDING," *FOUR QUARTETS* (1943)

ACCORDING TO MANY chronologies, 1996—the year in which
this book is being published—is the two thousandth anniversary of the
birth of Jesus. By any standards, Christianity has been a phenomenal
success in the first two millennia since its founder was born in Bethlehem. There are 1.8 billion Christians in the world today. More than 6
billion copies of the Bible are thought to have been sold since the turn of
the nineteenth century. The New Testament Scriptures, of which the
Magdalen papyrus is the earliest physical evidence on codex, have been
translated into hundreds of languages and dialects.

Needless to say, the scholarly battle to identify the nature and origin
of the Gospels is as pitched as ever. But the first Christian texts also
continue to play an absolutely central role in the moral life of the West.
The issues which divide biblical scholars in seminars and libraries are
still of fundamental importance to millions of ordinary people in their
daily lives.

In this final chapter, we assess the Magdalen Papyrus in the context of our own time and consider the broader implications of Carsten Thiede's research for scholars and ordinary readers. We look at the role played by the Gospels in the scholarship, culture and history of the twentieth century, and ask how the redating process may unsettle the orthodox view of how these books were written and what they are. We also look at the possible significance of this "new paradigm" for deeper faith questions which affect everyone born in our culture.

Christianity, wrote T. S. Eliot, is always adapting itself into something that can be believed. But it has found the process of adapting itself to the postmodern world of doubt and cultural relativism particularly traumatic. It might be said, indeed, that the most successful faith in history has become unsure of its own historic certainties. A bishop today is as likely to deny the reality of the Resurrection as to proclaim it. When Bishop John Spong wrote in 1992 that "a literalized myth is a doomed myth" and attacked those who clung to a "feeble religious security system,"[1] he spoke for more senior churchmen than might be expected. In the Church of England, David Jenkins, former Bishop of Durham, is only the most prominent critic of traditional Christian beliefs.

Why has Christianity suffered from this attack of nerves in the twentieth century? Its nightmare is Albert Camus's Meursault, the murderer who in the final pages of *The Stranger* realizes as he awaits execution that he can indeed find happiness in a God-less world. As a final act of spiritual defiance, he lays his heart "open to the benign indifference of the universe." To meet this challenge—the absolute skepticism and diffident atheism of our times—Christianity has made many compromises. Our purpose in this concluding chapter is not to judge these compromises but to examine the impact of modernity upon biblical scholarship and to consider the place of the Magdalen Papyrus in the context of this cultural conflict.

The Gospels in the Dock

Many books have changed the history of the West: Darwin's *Origin of Species,* Marx's *Das Kapital* and Freud's *Letters* are three of the most important of recent centuries. Yet the Gospels are the very building blocks of our civilization. Without them Giotto would not have painted his frescoes in the Arena Chapel at Padua; Dante would not have written the *Divine Comedy;* Mozart would not have composed his *Requiem;* and Wren would not have built St. Paul's Cathedral. The story and message of these four books—along with the Judaic tradition of the Old Testament—pervade not only the moral conventions of the West but also our systems of social organization, nomenclature, architecture, literature and education, as well as the rituals of birth, marriage and death which shape our lives. Though Christian belief has become a matter of personal choice, the key text which underpins it remains a handbook to the way we live, Christian and non-Christian alike. To ask how old the Gospels are and why they were written is to plumb the deepest wells of the social system which we inhabit. These questions are not the preserve of the theologian.

In spite of this extraordinary influence—or perhaps because of it—the New Testament has become an object of cultural suspicion. The instinct to undermine the Gospels has overtaken the premodern inclination to take their truth for granted. Today, indeed, some scholars and writers will go to almost any lengths to avoid the charge of credulity, just as their distant predecessors would have taken almost any action to avoid the opposite charge of skepticism. The post-Enlightenment world has no stakes at which it burns the heretics who dare to question its orthodoxy. It has instead the pressures of the academy, of media opinion and of a disapproving cultural elite, all of which can effectively be brought to bear on a scholar who breaks ranks. The New Testament is indeed worthy of objective analysis. Yet that is not the same thing as the instinctive distrust which it has come to inspire in many quarters.

In its most extreme form, this distrust can be absurd. In the early Church, a group of heretics known as Docetists denied that Christ ever had a real body or a narrowly "historical" existence. The Docetists have found their modern counterparts in the handful of scholars who have pursued doubt to its logical conclusions and presented the New Testament as defiantly unhistorical. In books such as *The Jesus of the Early Christians* (London, 1971) and *Did Jesus Exist?* (London, 1975), the author G. A. Wells argued that the Christ of history was an invention of the second century A.D.; until then, Christians worshipped only a mythical

Messiah or Savior figure. Quite apart from the obvious complaint that this puts the cart of history before the horse of faith, Wells's hypotheses simply do not match the evidence. His argument that the Gospels were not written until A.D. 100 is no longer tenable; nor, as we have seen, is his suggestion that they were invented in a distinctively "Hellenistic" setting. There was no sharp distinction between Jewish and Hellenistic culture. It is wrong to assume that what is Hellenistic is necessarily late.

Most biblical scholars would agree that this approach takes skepticism too far. By seeking to deny whatever is in its path, it makes the exercise of doubt a quasireligious responsibility. Few level-headed academics would endorse such a distortive approach to the problems of religious history. Nonetheless, it is interesting to note that the campaign to eradicate key Christian figures from the history books remains intellectually respectable. More recently than Wells, Herman Detering has argued in Der gefälschte Paulus (Düsseldorf, 1995) that not a single one of the allegedly Pauline letters is by St. Paul, that they were written by the heretic Marcion in the mid-second century and that the New Testament's St. Paul is an invention of early Catholicism. Thus, by academic sleight of hand, perhaps the most powerful human personality in the history of the Church disappears in a puff of skeptical smoke.

In a more general sense, the tendency of twentieth-century popular culture has been to present the historical Jesus as the victim of the Gospels' distortions as much as the subject of their narrative. In much popular art, literature and populist writing on Jesus, it has been insinuated that the Gospels are guilty of a form of treachery: that they disguise the real Jesus and mislead those who seek the truth about him. So deceptive is the New Testament, some allege, that the imagination is a better guide to the truth about Jesus. One writer mused recently that it was time to turn to poetry and fiction in search of the real Christ; he imagined a "quest for the post-historical Jesus" and admitted to a "secret hope" that his subject "might turn out to be a gentle left-wing revolutionary, correct on women and the environment."[2]

Fiction has played a vital role in reconditioning modern attitudes to the Gospels, often with impressive literary results. In his powerful novel The Last Temptation of Christ, Nikos Kazantzakis presented Jesus as a hesitant and troubled figure, far less the charismatic healer and spiritual leader of the New Testament than a tortured product of the post-

Freudian world. Kazantzakis wondered what might have happened if Christ

> had taken the smooth, easy road of men. He had married and fathered children. People loved and respected him. Now, an old man, he sat on the threshold of his house and smiled with satisfaction as he recalled the longings of his youth. How splendidly, how sensibly he had acted in choosing the road of men! What insanity to have wanted to save the world! What joy to have escaped the privations, the tortures, and the Cross![3]

By his own admission, Kazantzakis's purpose was to experiment, to turn sacred Scripture into (often dazzling) literature. "This book is not a biography," he wrote, "it is the confession of every man who struggles." Later—and with even more controversial results—the movie director Martin Scorsese was to attempt on film the same transformation of holy text into psychoanalysis.

In a more recent book, *Live from Golgotha* (New York, 1992), Gore Vidal has imagined a computer hacker eliminating the Gospels from human memory, visits by time travelers to the early Christian era and the possibility that Judas rather than Jesus died on the Cross. The story told in the New Testament and its principal characters become putty in the hands of computer operators and twentieth-century television executives. The novel ends with an outrageous parody of the Crucifixion, televised from Golgotha, in which Jesus is plucked from the Cross by a Japanese sun goddess—a sacrifice of doctrine to the tastes of modern television audiences.

Vidal's mischievous and sometimes entertaining book is merely the latest in a well-established science fiction genre exploring the use of advanced technology—usually time travel—to reclaim the real Jesus from the alleged myths of the New Testament, or indeed to reinvent him completely. What these books share is the cultural assumption that the Gospels are an essentially suspect source. This they have in common with much populist history of recent years. In their highly successful book, *The Holy Blood and the Holy Grail* (London, 1982), Michael Baigent, Richard Leigh and Henry Lincoln claimed that Jesus did not die on the Cross but lived to found a royal dynasty whose secrets have been protected for centuries by a Europe-wide conspiracy. The elusive Holy Grail of legend was in fact the holy blood of this sacred family.

Likewise, in *Jesus the Man: A New Interpretation from the Dead Sea Scrolls* (London, 1992), Barbara Thiering argued that Jesus was married to Mary Magdalene, that they had three children and that they were divorced prior to Jesus' remarriage. Making highly dubious use of a form of code allegedly found in the Dead Sea Scrolls, Thiering argued that the Gospels can be truly understood only if systematically deciphered. In so doing, she claimed to have discovered that Jesus was the "Wicked Priest" of the Essene sect referred to in the Scrolls; that he was crucified not in Jerusalem but at Qumran (where the first Scrolls were discovered by Bedouins in 1947); and—least plausibly—that Pontius Pilate journeyed to the Dead Sea specially to supervise his execution. Christianity, in other words, was an unlikely by-product of battles within the Essene community.

These fanciful claims are not, in fact, particularly novel. George F. Moore caused a greater scandal in 1916 with *The Brook Kerith,* which portrayed Jesus as the product of Essene ideas, a man who—having survived the Crucifixion—settled in an Essene community. What is most striking about Thiering's book, apart from its sensationalism, is the confidence with which it asserts that the Gospels are not all they seem. They speak in tongues. Their message can be understood only with the help of a literary codebreaker. And if not the Dead Sea Scrolls as a codebreaker, then why not Indian scriptures? By comparing Jesus' sayings to such texts, Elmar R. Gruber and Holger Kersten have recently argued in a book called *The Original Jesus* (Rockport, Mass., 1995) that Christ's teachings are rooted in Buddhism. He received, they allege, a Buddhist education from a sect of contemplatives called the Therapeutae in Alexandria while the Holy Family was in exile. Again, the vital premise of their work is that the Gospels can be understood only with the help of a quite separate navigation device. As it stands (it is suggested), the New Testament is profoundly unreliable and not fully comprehensible.

The connections between culture and scholarship are complex. But it is our belief that the profound mistrust of the Gospels detectable in some forms of popular culture has parallels in the world of serious scholarship. We believe, furthermore, that the redating of the Magdalen

Papyrus and the forthcoming work on other papyri have important implications for the future direction of biblical research; and that the forensic evidence of papyrology has a major contribution to make to a debate that has too often been governed by emotion. It is to this argument that we now turn.

The Gospels and Scholarship

There was a time when to question the literal truth of the Bible was to court death. In 1697, a young Scottish student named Thomas Aikenhead was hanged in Edinburgh for repeating Benedict Spinoza's rebellious claim that the author of the Pentateuch was not Moses but Ezra, who lived almost a thousand years later. Thomas Paine's denial of the Bible's truthfulness in the late eighteenth century led to his English publisher's imprisonment. In the premodern West, the authenticity and truthfulness of Scripture—its "verbal inerrancy"—were taken for granted.[4]

Slowly, however, the doctrine of verbal inerrancy was eroded by time and the triumph of the Enlightenment worldview. Partly, this was a matter of gut distaste, the revulsion which many scholars felt for the Evangelicals who inspired Charles Huleatt: for example, Herbert Marsh (1757–1839), Professor of Divinity at Cambridge, who drew up eighty-seven questions as "a trap to catch Calvinists." In a broader sense, the new, more skeptical approach to Scripture reflected the development of the modern critical methods which characterize today's scholarship.[5] Following the Göttingen academic Johann David Michaelis (1717–91), scholars began to confront seriously the possibility that there might be contradictions within Scripture. They also dared to ask whether the Jesus of history was quite the same as the Christ of orthodox faith.

One of the first to pose this question was Hermann Samuel Reimarus (1694–1768), a professor at Hamburg. His groundbreaking book on the aims of Jesus and his disciples questioned Christ's divinity. It remained secret till the author's death but eventually launched the long historical quest. Perhaps the most influential of the seekers who followed Reimarus was David Friedrich Strauss (1808–74), whose two-volume *Life of Jesus (Das Leben Jesu)* advanced the theory that the supernatural events described by the Gospels are mythical—a theory which, as we have seen, outraged Evangelicals such as Charles Huleatt.

In 1860, the English publication of the collection *Essays and Reviews* by seven scholars (mostly from Oxford) sounded the death knell of the old approach to Scripture. Legal proceedings were started against the book; ten thousand Anglican clergymen signed a petition condemning it. Yet the critical methods of scholarly investigation which the collection endorsed were here to stay. The inerrancy of the Bible as a product of divine inspiration could no longer be taken for granted. A new era of religious history and scholarship had begun.

This victory is one of the greatest in the history of Western ideas. In a sense, it completed the project begun by the Renaissance humanists, the first Protestant reformers and the earliest printers to release the Word of God from the control of the Church. The next phase, carried out by the thinkers of the Enlightenment and their successors, was to ask what the Word of God actually *was;* to question whether it was, indeed, divinely inspired; and to suggest what its textual history might have been. The Gospels, the great building blocks of our civilization, were at last to be analyzed, their structure scrutinized, the builders' identities and intentions questioned.

The legacy of this great leap forward has been troubled, however. The twentieth century's most influential biblical scholar, Rudolf Bultmann (1884–1976), transformed the modern approach to the Gospels. "I am of the opinion," he wrote, "that we can know practically nothing about Jesus' life and personality, since the Christian sources had no interest in such matters." Bultmann and other scholars of the "form criticism" school argued that the Gospels are not historical narratives but intensely stylized collections of traditional "forms." These collections had arisen over time, evolving from the life, worship and oral traditions of early Christian communities. They reflected the needs of the post–Easter Church—preaching, instruction and prayer—rather than the historical reality of the pre–Easter Jesus. They proclaimed a "kerygma," or theological truth, rather than a series of historical reminiscences.[6] Rejecting the view of Justin Martyr in the second century A.D. that these books were "memoirs of the apostles," Bultmann believed that the authors of the Gospels were so far removed from the historical Jesus that they could hear only the faintest whisper of his voice.

Bultmann's work encouraged the view that the Gospels were written later rather than earlier and that they were to be understood as primitive ecclesiastical manuals rather than biographies or eyewitness accounts. It focused attention upon the Christ of faith rather than the Jesus of history. From Bultmann's enormously influential perspective, the "that-ness" of Jesus mattered rather than the "whatness": the fact that he existed rather than what he did and how he lived. Why, then, continue the search for the historical Jesus?

The school of form criticism focused much-needed attention upon the theological and early ecclesiastical role of the Gospels. Nonetheless, it has been seriously challenged since the Second World War. In particular, every respectable scholar and theologian has rejected the claim that the quest for the historical Jesus is pointless. In the 1950s, a "second quest" was under way, led by that generation's best minds—Ernst Kaseman, Günther Bornkamm and James Robinson—with inconclusive results. A "third quest" gathered pace in the late 1970s and 1980s in the work of scholars such as E. P. Sanders, Burton Mack, Marcus J. Borg and—perhaps most obviously—John Dominic Crossan and the Jesus Seminar. The seminar put the search for the historical Jesus back into the news and Crossan vaulted onto the best-seller lists in 1994 with his short book *Jesus: A Revolutionary Biography* (San Francisco).[7] The tendency of this new wave of scholarship has been to present Jesus as a teacher of subversive wisdom whose message would have had profound implications for the social world in which he lived, as well as the souls of those to whom he preached. The view of many earlier historians—led by Albert Schweitzer (1875–1965)—that Jesus was an apocalyptic prophet declaring the imminent end of the world has tended to fade away, although it has not died entirely.

This is a healthy and inclusive debate, of significance to anyone with the remotest interest in Christianity's origins. The search for the historical truth about Jesus—his "whatness"—survived the onslaught of form criticism and still has much to tell us about the world in which Christ ministered and the possible significance his ideas may have had for his contemporaries. Yet Bultmann's influence has persisted surreptitiously in ways which are not necessarily positive; in a lucid survey of Jesus scholarship, one scholar wrote recently—and aptly—of the "post-Bultmannian anguish" which continues to grip the academy.[8]

Many theologians continue to be scandalized by the straightforward suggestion that their ancient sources are early and reasonably reliable. They prefer the notion that the Gospels are late community creations, legendary texts which may be freely interpreted by theorists in our own time. Posturing as historians, many theologians employ methods that are often very different from those of the open-minded historical re-searcher. The result has been the survival of several key Bultmannian orthodoxies.

It is still assumed, for example, that a thick veil of tradition stood between the man who wandered through Galilee and the communities which later worshipped him. They could not see him clearly as a flesh-and-blood human being; nor did they necessarily wish to. According to this analysis, the Gospels were not an attempt to describe an awesome series of events which occurred in Palestine during the first part of the first century A.D. but an expression of a religious tradition which had already evolved over many years before it was written down. It has recently been described as a "foundational claim" of the modern quest that "Jesus of Nazareth was quite different from how he is portrayed in the gospels and creeds of the church."[9]

The clearest proof that this is indeed the consensus among academics is the work of the Jesus Seminar. This loose-knit group of about a hundred scholars, mostly from North America, first met in 1985 at the Pacific School of Religion in Berkeley, California. Organized by the Jesus scholar Robert Funk, the seminar sought to establish by a complex voting procedure which of the many sayings attributed to Christ reflect his authentic voice. Each saying was put before the assembled experts, who collectively judged the likelihood that it represented the real Jesus—his *ipsissima vox* ("very own voice"). The findings of this curious electoral college were published in 1993, amid great media excitement, as *The Five Gospels: The Search for the Authentic Words of Jesus* (New York). As a snapshot of academic opinion, the book reveals dramatically how untrustworthy most scholars consider the New Testament to be. By the reckoning of the seminar, only 20 percent of the sayings in the Gospels are authentic or near approximations, almost all of St. John is inauthen-tic. Jesus never spoke of himself as "son of God." Nor, in fact, did he regard his own death as the purpose of his life. Rarely has there been a more comprehensive rejection of the Gospels as historical sources.

One consequence of this, as we have already noted in this chapter, has been the tyranny of theory and interpretation. If the Gospels are assumed to be unreliable, then the theorist becomes our only guide to the life of Jesus. It follows from this that almost anything can be—and has been—said about Jesus. If Jesus was not an Essene, then he was a Buddhist; or a protofeminist and worshipper of the goddess "Sophia"; or a Marxist revolutionary; or a politically correct left-winger who would feel at home on a university campus. It does not take much imagination to see that excessive use of theory makes us see Jesus as we want to see him, as a reflection of us, not as he was.

Some academics, such as the American Catholic biblical scholar John P. Meier, have resisted this orthodoxy bravely—arguing, for instance, that the miracle tradition was not a fabrication of the early Church but should be traced back to the historical Jesus himself.[10] In his monumental study of the life of Christ, Meier is commendably wary of grand theory and reductionism; he makes intelligent use of the Gospel sources. Too often, however, scholars who question the above consensus in their approach to the Gospels are accused of fundamentalism. We no longer—thankfully—inhabit a world in which the literal sense of the Gospels is taken for granted. In our post-Enlightenment civilization, to argue that the Gospels are meant to be taken (at least in part) literally is a conscious intellectual decision. Paul Tillich described this transition evocatively as the shift from "natural literalism" of the old world to the "conscious literalism"[11] of the modern era. The trouble is that "conscious literalism" is no longer regarded as intellectually respectable. To suggest that the Evangelists meant what they said in anything like a literal sense is to court the charge of fundamentalism or unthinking and uncritical conservatism.

A good illustration of this tendency is Bishop John Shelby Spong's best-selling book, quoted above, *Rescuing the Bible from Fundamentalism*. In many ways, this short study is an honorable attempt to reclaim the Bible from bigots who sometimes turn it to socially oppressive ends. Yet the language Bishop Spong uses is revealing in a more general sense. For him, literalism is ipso facto "mindless"; it appeals to "deeply insecure and fearful people." Those who show an interest in the literal sense of the Gospels are "anti-intellectual." They have consigned the Bible to the "Babylonian captivity of the fundamentalists." Bishop Spong is richly entitled to his views on the nature and origins of the Bible. Less acceptable is the contemptuous language he reserves for scholars and believers who hold a different opinion.

We have encountered similar resistance ourselves in the visceral anger which Carsten Thiede's thesis about the Magdalen fragments has prompted among many in the academy. The vehement response to the front-page exclusive in *The Times* was quickly apparent in the letters column of the newspaper and elsewhere. The story seemed to have struck any number of nerves. As the months passed, more and more scholars who had first been hostile became intrigued and then increasingly sympathetic as they grasped the dispassionate rigor with which the new claim was being made. The hard facts were mounting, presenting a convincing case. Yet it was clear that many found the mere suggestion that Matthew had been written so early in the first century unsettling to their own academic and theological convictions. The battle lines between "conservative" and "liberal" remain stark in the world of biblical scholarship. Indeed, many academics have found their progress up the academic ladder thwarted because of their conservative views; in some extreme cases, such scholars have been barred from the more senior professorships. For many academics, the redating of the Magdalen Papyrus has become a symbol of the squabbles between conservatives and the liberal establishment. More is at stake than the mere date of a papyrus.

We believe that the coming debate on the redating of the New Testament using papyrological research is badly needed and will draw some of the poison from the argument. In 1976, John Robinson was struck by "how *little* evidence there is for dating *any* of the New Testament writings . . . there are no fresh facts—like the introduction of carbon-14 datings into archaeology—which have clearly changed the picture."[12] It is a shame that Robinson, whose instincts were so sound, was unable to incorporate papyrus research into his work. The whole business of dating the Gospels is, as he readily acknowledged, fraught with difficulty. The external and internal evidence is limited. Speculation tends to follow inclination. Skeptics will look for later dates; theological conservatives will do the opposite.

This is why forensic evidence is so important. There is a desperate need for an open-minded scholarly debate on the dating of the New

Testament based on papyrological data rather than conjecture rooted in bias. We hope that this book is only the first salvo in that debate.

The Importance of the Redating

Where might such a debate lead? As we have seen, the argument that St. Matthew's Gospel was written before A.D. 70 would be powerful even without the evidence of the Magdalen fragments. With this new information included in the analysis, the case becomes extremely strong. Crossan, for instance, suggests that the Matthean source known as "Q"—some sayings of Jesus and a few other minor sources—first circulated between A.D. 30 and 60. That may be so. But it now appears that the finished Gospel according to St. Matthew was also circulating in codex form at that time. It could conceivably have been read and handled by an eyewitness to the Crucifixion.

This suggests a great deal about the precocious development of the early Church before the destruction of the Temple. The men and women who founded the first Christian communities did so with remarkable speed and organizational skill, driven no doubt by a sense of daunting mission and absolute spiritual responsibility. It also enables us to speculate in a different way about the nature of the Gospels, their character and their purpose. Many criteria have been proposed as ways of establishing the authenticity of statements in the New Testament, such as the "criterion of multiple attestation"—material repeated in different Gospels is more reliable—or the "criterion of dissimilarity"— sayings which are clearly alien to Judaism are more trustworthy. The objections are obvious. Since the Gospels are interdependent, the fact that a saying appears in more than one does not prove its authenticity. Likewise, the idea that only non-Judaic utterances can be reliably attributed to Jesus arbitrarily ignores the fact of his Jewishness. As a man who lived and died a Jew, why should he not draw extensively upon Jewish wisdom? Indeed, how could he not?

No completely satisfactory criterion or set of criteria has been established. But surely a simpler criterion—the "criterion of antiquity"— has been overlooked? If material is older, it is prima facie more likely to be a reliable account of what happened. A diary written on the day of an event is—in most cases—better evidence than a memoir written forty years later. That does not mean the diary entry should be read any less critically or thoughtfully than the memoir. But it must be treated in a different way, as a document written in the heat of the moment rather than the cool light of hindsight. In the same way, a religious text written twenty years after the events it describes is radically different from one written forty years after. There is, as Robinson notes, "less likelihood of distortion the shorter the interval."[13]

If the so-called "tunnel" separating the life of Jesus from the work of the Evangelists was short—perhaps years rather than decades—then we need not *assume* that their recollections were faulty or fabricated. This does not mean that the Gospels are biographies or historical accounts in the twentieth-century sense. To claim as much would be a grotesque anachronism. Nor does the redating of St. Matthew's Gospel invalidate the argument that its structure reflects the practical liturgical needs of an early "Matthean" community. But the redating does strengthen the view that, in the words of one biblical scholar, "the Gospels are not a doctrinal speculation but the attestation of a fact."[14]

And what more practical need could the early communities have possibly felt than the need for authentic information about their Lord and Savior? It is odd that the question of accurate witness has been accorded so little significance by recent scholars, given that it was clearly so important to the New Testament authors themselves. The Lucan Evangelist says that his history was handed to him "by those who from the beginning were eyewitnesses and servants of the word" (Luke 1:2). The author of St. John, likewise, stresses that his account of the soldier piercing Jesus' side when he was on the Cross is based on eyewitness evidence: "He who saw this has testified so that you also may believe. His testimony is true, and he knows that he tells the truth" (St. John 19:35). Later the Evangelist is identified as "the disciple who is testifying these things and has written them, and we know that his testimony is true" (St. John 21:24). This suggests, like St. John 1:14, that the author also included many of his *readers* among the eyewitnesses of Jesus' life and Resurrection.

This, it might be said, is merely a literary device to establish the credentials of the Evangelist. Yet, at the very least, the use of this particular device indicates that the communities for whom the Gospels were written placed a premium on accurate testimony. To be a witness to Christ was to be part of a spiritual elite, however humble their beginnings. In Acts 10:41, Jesus is said to have appeared "not to all the people but to us who were chosen by God as witnesses." It was not a claim made lightly or simply for show.

The question of being a reliable witness was evidently one of deadly seriousness. In a series of influential books, the textual scholar Birger Gerhardsson—following his mentor Harald Riesenfeld—has shown how important the accurate transmission and learning by heart of holy tradition were in the Jewish milieu of the first century A.D. Diligent memorization of important texts and sayings, he argues, was a sacred task. Paul speaks often of a tradition which was handed over and received between Christians.[15] So does Matthew in chapter 15 of his Gospel. The transmission of the good news from witness to witness, from witness to convert, from convert to scribe, was probably "conscious, deliberate, and programmatic."[16] This, as Gerhardsson is the first to point out, does not mean the Gospels were a stenographer's account of the life and work of Jesus. Equally, however, "there is no reason to suppose that any believer in the early church could create traditions about Jesus and expect that his word would be accepted."[17]

Gerhardsson's work has not been unreservedly accepted. Yet it still has much to tell us about the formal relationship between memory and text in the first decades of Christianity.[18] The redating of the Magdalen Papyrus should be considered in this context. If St. Matthew was written before the destruction of the Temple in A.D. 70—perhaps many years before—it was written for men and women who would look upon the events it described as recent reality rather than generations-old folklore. Some of them would have had direct experience of Jesus' ministry; many more would know those who claimed to have seen the miracles, the raising of the dead, even the risen Christ.[19] Their faith was a tradition in the sense that it was a shared, recent experience rather than a body of folklore that had taken decades to evolve.

Even if the Gospel according to St. Matthew was not written by an eyewitness, it was almost certainly written for—and using the testimony of—people who were. Why should we assume a priori that the description of Jesus' visit to Bethany in the Magdalen fragments does not describe a real event which might be recalled by believers to whom these verses were later read out loud? To suggest as much is of course conjecture. But it is not inherently impossible.

Nor should we dismiss the biographical function of the Gospels. They do not resemble modern biography at all. Indeed, their authors and readers would have found the idea of a book exploring the depths of an individual's psychology, motives and character development from birth to death, *wie es eigentlich gewesen* ("as it really was"), quite mystifying. The sentimental "Lives of Jesus" which proliferated in the nineteenth century were based upon a complete misassumption about their biblical sources. That does not mean, however, that the Gospels are not, in a strictly defined sense, biographical texts. The belief of the form critics that these books were merely "unliterary writings"—*Kleinliteratur*—and "folk books" drawn from the ether of oral tradition has been seriously undermined.

Recently, scholars have begun to explore once more the idea that the Gospels *were* biographies in the Graeco-Roman sense and to observe their similarities with that particular, extremely stylized genre as it expressed itself in works such as Suetonius's *Lives of the Caesars* and Tacitus's *Agricola*.[20] This process of reassessment is shedding light on the way in which the Evangelists might have mingled the real and the conventional, the naturalistic and the stereotyped, in an attempt to recall actual events in an ordered and polemical fashion. It also illustrates the extent to which Jewish and Hellenistic cultures may have intermingled. This new approach does not pretend that the Gospels were diaries or memoirs in the modern sense; nor, however, does it rule out the likelihood that they were meant to relate factual information about the life of a real man.[21] The fact that they were written in a particular literary style does not mean that they are utterly unreliable as historical sources.

The modern mind gets confused when it tries to understand what literal truth meant to the people of this era. The peasants and villagers of first-century Palestine believed in demons, miracles and charismatic healing. They saw the numinous, the divine and the supernatural at work in their daily lives; the "open door" to heaven (Revelation 4) was always ajar. Reality was permanently subject to moments of petty transfiguration when the difference between the natural and the supernatural would appear blurred.[22]

Their writings and what they said reflected this belief; they spoke and wrote in a language steeped in metaphor, allusion and reference to the supernatural. They were used to speaking in a way that allowed the possibility of magic and divine intervention. The purpose, indeed, of Scripture was to explain the relationship between the two worlds. John Donne understood this better than we do. "The literall sense is not alwayes that, which the very Letter and Grammar of the place presents," he wrote, "as where it is literally said *That Christ is a Vine,* and literally *That his flesh is bread* . . . in many places of Scripture, a figurative sense is the literall sense."[23] All Scriptural writing was literal in the sense that it spoke of real experience.

In the writing of the Gospels, this mixture of myth and empirical information was probably taken for granted. The modern partition between natural and supernatural was not respected; the authors did not think it odd to juxtapose the figurative with the actual, the spiritual with the down-to-earth.[24] Only recently have we started to expect our historical writings to be entirely objective, free of genre and free of mythic language. We need to read the Gospels as descriptions of the world *as it seemed to their writers* and to understand that these books describe a form of reality, however alien or confused it may appear to the modern rationalist reader.[25]

Whether or not one believes these events happened is entirely a matter of personal faith. What should not be doubted is that the authors of the Gospels considered them of overwhelming, awe-inspiring and perhaps even terrifying significance. We need to imagine men and women breathless with history and overcome by the impulse to record a quite exceptional occurrence. They felt a divinely inspired obligation to tell the world and posterity (if there was to be a posterity) that God had been made flesh, died on a Cross and risen from the dead. The validity of these accounts was never in question. The only issue was whether or not people who heard this "good news" would become followers of Jesus the Christ. All this had happened to ordinary people in occupied Galilee. If we lose sight of this elemental truth about the origin of the Gospels—if we become too far drawn into questions of theory and genre and forget their sheer *urgency*—we lose sight of what these extraordinary books really are. In so doing, we forget what we behold: the ancient building blocks beneath our very feet.

The Magdalen Papyrus and Faith

We have tried to sketch out the beginnings of a new paradigm in New Testament scholarship: its essence is a renewed attention to the date of the Gospels, rooted in the forensic evidence of papyrology, and an open-mindedness to the potential implications of redating for our understanding of the Gospels' origins. Our approach does not answer the question "What is a Gospel?" Nonetheless, it makes some answers more plausible than others. It is our hope that this will stimulate a long and productive academic debate, and also inspire a more general interest in these themes outside the academic world. The possibilities are endless and the journey has only just begun.

Thus far we can go as a scholar and a journalist, observers and interpreters of fact, with no axe to grind. Yet—as observers of people rather than of papyri—we cannot ignore the powerful emotions and arguments which have already been triggered by this claim among ordinary believers and nonbelievers with no prior interest in papyrus research or Jesus scholarship.

Bultmann was wrong: the authors of the Gospel could hear far more than the faintest whisper of Jesus' voice. Indeed, the first readers of St. Matthew may have heard the very words which the Nazarene preacher spoke during his ministry; may have listened to the parables when they were first delivered to the peasant crowd; may even have asked the wise man questions and waited respectfully for answers. The voice they heard was not a whisper but the passionate oratory of a real man of humble origins whose teaching would change the world.

To say as much has implications beyond the scope of biblical scholarship, wide as that is. Indeed, the redating of the Magdalen Papyrus speaks to those who have never heard of or cared about the centuries-old academic rows over the historical Jesus or the textual development of the Gospels. Up to now, ordinary people have had little reason to concern themselves with the dates of ancient papyri. In the course of everyday conversation and correspondence, we have come to realize the extent to which this new claim is directly relevant to the fundamental faith questions which all people, Christian and non-Christian, atheist and

agnostic, must ask themselves. The redating of the St. Matthew fragments, in other words, has a life beyond the confines of the academy.

Where will this lead? We live in an age consumed by doubt but
desperate for certainty. In the West, there is a faltering search across the
political spectrum for new "values," or ways of reinstating traditional
Judaeo-Christian morality. There is a general weariness with secularism
and its aversion to clear morality. There is a corresponding hunger for
ideas and policies which will assert some sort of moral framework. In
the memorable words of one *Wall Street Journal* editorial, there is a desire
for "guard-rails," the certainties which protect us from moral anarchy.
The key questions asked by ordinary people today—about family values
and permissiveness, crime and punishment, duty and freedoms—are not
so very different from the questions asked of Jesus more than nineteen
centuries ago. The New Testament remains a fundamental text for those
seeking answers to these basic problems of the human experience.

In this context, the redating of the Gospels—a process which is only
now beginning in earnest—may seem an enterprise appropriate to its
times, to the mood of the millennium's end. There is now good reason
to suppose that the Gospel according to St. Matthew, with its detailed
accounts of the Sermon on the Mount and the Great Commission, was
written not long after the Crucifixion and certainly before the destruction of the Temple in A.D. 70; that the Gospel according to St. Mark was
distributed early enough to reach Qumran; that the Gospel according to
St. Luke belonged to the very first generation of Christian codices; and
that internal evidence suggests a date before A.D. 70 even for the non-
synoptic Gospel according to St. John (as the highly respected German
academic Klaus Berger argued in 1994[26]). These are the first stirrings of
a major process of scholarly reappraisal. It concerns all of the Gospels. It
affects everyone who has read them or will read them.

Two thousand years after the birth of Jesus, the books that tell of his
life are being analyzed once more—not by priests, theologians and literary critics but by scientists. For centuries, science has often seemed the
enemy of faith. Galileo was condemned by the Church as a heretic;
Darwin's evolutionary theory made nonsense of the Creation myth; and
Freud's research into the inner promptings of the human psyche undermined the Christian belief in personal moral responsibility. For Huleatt's
generation, the science of Darwinism and the science of textual criticism

(as epitomized by Renan and Strauss) were unequivocally hostile forces. Yet, in the case which is this book's subject, empirical science may prove to be the handmaiden of faith rather than its archenemy.

This process of reevaluation, then, is an opportunity for ordinary people to look afresh at the New Testament and its relevance to their lives. No scientist can say that the Gospels are *true*. But he or she can form a judgment as to whether they are *authentic*. Responding to such claims, some people will say that evidence—the empirical findings of a science like papyrology—has nothing to do with faith and morality. Like Charles Huleatt, they do not need shrouds, miracles or even the sources of history to buttress their belief. Others may take the opposite point of view and find their beliefs profoundly affected by the redating. They may see in the redating process an unexpected convergence of faith and history, a filling in of what Gotthold Lessing called the "ugly ditch" between the two. The gap between the university and the church, between science and faith, may at last be overcome.

For if the Gospels are more authentic than we thought, then perhaps the gap between the Jesus of history and the Christ of faith is not as great as academics have claimed and Christians feared. These extraordinary books stand before us bathed in a new light of understanding. Jesus' voice seems anything but a whisper. In this sense, the Magdalen Papyrus speaks not only to the minds of scholars but to the hearts of all people.

"When you read God's word," wrote Søren Kirkegaard, "you must constantly be saying to yourself, 'It is talking to me, and about me.' " Nobody who pursues this subject for long can fail to be moved and challenged by it. Our research has taken us all over the world: from Germany to America, to Egypt and Israel, and across Europe. These travels are not yet done. However, the story of the papyrus must end where it began, at Magdalen, the college which has been home to these precious fragments for most of this century. For it is this five-hundred-year-old institution—founded fourteen hundred years after the papyrus was written—that stands at the center of the tale: that sent Charles Huleatt forth, that inspired the devotion which drove him to send the papyrus back a few years before his death. And it was to Magdalen that Carsten Thiede would later come to redate the fragments.

Today, the college is thriving. It has lost none of its medieval majesty. Indeed, it has been lovingly restored in recent years so that future generations may continue to enjoy its unique beauty. Huleatt's old mentor, Herbert Warren, would be proud of what Magdalen has become. As in his day, few experiences in Oxford compare with an afternoon walk from the High Street through the porter's lodge, past the President's lodgings and the chapel, where the School of Leonardo's *Last Supper* now hangs, through the ancient cloisters and out toward the deer park. It is a place to enjoy the fruits of intellect and the mason's skill and to consider what has been accomplished within its walls.

Standing in the Old Library, amid the books and manuscripts and carved wooden gargoyles, one can only guess what tricks of fortune saved the papyrus from destruction and brought it here. Looking out of the window to the splendor of the Magdalen New Buildings—as Gibbon did two centuries ago—it is odd to reflect that this tiny object ever reached this place at all. For what would the scribes have thought if they had known that their work would one day be brought here? Laboring in the blazing sun of the Near East, committing their story to fragile paper, they would have been amazed to learn that it would travel so far and mean so much.

ENDNOTES

Chapter 2: Dates and Debates: St. Matthew and the Controversy over the Origins of the New Testament

1. M. Hengel, *Studies in the Gospel of Mark* (London, 1985), pp. 85–113.

2. There are no historical writings without an "interest" in antiquity; the Gospels are certainly not any more tendentious than, say, the Roman historian Tacitus's book *Agricola*, a selective biography of his father-in-law Cn. Iulius Agricola written in A.D. 98. The first four sentences are an uninhibited declaration of partisanship. At the beginning of Livy's history of Rome, *Ab urbe condita* (c. A.D. 9), the author states that he writes in order to praise the glorious deeds of the one people "leading on earth," i.e., the Romans. It was customary to admit one's interests—and to have them in the first place. St. Luke, writing that he published his Gospel so that Theophilus "may know the truth concerning the things of which you have been informed" (St. Luke 1:4), was in the very best company of ancient historians.

3. Hengel, *Studies in the Gospel of Mark*, p. 110.

4. A widespread misunderstanding of this verse has been caused by the expression "some standing here who will not taste death before . . . ," as though it was stressing the word "some." Jesus does not imply that others will die. All the sentence does say is that some, not all, of those present will see a revelation of his glory. And indeed, only a few of them were present at the Transfiguration.

5. This is a literal translation from the original Greek.

6. Cf. Romans 11:26!

7. Interestingly, the Greek word used in St. Matthew 10:23 for this act of "completing," *teléo*, is used in exactly the same sense at the beginning of St. Luke's Gospel: "When his parents had completed everything which the Law of the Lord prescribes, they returned to Galilee, to their town of Nazareth."

8. See Chapter 3 of this book.

9. Th. Zahn, *Das Evangelium des Matthäus* (Leipzig/Erlangen, 1903; 4th ed., 1922; repr. Wuppertal/Zürich, 1984), p. 407.

10. "Awake or asleep" = "whether we live or die"; cf. Romans 14:8. In other words, Paul himself was prepared for death prior to the Second Coming, as others had died before—including such eminent figures as Stephen, the leader of the Hellenists among the Christian community at Jerusalem as early as c. A.D. 33—an event Paul had witnessed and supported before his conversion.

An alternative explanation assumes that the Second Coming had already happened fifty days after Easter, at Pentecost, in the outpouring of the Holy Spirit, the "paraclete" or "helper" prophesied by Jesus in St. John 14:16–26, 15:26 and 16:9–11.

11. *Novum Testamentum Graece*, Nestle-Aland²⁷ʳᵉᵛ·, p. 453.

12. St. Mark is sometimes excepted from this "rule," as the prophecy is slightly abbreviated, less detailed, than in the other Gospels. Thus, "generous" scholars would grant St. Mark a date of "about A.D. 70." Remarkably, the late Günther Zuntz, Professor of Hellenistic Greek (which is the period including the New Testament) at Manchester University, and an internationally recognized authority on the subject, thought nothing of such artificial argumentations and opted for the other end of the spectrum: A.D. 40 was, for him, the most likely date of composition of St. Mark. See G. Zuntz, "Wann wurde das Evangelium Marci geschrieben" and "Ein Heide las das Markusevangelium," in H. Cancik, ed., *Markus-Philologie. Historische, literargeschichtliche und stilistische Untersuchungen zum zweiten Evangelium* (Tübingen, 1984), pp. 47–71 and pp. 205–22.

For St. Matthew's Gospel, the earliest dates suggested by scholars who were not impressed by the theory of a prophecy made up after the event are c. A.D. 40–60 (J. A. T. Robinson,

Redating the New Testament [London, 1976]), c. A.D. 43 (B. Orchard and H. Riley, *The Order of the Synoptics* [Macon, 1987]), c. A.D. 50–64 (B. Reicke, "Synoptic Prophecies on the Destruction of Jerusalem," in *Studies in New Testament and Early Christian Literature. Essays in Honour of Allen P. Wikgren*, ed. D. E. Aune [Leiden, 1972], pp. 121–34).

13. As the Anchor Bible, vol. 26, W. F. Albright and C. S. Mann, *Matthew, Introduction, Translation and Notes* (New York, 1971), puts it: "A Messiah without a Messianic Community would have been unthinkable to any Jew," p. 195.

14. M. Hengel, "The Titles of the Gospels and the Gospel of Mark," in idem, *Studies in the Gospel of Mark* (London, 1985), pp. 64–84.

15. See, e.g., Th. Birt, *Die Buchrolle in der Kunst* (Leipzig, 1907; repr. 1976); E. Schmalz-riedt, *Peri Physeos. Zur Frühgeschichte der Buchtitel* (München, 1970); and G. Cavallo, *Libri, Scritture, Scribi a Ercolaneo* (Naples, 1983).

16. Hengel, *Studies in the Gospel of Mark*, pp. 81–82.

17. For the archaeology of Capernaum with its enormous surfaced jetty (700 m [2,298 ft.] long and 2 m [6¹/₂ ft.] wide), see M. Nun, *Anchorages and Harbours Around the Sea of Galilee*, En Gev, 1988, pp. 24–26; cf. also B. Pixner, *Wege des Messias und Stätten der Urkirche. Jesus und das Judenchristentum im Licht neuer archäologischer Erkenntnisse*, 2nd enl. ed. by R. Riesner (Giessen, 1994), pp. 65–66.

18. See F. Herrenbrück, *Jesus und die Zöllner* (Tübingen, 1990).

19. C. F. D. Moule, "St. Matthew's Gospel: Some Neglected Features," in idem, *Essays in New Testament Interpretation* (Cambridge, 1982), pp. 67–74. Moule does not think that this disciple then went on to write the whole Gospel himself, but he argues in favor of his role in the collection of the original source material.

20. Quoted by Eusebius in his *Church History* 3.39.16 (written in c. A.D. 325). See Chapters 3 and 6 of our book.

21. Told by Clement of Alexandria (c. A.D. 150–219), *Stromateis* 4.9.

22. An excellent, exhaustive survey of opinions and publications on this Gospel and all New Testament writings can be found in the most comprehensive study of the New Testament, the 1,160 pages of D. Guthrie's *New Testament Introduction* (Leicester, 4th rev. ed., 1990).

23. J. A. T. Robinson, *The Priority of John* (London, 1985), pp. 1–122.

24. K. Berger, *Theologiegeschichte des Urchristentums. Theologie des Neuen Testaments* (Tübingen/Basel, 1994), here in particular pp. 653–57 (on St. John) and pp. 568–71 (on Revelation). Berger remains more conservative and closer to the traditional consensus on the dates of other New Testament writings, mainly without going into chronological details.

25. D. L. Sayers, "A Vote of Thanks to Cyrus," in her *Unpopular Opinions* (London, 1946; 2nd ed., 1951), pp. 23–28, here p. 25.

Chapter 3: Investigating the Magdalen Papyrus

1. A story preserved by the German papyrologist U. Wilcken, *Die griechischen Papyrusurkunden* (Berlin, 1897), p. 10.

2. Most of the Codex Sinaiticus is now at the British Library, London; several leaves are kept at the University Library of Leipzig (Tischendorf's home university), and a further twelve, recently discovered at the monastery, have so far remained there. The other, equally important codex, also of a mid-fourth century date, is the Codex Vaticanus, at the Vatican Library.

3. A good description of the technique can be found in P. W. Pestman, *The New Papyrological Primer* (Leiden/New York, 1990).

4. Gaius Plinius Secundus, *Natural History* 13.74–82.

5. See I. Gallo, *Greek and Latin Papyrology, Classical Handbook I* (London, 1986), p. 14, and Chapter 5 of this book.

6. For this and for further material, cf. Th. Birt, *Die Buchrolle in der Kunst* (Leipzig, 1907), here pp. 254 and 326.

7. Thus, the later one tries to date the Pastoral Epistles, the more likely it becomes,

theoretically at least, that *biblia* already means "codices" rather than "scrolls." Against the tendency to postdate 2 Timothy to the late first or early to mid-second century, see recently (among others) G. D. Fee, *1 and 2 Timothy, Titus* (San Francisco, 1984); M. Prior, *Paul the Letter-Writer and the Second Letter to Timothy* (Sheffield, 1989).

8. C. H. Roberts and T. C. Skeat, *The Birth of the Christian Codex* (London, 1983), pp. 21–23, here p. 22.

9. See J. Genoth-Bismuth, *Un Homme nommé Salut. Genèse d'une "hérésie" à Jérusalem,* 2nd ed. (Paris, 1995), pp. 205–7, here p. 205, analyzing the tracts Sabbat 16:1 and 116a.

10. J. O'Callaghan, "Papiros neotestamentarios en la cueva 7 de Qumrân?," *Biblica* 53 (1972), pp. 91–100; authorized English translation by W. L. Holladay in *Journal of Biblical Literature* 91 (1972), Suppl., pp. 1–14. O'Callaghan published in-depth studies of the 7Q papyri in many subsequent issues of specialist journals, answering his opponents. A good summary of his investigations is contained in his monograph *Los Papiros Griegos de la Cueva 7 de Qumrân* (Madrid, 1974). See also his *Los primeros testimonios del Nuevo Testamento* (Córdoba, 1995), pp. 95–145.

11. For the recent debate about this date and the deficient nature of attempts to question it, see Chapter 5, note 14.

12. K. Schubert, "Die Religion der Qumranleute," in *Qumran. Ein Symposion,* ed. J. B. Bauer et al. (Graz, 1993), pp. 73–85, here pp. 84–85.

13. For further literature and sources, see J. A. Fitzmyer, *The Dead Sea Scrolls. Major Publications and Tools for Studies,* rev. ed. (Atlanta, 1990), and in this book Chapter 5, note 14.

14. C. P. Thiede, "7Q—Eine Rückkehr zu den neutestamentlichen Papyrusfunden in der siebten Höhle von Qumran," *Biblica* 65 (1984), pp. 538–59.

15. Thiede's latest monograph in English, a full discussion of the arguments pro and con, was published in 1992: C. P. Thiede, *The Earliest Gospel Manuscript? The Qumran Fragment 7Q5 and Its Significance for New Testament Studies* (Exeter/Carlisle, 1992). See also the most up-to-date summary in C. P. Thiede, "7Q5—Facts or Fiction?," *The Westminster Theological Journal* 57 (1995), pp. 471–74.

16. S. Talmon, "Streit um die Rollen von Qumran," *Zur Debatte,* 22/5, 1992, pp. 1–3.

17. "No credo possano esserci dubbi circa l'identificazione del 7Q5"; O. Montevecchi, "Ricerchiamo senza pregiudizi" ("Let us research without prejudices"), interview with S. Paci, *30 Giorni* XII/7–8 (1994), pp. 75–76.

18. G. Stanton, *Gospel Truth? New Light on Jesus and the Gospels* (London, 1995), pp. 20–32 and pp. 11–20, respectively.

19. M. Baillet, J. Milik and R. de Vaux, eds., *Discoveries in the Judaean Desert of Jordan, III: Les "Petites Grottes" de Qumrân,* 2 vols. (Oxford, 1962).

20. H. Hunger, "7Q5: Markus 6,52–53—oder? Die Meinung des Papyrologen," in B. Mayer, *Christen und Christliches in Qumran?* (Regensburg, 1992), pp. 33–56, here p. 39.

21. Comparatively speaking, omissions (or rather, noninclusions) can be found in other very early papyri, such as in the 𝔓[46] or, in a particularly striking case, in the oldest known papyrus of St. John's Gospel, the famous 𝔓[52] at the John Rylands University Library, Manchester (Gr.P. 457). Chapter 18:37 has only one *eis touto* ("for this") instead of two, as is the case in all other St. John manuscripts without exception. A singular phenomenon, and yet, no one has batted an eye—indeed, it is not even mentioned in the apparatus of the critical Greek New Testament editions.

22. P. Segal, "The Penalty of the Warning Inscription from the Temple of Jerusalem," *Israel Exploration Journal* 39 (1989), pp. 79–84.

23. H.-U. Rosenbaum, "Cave 7Q! Gegen die erneute Inanspruchnahme des Qumran-Fragments 7Q5 als Bruchstück der ältesten Evangelien-Handschrift," *Biblische Zeitschrift* 51 (1987), pp. 189–205, here p. 200. Rosenbaum's paper is marked by factual errors, invectives and lack of expert knowledge.

24. F. T. Gignac, *Grammar of the Greek Papyri of the Roman and Byzantine Periods,* vol. 1, *Phonology* (Milan, 1976), pp. 80–83.

25. Hunger, "7Q5: Markus" (see note 20).

26. The official report on this investigation was published by C. P. Thiede, "Bericht über die kriminaltechnische Untersuchung des Fragments 7Q5 in Jerusalem," in B. Mayer, Christen und Christliches in Qumran? (Regensburg, 1992), pp. 239–45, with 4 plates, including a video printout of the nu–detail.

27. Stanton, Gospel Truth?, plate 8. On pp. 28–29, he claims that "although it is most unlikely that an early copy of Mark's Gospel found its way to Cave 7, this is not completely impossible. The theory that 7Q5 is part of Mark's Gospel does not collapse for this reason, but simply because the crucial damaged letter on line 2 of 7Q5 cannot be a nu." As our Chapter 3 demonstrates at length, an early copy of St. Mark's Gospel at Qumran is anything but unlikely, and Stanton would even be prepared to accept this, it seems. So why does he insist on the impossibility of the Nu, in the face of the Jerusalem microscope and of Hunger's comparative analysis? His belittling of the perfectly clear evidence from Jerusalem is incomprehensible, all the more so as he himself quotes from a letter sent to him by the critical American Qumran scholar J. A. Fitzmyer, who has been impressed by the evidence of the photograph of the Jerusalem analysis (Stanton, p. 198, note 16).

28. F. Rohrhirsch, "Das Qumranfragment 7Q5," Novum Testamentum 30/2 (1988), pp. 97–99; idem, Markus in Qumran? Eine Auseinandersetzung mit den Argumenten für und gegen das Fragment 7Q5 mit Hilfe des methodischen Fallibilismusprinzips (Wuppertal/Zurich, 1990).

29. The latest two attempts, imaginative but unrelated to the visible evidence on the papyrus, have come from Vittoria Spottorno and Daniel B. Wallace; see C. P. Thiede, "Greek Qumran Fragment 7Q5: Possibilities and Impossibilities," Biblica 75 (1994), pp. 394–98; and idem, "7Q5—Facts or Fiction?," Westminster Theological Journal 57 (1995), pp. 471–74.

30. See C. P. Thiede, "Papyrologische Anfragen an 7Q5 im Umfeld antiker Handschriften," in B. Mayer, Christen und Christliches in Qumran? (Regensburg, 1992), pp. 57–72.

31. E. G. Turner, "Menander, Samia 385–390 Austin (170–175 Koe)," Aegyptus 47 (1967), pp. 187–90.

32. F. H. Sandbach, Menandri Reliquiae Selectae, rev. ed. (Oxford, 1990).

33. H. M. Cotton and J. Geiger, eds., Masada II. The Latin and Greek Documents (Jerusalem, 1989), pp. 31–34, with plate.

34. K. Aland, "Über die Möglichkeit der Identifikation kleiner Fragmente neutestamentlicher Handschriften mit Hilfe des Computers," in Studies in New Testament Language and Text, ed. J. K. Elliot (Leiden, 1976), pp. 14–38, here pp. 21–22 and 32–33, plus subsequent literature.

35. Albert Dou, professor of mathematics at Madrid University and member of the Royal Academy of Sciences, has recently added yet another element to the corroboration of 7Q5 = St. Mark 6:52–53. Having analyzed every single possible (and impossible) reading of complete and fragmentary letters on 7Q5, and every attempt at identifying the fragment, regardless of the papyrological plausibility, and on the basis of the available stichometry, he came to a truly breathtaking conclusion: the possibility that 7Q5 is not identical with St. Mark 6:52–53 is 1:900,000,000,000 (A. Dou, "El cálculo de probabilidades y las posibles identificaciones de 7Q5," in J. O'Callaghan, Los primeros testimonios del Nuevo Testamento [Córdoba, 1995], pp. 116–39).

36. This is not the place to discuss the other fragments in Cave 7, one of which has been identified as 1 Timothy 3:16–4:3; see J. O'Callaghan, Los Papiros Griegos de la Cueva 7 de Qumrân (Madrid, 1974); C. P. Thiede, "Papyrologische Anfragen an 7Q5 im Umfeld antiker Handschriften," in B. Mayer, Christen und Christliches in Qumran? (Regensburg, 1992), pp. 57–72, here pp. 59–65; idem, The Earliest Gospel Manuscript? The Qumran Fragment 7Q5 and Its Significance for New Testament Studies (Exeter/Carlisle, 1992), pp. 46–54; idem, "Das unbeachtete Qumran-Fragment 7Q19 und die Herkunft der Höhle 7," Aegyptus 74 (1994), pp. 123–28.

37. Reported by Hegesippus and quoted by Eusebius, Church History 2.23.3–18.

38. Tacitus, Annals 15.38–44.

39. Cf. Acts 18:2; Suetonius, Claudius 25.4; Dio Cassius, History 60.6.6.

40. For a summary of the archaeological evidence and the date, see É. Puech, "La Synagogue judéo-chrétienne du Mont Sion," *Le Monde de la Bible* 57 (1989), pp. 18–20; B. Pixner, *Wege des Messias und Stätten der Urkirche. Jesus und das Judenchristentum im Licht neuer archäologischer Erkenntnisse,* 2nd ed., ed. R. Riesner (Giessen, 1994), pp. 287–326. Recently, J. E. Taylor launched an attempt at doubting most early Jewish-Christian sites in Jerusalem (*Christians and Holy Places, The Myth of Jewish-Christian Origins* [Oxford, 1993]). However, her methods and results are based on a deficient historical and linguistic awareness of the sources and their meaning, as well as a lack of archaeological carefulness. See B. Pixner, op. cit., chapter 32, "Bemerkungen zum Weiterbestehen judenchristlicher Gruppen in Jerusalem," pp. 402–11.

41. For the date and the historical context, see the most circumspect study on the subject, F. Manns, *John and Jamnia: How the Break Occurred Between Jews and Christians* (Jerusalem, 1988), in particular pp. 15–30.

42. Cicero refers to copies of letters preserved in such notebooks: *Epistulae ad Familiares* 9.26.1; cf. E. R. Richards, *The Secretary in the Letters of Paul* (Tübingen, 1991), pp. 3–4, 65, 164. For the role of the Roman poet Martial in the introduction of the codex to classical literature, see Chapter 5.

43. The manifold advantages of the codex for the early Christians have been described and analyzed by many scholars and from various viewpoints; see, e.g., C. H. Roberts and T. C. Skeat, *The Birth of the Codex* (London, 1983); G. Cavallo, "Codice e storia dei test greci antichi. Qualque riflessione sulla fase primitiva del fenomeno," *Bibliologia* 9 (1989), pp. 13–35; T. C. Skeat, "The Origin of the Christian codex," *Zeitschrift für Papyrologie und Epigraphik* 102 (1994), pp. 263–68; S. R. Lewellyn and R. A. Kearsley, *New Documents Illustrating Early Christianity* (Sydney, 1994, vol. 7), pp. 250–56; and many others.

44. Eusebius, *Church History* 2.15.2.

45. C. H. Roberts, "An Early Papyrus of the First Gospel," *Harvard Theological Review* 46 (1953), pp. 233–37.

46. C. P. Thiede, "Papyrus Magdalen Greek 17 (Gregory-Aland p64). A Reappraisal," *Zeitschrift für Papyrologie und Epigraphik* 105 (1995), pp. 13–20 + plate ix, here p. 19.

47. Codex D's outstanding importance for the textual tradition of the New Testament was recently emphasized by D. C. Parker's monograph *Codex Bezae. An early Christian manuscript and its text* (Cambridge, 1992).

48. J. M. Bover and J. O'Callaghan, eds., *Nuevo Testamento Trilingüe,* 3rd ed. (Madrid, 1994), p. 152.

49. The order of the Magdalen Papyrus, *autōn* before *meti,* is also favored, albeit in brackets, by the main text of A. Merk, *Novum Testamentum Graece et Latine,* 11th ed. (Rome, 1992), p. 94.

50. Apparently, Wachtel's article was written under pressure to mount an immediate counterattack without paying due—and time-consuming—attention to detail. His paleographic description of the Magdalen Papyrus and some Qumran scrolls from Cave 4, and hence his conclusions as to the dating of these scripts, are thus marred by factual errors. As for St. Matthew 26:22, his misjudgment may be attributed to his ignorance of the microscopal analysis of the line. K. Wachtel, "P64/P67: Fragmente des Matthäusevangeliums aus dem 1. Jahrhundert?," *Zeitschrift für Papyrologie und Epigraphik* 107 (1995), pp. 73–80. B. Aland underscored the hesitancy in coming to terms with the textual challenge of the earliest papyri in a recent essay published before the redating of the Magdalen Papyrus and its textual reappraisal. B. Aland, "Das Zeugnis der frühen Papyri für den Text der Evangelien diskutiert am Matthäusevangelium," in *The Four Gospels 1992. Festschrift Frans Neirynck,* ed. F. Van Segbroeck et al. (Leuven, 1992), vol. 3, pp. 325–35.

51. C. H. Roberts, "Complementary Note" (dated "9.6.60"), in R. Roca-Puig, *Un Papiro Griego del Evangelio de San Mateo* (Barcelona, 1962), pp. 58–60.

52. For stichometrical reasons only, Roca-Puig assumed that *patéra* ("father") was abbreviated *PRA* in line 2 of fragment 1, verso. This is unlikely, since "Father" may be treated as a "holy name," but originally only when referring to God himself, not to Abraham, as it does in St. Matthew 3:9. A full, unabbreviated *pater* could easily be fitted into the stichometrical

structure of the papyrus if the word was divided between lines 1 and 2! Conversely, "God" (*theos*) would have been abbreviated by the first and last letters, *theta* + *sigma*, in a reconstructed line 5 (St. Matthew 3:9)—a line of which only one letter, a *tau*, is legible; and on the recto of the same fragment, we may assume for the same reason that *iesous* in line 2 (St. Matthew 3:15) was abbreviated to read *IS*.

53. Roca-Puig, *Papiro Griego*, p. 55.

54. C. P. Thiede, "Papyrus Bodmer L. Das neutestamentliche Papyrusfragment $\mathfrak{P}^{73}$ = Mt 25,43/26,2–3," *Museum Helveticum* 47/1 (1990), pp. 35–40, with plate.

55. See P. A. Kuhlmann, *Die Giessener literarischen Papyri und die Caracalla-Erlasse. Edition, Übersetzung und Kommentar* (Giessen, 1994), pp. 116–30.

56. K. Aland, "Neue Neutestamentliche Papyri II," *New Testament Studies* 12 (1965/66), here pp. 193–95.

57. J. van Haelst, *Le Catalogue des Papyrus littéraires juifs et chrétiens* (Paris, 1976), p. 146; C. H. Roberts and T. C. Skeat, *The Birth of the Codex* (London, 1983), pp. 40–41, 65–66.

58. K. Aland, *Studien zur Überlieferung des Neuen Testaments und seines Texts* (Berlin, 1967), p. 109.

59. K. Aland and B. Aland, *Der Text des Neuen Testaments* (Stuttgart, 1981; 2nd enl. ed., 1989), pp. 105, 106, 110.

60. Ph. W. Comfort, *The Quest for the Original Text of the New Testament* (Grand Rapids, 1992), pp. 81–83.

61. Ph. W. Comfort, "Exploring the Common Identification of Three Manuscripts: P4, P64, and P67," *Tyndale Bulletin* 46.1 (1995), pp. 43–54; C. P. Thiede, "Notes on $\mathfrak{P}^4$ = Bibliothèque Nationale Paris, Supplementum Graeccum 1120/5," *Tyndale Bulletin* 46.1 (1995), pp. 55–57. Comfort's paper is also most valuable for its summary of arguments in favor of the undisputed codex identity of the Magdalen and the Barcelona papyri.

62. J. Morell, "Nouveaux fragments du papyrus 4," *Revue biblique* 47 (1938), pp. 5–22 and plates I–VIII.

63. For the importance of the *tau*, cf. also Comfort, "Exploring the Common Identification," p. 50.

64. It was first published and annotated by C. P. Thiede in his paper "Die Datierung von antiken Handschriften als Beispiel für interdisziplinäre Zusammenarbeit in der Papyrologie," in C. P. Thiede and G. Masuch, *Wissenschaftstheorie und Wissenschaftspraxis. Reichweiten und Zukunftsperspektiven interdisziplinärer Forschung* (Paderborn, 1995), pp. 205–21, with six photographs. The material presented in that paper is fully integrated and expanded in Chapter 5 of this book.

65. See Comfort, *Quest for the Original Text*, pp. 31–33. For Kim's dating of $\mathfrak{P}^{46}$, the oldest surviving codex of St. Paul's letters, see Y.-K. Kim, "Paleographic Dating of $\mathfrak{P}^{46}$ to the Later First Century," *Biblica* 69 (1988), pp. 248–57. On the issue of dating the Bodmer papyrus, the oldest surviving near complete codex of St. John's Gospel, see H. Hunger, "Zur Datierung des papyrus Bodmer II ($\mathfrak{P}^{66}$)," *Anzeiger der Österreichischen Akademie der Wissenschaften, Phil.-hist. Klasse* 4 (1960), pp. 12–23. Both of these papyri are commonly dated to ca. A.D. 200, which is between seventy-five and one hundred years later than the dates proposed by Hunger and Kim, respectively.

66. G. Bonani, M. Broshi, I. Carmi, S. Ivy, J. Strugnell and W. Woelfli, "Radiocarbon Dating of the Dead Sea Scrolls," *Atiqot* 20 (1991), pp. 27–32; G. A. Rodley, "An Assessment of the Radiocarbon Dating of the Dead Sea Scrolls," *Radiocarbon* 35 (1993), pp. 335–38. Recently, eighteen further Dead Sea Scrolls were radiocarbon-dated, using ragged parts of top or bottom edges and two pieces of linen that had allegedly wrapped the scrolls. This new test confirmed previous datings, but caused one major upheaval: one scroll fragment from Cave 4, 4Q258, had previously been dated to c. 100 B.C. by paleographical means, whereas the carbon-14 result was "A.D. 119–245." This dating, archaeologically and paleographically impossible and therefore to be ruled out straightaway, is "difficult to explain," according to a preliminary report (see "New Carbon-14 Results Leave Room for Debate," *Biblical Archaeology Review* 21/4 [July/August 1995], p. 61). The explanation, however, is as simple as it is well known: even allowing for the

general effectiveness of "calibration" (the empirical adjustment of the data on the basis of independent information), external influences on the state of a piece of papyrus or leather, etc., may hopelessly distort the c-14 result. Given such vagaries (who knows when and how a fragment was subjected to what kind of influence?), and the almost useless time span inherent in the method (even the latest analysis allowed for a range of 170 years in one case), radiocarbon dating can, at best, be used as a control mechanism, but definitely not as a tool for conclusive results in papyrology.

Chapter 4: The Discovery of a Lifetime

1. G. W. Steevens, *Egypt in 1898* (London, 1898), p. 225.

2. The authors are deeply indebted to Captain Julian Williams and Thomas Huleatt-James, both indirect descendants of Charles Bousfield Huleatt, for their help in the writing of this chapter.

3. See W. G. Rutherford, *St. Paul's Epistles to the Thessalonians and to the Corinthians* (London, 1908). This posthumous publication includes a helpful prefatory memoir by Spenser Wilkinson.

4. *The Oxford Magazine,* January 21, 1909, p. 132.

5. W. G. Rutherford, *St. Paul's Epistle to the Romans—A New Translation with a Brief Analysis* (London, 1900), p. xi.

6. This aspect of the university's history is well explored in R. Symonds, *Oxford and Empire: The Last Lost Cause?* (London, 1986).

7. T. Hughes, *Tom Brown at Oxford* (1861), quoted in M. Graham, *Images of Victorian Oxford* (Oxford, 1992).

8. J. R. Green, *Oxford Studies* (Oxford, 1901), p. xi, cited in Graham, *Images of Victorian Oxford,* p. 9.

9. See L. Magnus, *Herbert Warren of Magdalen—President and Friend 1853–1930* (London, 1932); T. H. Warren, *Magdalen College, Oxford* (London, 1907); H. A. Wilson, *Magdalen College, Oxford* (London, 1899). For a fictional portrait of Magdalen during the Warren era, see Compton Mackenzie's 1913 novel *Sinister Street.*

10. Magnus, *Herbert Warren,* pp. 86 and 55.

11. *Lecture Given by T. H. Warren to Undergraduates of Magd. on the last Sunday of the Summer Term of 1885* (Oxford, 1885).

12. Ibid., p. 21.

13. Ibid., p. 22.

14. Guildhall Library MS.

15. *The Greater Britain Messenger,* 1909, p. 21.

16. For a useful account of Strauss's work and influence, see S. Neill, *The Interpretation of the New Testament 1861–1961* (Oxford, 1964), pp. 12ff.

17. Cited in ibid., p. 194.

18. Cited in B. M. G. Reardon, *Religious Thought in the Victorian Age: A Survey from Coleridge to Gore* (London, 1980), p. 259.

19. Cited in Neill, *Interpretation of the New Testament,* p. 193.

20. *Anglican Church Magazine,* 1904, pp. 15–17.

21. *Anglican Church Magazine,* 1906, pp. 44–45, 70–72.

22. Obituary notice of Charles B. Huleatt in *The Times* (London), January 1909.

23. *Annual Report of the C&CCS 1898–99.*

24. *Annual Report of the C&CCS 1906–1907.*

25. See J. S. Reynolds, *The Evangelicals at Oxford 1735–1871: A Record of an Unchronicled Movement* (Oxford, 1973); the authors are grateful to the Reverend J. S. Reynolds for his assistance on Huleatt's years at Wycliffe Hall.

26. Ibid., p. 159.

27. See F. W. B. Bullock, *History of Ridley Hall, Cambridge* (Cambridge, 1941), for the origins of both halls.

28. *Wycliffe Hall, Oxford* (Oxford, 1878).

29. See Symonds, *Oxford and Empire,* Chapter 11.

30. For an account of a near contemporary of Huleatt's who became a missionary in Egypt, see C. E. Padwick, *Temple Gairdner of Cairo* (London, 1929).

31. Symonds, *Oxford and Empire,* p. 227.

32. For a survey of the society's history, see B. Underwood, *Faith at the Frontiers: Anglican Evangelicals and Their Countrymen Overseas* (London, 1974).

33. *The Greater Britain Messenger,* August 1891, pp. 10–11.

34. *Minutes of the C&CCS,* July 29, 1891.

35. *Programme of Cook's International Tickets to Egypt 1898–99.*

36. Published in *Greater Britain Messenger,* August 1891, pp. 10–11.

37. See P. Brenden, *Thomas Cook—150 Years of Popular Tourism* (London, 1991).

38. Quoted in C. A. Cooper, *Seeking the Sun: An Egyptian Holiday* (Edinburgh, 1892).

39. As reported in *Greater Britain Messenger,* August 1891, pp. 10–11.

40. *The Times,* May 21, 1909, p. 12.

41. *Greater Britain Messenger,* August 1891, pp. 10–11.

42. Quoted in I. Wilson, *Jesus the Evidence* (London, 1984), p. 16.

43. This contrast is still a striking feature of modern papyrology. The Isaiah scroll discovered at Qumran is more than 7 m (23 ft.) long, while the oldest extant fragment of Virgil found on Masada is only 16 cm × 8 cm (6¹/₄ in. × 3¹/₈ in.).

44. See "Arthur Surridge Hunt 1871–1934," in *Proceedings of the British Academy,* vol. 20.

45. See A. H. Sayce, *Reminiscences* (London, 1923).

46. A. H. Sayce, *The Egypt of the Hebrews and Herodotos* (London, 1896).

47. Quoted in A. Sattin, *Lifting the Veil: British Society in Egypt 1768–1956* (London, 1988).

48. See, for instance, Sayce, *Reminiscences,* pp. 332–34.

49. Magdalen College Librarian's Report, 1901.

50. C. Roberts, "An Early Papyrus of the First Gospel," *Harvard Theological Review* 46 (1953), pp. 233–37.

51. *Annual Report of the C&CCS 1901–02.*

52. *Anglican Church Magazine,* March-April 1909, p. 44.

53. *Annual Report of the C&CCS 1903–04.*

54. Obituary notice in *The Guardian,* January 13, 1909.

55. For an account of the earthquake, see J. W. Wilson and R. Perkins, *Angels in Blue Jackets: The Navy at Messina, 1908* (Chippenham, 1985); for Collins's part in it, see his account in *Anglican Church Magazine,* March-April 1909, and A. J. Mason, *Life of W. E. Collins, Bishop of Gibraltar* (London, 1912).

56. *Anglican Church Magazine,* March-April 1909.

57. Ibid.

58. *Oxford Magazine,* January 21, 1909, p. 132.

Chapter 5: Redating the Magdalen Papyrus

1. H. C. Youtie, *The Textual Criticism of Documentary Papyri. Prolegomena* (London, 2nd ed., 1974), p. 66.

2. *The Oxyrhynchus Papyri Part I* (London, 1898), pp. 59–60; kept at the British Library, London, under the inventory number P. 745.

3. Librarian's Report 1901, Archives of Magdalen College, Oxford. Hunt may have been influenced by the lack of corroborative codices from the first century; he and Grenfell had already misdated the fragment from the *History of the Macedonian Wars* for the same reason. Given the popularity of the Latin codex at the end of the first century and into the early second century, during Martial's lifetime (with codex "paperback" editions of classics like Homer, Virgil, Cicero, Livy, Martial and Ovid, all mentioned by Martial himself), one may indeed ask why it did not catch on during the second and third centuries, and why it was only in the mid to

late fourth century that the codex format became the majority format for non-Christian literature as well. The answer probably lies in the fact that the codex was being used by Christians to
such an extent that it was identified with them: the codex was "the" Christian format. Decent
Roman *litterati* would not want to be seen copying the scribal habits of an illicit religion. Only
with Constantine and the Christianization of the Roman Empire would the codex begin to enjoy
an accepted and acceptable position.

A similar phenomenon occurred at the same time, the late first, early second century, when
the Jews began to discontinue the use of their own Greek translation of the Old Testament, the
Septuagint of the third century B.C. The Christians had been using it, for quotations and in their
missionary activities, to such an extent that it had become Christian property in Jewish eyes.
Alternative Jewish translations were produced so that the "soiled" Septuagint could be avoided.

4. Masada papyrus 721A, one line of fifteen fragmentary letters, containing *Aeneid* 4.9 and
dated to A.D. 73/74. H. M. Cotton and J. Geiger, eds., *Masada II. The Latin and Greek Documents*
(Jerusalem, 1989), pp. 31–35 + plate I, 721 a/b. For the use of Latin in first-century Palestine,
particularly among New Testament authors, see A. Millard, "Latin in First-Century Palestine; in
*Solving Riddles and Untying Knots. Biblical Epigraphic, and Semitic Studies in Honor of Jonas C.
Greenfield*, ed. Z. Zevit et al. (Winona Lake, 1995), pp. 451–58.

5. In a major treatise, *Against the Heresies*, the second-century theologian Irenaeus recorded
the information that St. Mark wrote his Gospel after the *exodos* of St. Peter (and St. Paul). Many
commentators have assumed that Irenaeus was referring to St. Peter's death—comparatively late
in other words, some time after A.D. 65/67, rather than during St. Peter's lifetime. G. Stanton,
in his latest monograph, *Gospel Truth? New Light on Jesus and the Gospels* (London, 1995), pp. 49–
50, repeats this old mistake. *Exodos* can in fact mean "death," although most examples in biblical
Greek mean "departure," as in the title of the second book of the Old Testament. In 1991, the
American scholar E. Earle Ellis presented a paper at the International Qumran Congress, Eich-
stätt University, demonstrating from a computer analysis of Irenaeus's works that he always used
thanatos (or, in Latin, *mors*) when he meant "death," and that he was thus in complete agreement with other early Church historians like Eusebius that St. Mark's Gospel was written during
the lifetime of St. Peter. (E. E. Ellis, "Entstehungszeit und Herkunft des Markus-Evangeliums,"
in B. Mayer, *Christen und Christliches in Qumran* [Regensburg, 1992], pp. 195–212, here 198–
201.)

6. Eusebius, *Church History* 2.15.2.

7. *The Times* (London), December 24, 1994.

8. O. Murray, P. Parsons, T. W. Potter and P. Roberts, "A 'stork-vase' from the Mola di
Monte Gelato," *Papers of the British School of Rome*, vol. 59 (London, 1991), pp. 177–95, here p.
195.

9. Ibid., p. 193.

10. G. Cavallo, *Ricerche sulla maiuscola biblica* (Florence, 1967). There are of course other
important handbooks with useful material, such as C. Roberts, *Greek Literary Hands, 350 B.C.–
A.D. 400* (Oxford, 1955); E. G. Turner, *Greek Manuscripts of the Ancient World* (Oxford/Prince-
ton, 1971; 2nd rev. enl. ed. by P. Parsons [London, 1987]), the indispensable R. Seider,
Paläographie der griechischen Papyri, I/II (Stuttgart, 1967/1970); G. Cavallo and H. Maehler, *Greek
Bookhands of the Early Byzantine period, A.D. 300–800* (London, 1987); and many, many others.

11. G. Stanton, in his *Gospel Truth? New Light on Jesus and the Gospels* (London, 1995), p. 14,
states that he cannot see the reasons why Thiede "was no longer satisfied by the arguments
advanced by Roberts in favour of a late second century date." In fact, the reasons are clearly set
out. But Stanton, in any case, misses the point of the original article, which was to explore fresh
arguments rather than to criticize old ones.

12. C. H. Roberts, "An Early Papyrus of the First Gospel," *Harvard Theological Review* 46
(1953), pp. 233–37, here p. 237.

13. R. Roca-Puig, *Un Papiro Griego del Evangelio de San Mateo*, (Barcelona, 2nd ed., 1962),
with Roberts's "Complementary Note" on pp. 59–60.

14. This year, A.D. 68, has been accepted by scholars since the publication of the archaeologi-

cal report by the leader of the excavation team, Roland de Vaux (*Archaeology and the Dead Sea* [London, 1973]). Occasionally, doubts have been raised, but without solid archaeological or historical foundation. For a reliable summary, see J. Murphy-O'Connor, "Qumran," in *The Anchor Bible Dictionary*, vol. 5 (New York, 1992), pp. 590–94; and O. Betz and R. Riesner, *Jesus, Qumran and the Vatican. Clarifications* (London, 1994), pp. 50–68.

15. See his monograph *Manuscripts, Society and Belief in Early Christian Egypt* (London, 1979), pp. 26–48, here p. 46.

16. The historicity of the so-called Flight to Pella, mentioned by the Church historian Eusebius (*Church History* 3.5.3, written in c. A.D. 325), has been doubted by skeptics; the debate and the conclusive arguments in its favor are summed up in B. Wander, *Trennungsprozesse zwischen Frühem Christentum und Judentum im 1. Jahrhundert n. Chr.* (Tübingen/Basel, 1994), pp. 272–75.

17. I. Gallo, *Greek and Latin Papyrology* (London, 1986), p. 14.

18. P. W. Skehan, E. Ulrich and J. E. Sanderson, eds., *Qumran Cave 4, IV, DJD IX* (Oxford, 1992).

19. Ibid., p. 8.

20. April 7, A.D. 30, appears to be the only date that fulfills all relevant criteria for the day of the Crucifixion. There are minority votes in other directions, such as A.D. 28 or, more vigorously, A.D. 33. But even these variations would not decisively deflect from the short span that determines the period after which the first papyrus of a completed gospel could be expected.

21. The papyri from Cave 7 were first published in 1962: M. Baillet, J. T. Milik and R. de Vaux, eds., *Les "Petites Grottes" de Qumran, DJD III* (Oxford, 1962).

22. This, at any rate, is the present majority consensus expressed, among others, by D. Barthélemy, W. Schubart, E. Würthwein, C. H. Roberts, E. Hanhart. See E. Würthwein, *Der Text des Alten Testaments* (Stuttgart, 5th ed., 1988), p. 184, with plate; W. H. Schmidt, W. Thiel, R. Hanhart, *Altes Testament*, (Stuttgart et al., 1989), p. 194–95, with plate. Peter Parsons, again commenting on the date on behalf of the Dead Sea Scrolls editorial team, did not object to such a date, but somewhat hesitatingly preferred a date toward the end of the first century B.C.: E. Tov, ed., *The Greek Minor Prophets Scroll 8HevXIIgr* (Oxford, 1990), 19–26.

23. H. M. Cotton and J. Geiger, eds., *Masada II. The Latin and Greek Documents* (Jerusalem, 1989), pp. 123–24, and plate 15, no. 784.

24. An example of inappropriate and palpably incorrect statements on paleographic details, meant to serve the purpose of refuting Carsten Thiede's redating, can be found in K. Wachtel's paper "𝔓64/67: Fragmente des Matthäusevangeliums aus dem 1. Jahrhundert?," *Zeitschrift für Papyrologie und Epigraphik* 107 (1995), pp. 73–80, here 76–79.

25. A. M. Farrer, *The Revelation of St John the Divine* (Oxford, 1964), p. 37.

26. A. E. Housman, "The Application of Thought to Textual Criticism," *Proceedings of the Classical Association, August 1921* 18 (1922), here pp. 68–69; reprinted in J. Carter, ed., *A. E. Housman, Selected Prose* (Cambridge, 1961), pp. 131–50, here pp. 132–33.

27. P. Oxy. II 246, plate vii, now at the Cambridge University Library.

28. L. Ingrams, P. Kingston, P. J. Parsons and J. R. Rea, in *Oxyrhynchus Papyri XXXIV* (London, 1968), pp. 1–3, with 2 plates; Ph. W. Comfort, *The Quest for the Original Text of the New Testament* (Grand Rapids, 1992), p. 188.

29. See B. P. Grenfell and A. S. Hunt, *Oxyrhynchus Papyri I* (London, 1892), pp. 4–7, with 1 plate; E. M. Schofield, "The Papyrus Fragments of the Greek New Testament." Ph.D. thesis, Southern Baptist Theological Seminary (Louisville, 1936), pp. 86–91.

30. B. P. Grenfell and A. S. Hunt, *Oxyrhynchus Papyri II* (London, 1899), pp. 1–8, and *Oxyrhynchus Papyri XV* (London, 1922), pp. 8–12.

31. E. Lobel, C. H. Roberts, E. G. Turner and J. W. R. Barns, in *Oxyrhynchus Papyri XXIV* (London, 1957), pp. 1–4, with 1 plate; K. Aland, "Alter und Entstehung des D-Textes im Neuen Testament. Betrachtungen zu 𝔓69 und 0171," in *Miscellánea papirológica Ramón Roca-Puig*, ed. J. Janeras (Barcelona, 1987), pp. 37–61.

32. T. C. Skeat, in *Oxyrhynchus Papyri L* (London, 1983), pp. 3–8, with 1 plate.

Chapter 6: Scribes and Christianity

1. K. Laub, "City linked to Jesus is unearthed," *Philadelphia Inquirer,* July 2, 1995.

2. This is the only philologically correct understanding of the term and the point St. Mark is trying to make. The common modern translation, "She was a pagan" or "She was a gentile," would be a nonsensical pleonasm if applied to a woman explicitly described as a Syro-Phoenician. Cf. J. N. Sevenster, *Do You Know Greek?* (Leiden, 1967), p. 190; M. Hengel, *Studies in the Gospel of Mark* (London, 1985), p. 29; R. Rieser, *Jesus als Lehrer. Eine Untersuchung zum Ursprung der Evangelien-Überlieferrung,* 3rd enl. ed. (Tübingen, 1992), p. 391. Riesner also refers to the dialogues of Jesus with Pilate, in the apparent absence of an interpreter.

3. B. Schwank, "Ein griechisches Jesuslogion?", in *Anfänge der Theologie. Festschrift J. B. Bauer,* ed. N. Brox et al. (Graz, 1987), pp. 61–63.

4. As always in New Testament criticism, there are those who prefer to think that such historical cameos are legends, made up by the author. But even if we were to assume, for the sake of argument and in contradiction to the comparative experience of historiography, that St. Luke (or whoever) made it all up, we would still have to live with the fact that a first-century Christian document has Jesus quoting from a classical play.

5. R. O. P. Taylor, *The Groundwork of the Gospels* (Oxford, 1946), pp. 21–30.

6. Other examples include 1 Corinthians 1:1 ("Paul . . . and Sosthenes"), 2 Corinthians 1:1 ("Paul . . . and Timothy"), Philippians 1:1 ("Paul and Timothy"), Colossians 1:1 ("From Paul . . . and from our brother Timothy"), 1 Thessalonians 1:1 ("Paul, Silvanus and Timothy"), 2 Thessalonians 1:1 ("Paul, Silvanus and Timothy") and Philemon 1 ("From Paul . . . and from our brother Timothy").

7. G. Burge, "The Real Writer of Romans," *Christian History* 47/XI, no. 3 (1995), p. 29.

8. The best recent investigative summary of this difficult subject can be found in E. R. Richards, *The Secretary in the Letters of Paul* (Tübingen, 1991), pp. 26–47, 169–172. Richards suggests that the shorthand qualities of Tertius may have qualified him for the job of taking down and editing the long Letter to the Romans (p. 171), but he does not comment on the Greek Old Testament reference to shorthand writing (Psalm 45:1) or on St. Matthew's qualifications in this respect, analyzed by others—see note 9, below.

9. On St. Matthew (Levi-Matthew) as shorthand writer, see, among others, E. J. Good-speed, *Matthew, Apostle and Evangelist* (Philadelphia, 1959), p. 16–17; R. H. Gundry, *The Use of the Old Testament in St. Matthew's Gospel* (Leiden, 1967), pp. 182–84. On shorthand writing as a basis for St. Mark's Gospel, see B. Orchard and H. Riley, *The Order of the Synoptics* (Macon, Ga., 1987), pp. 269–73.

10. A useful commentary on this verse in its stenographical context can be found in A. Wikenhauser, "Der heilige Hieronymus über Psalm 45(44), 2," *Archiv für Stenographie* 59/III (1908), pp. 187–89.

11. P. Benoit, J. T. Milik and R. de Vaux, eds., "Les Grottes de Murraba ͨat," *Discoveries in the Judean Desert of Jordan,* vol. 2 (Oxford, 1961), pp. 275–79.

12. When one of the present authors, who had seen the original years ago, applied for its loan to an archaeological exhibition in Italy which he was helping to prepare at the time of writing, as head of the scientific committee, he was told by the John Rockefeller Museum, Jerusalem, where it is kept, that it had been put aside for restoration.

13. Most people almost automatically assume that the Christ monogram was introduced by Emperor Constantine, through his vision prior to the decisive battle against Maxentius in A.D. 312, where it is described (Lactantius, *On the Deaths of the Persecutors* 44.5; Eusebius, *Life of Constantine* 1.28). However, the *Chi-Rho* had been popular long before, and the vision merely authorized it, as it were, persuading Constantine to "affix Christ to the shields" of his soldiers (*"Facit ut iussus est et transversa X littera summo capite circumflexo,* Christum in scutis notat," Lactantius).

14. See, e.g., J. Finegan, *Encountering New Testament Manuscripts. A Working Introduction to Textual Criticism* (Grand Rapids, Mich., 1974), p. 32.

15. See Chapter 3, note 65.

16. See, recently, B. M. Metzger, *The Canon of the New Testament. Its Origin, Development, and Significance* (Oxford, 1987), pp. 167–69; J. Jeremias and W. Schneemelcher, "Papyrus Egerton 2," in *Neutestamentliche Apokryphen in deutscher Übersetzung,* 5th ed., ed. W. Schneemelcher (Tübingen, 1987), pp. 82–85. A few years ago, a new fragment unknown to H. I. Bell and T. C. Skeat, the first editors of the Egerton Papyrus in 1935, was discovered and edited as part of the Cologne collection of papyri, P. Köln No. 255; the new fragment confirmed the paleographic similarities with $\mathfrak{P}^{66}$ (St. John), which, according to H. Hunger, must be dated c. A.D. 125.

17. Examples and comparisons with biblical usage can be found in E. Nachmanson, "Die schriftliche Kontraktion auf den griechischen Inschriften," *Eranos* 10 (1910), pp. 100–41; G. Rudberg, *Neutestamentlicher Text und Nomina sacra* (Uppsala, 1915); and other publications, particularly by Rudberg.

18. L. Traube, *Nomina Sacra: Versuch einer Geschichte der christlichen Kürzung* (München, 1907). For the technical differences between "abbreviation," "contraction" and "suspension," further material and occasionally differing assessments, see also A. H. R. E. Paap, *Nomina Sacra in the Greek Papyri of the First Four Centuries A.D.—The Sources and Some Deductions* (Leiden, 1959). Cf. also F. Bedodi, "I 'nomina sacra' nei papiri greci veterotestamentari precristiani," *Studia Papyrologica* 13 (1974), pp. 89–103; and A. Pietersma, "Kyrios or Tetragram: A Renewed Quest for the Original LXX," in *De Septuaginta. Studies in Honor of John William Wevers,* ed. A. Pietersma and C. Cox (Mississauga, Ontario, 1984), pp. 85–101. See also A. Millard, "Ancient Abbreviations and the Nomina Sacra," in *An Unbroken Reed. Essays in Honour of A. F. Shore,* ed. A. Leany and E. J. Eyre (London, 1995), pp. 221–26.

19. See, for a summary of the debate, C. P. Thiede, "Papyrologische Anfragen an 7Q5 im Umfeld antiker Handschriften," in B. Mayer, *Christen und Christliches in Qumran?* (Regensburg, 1992), pp. 57–72, here pp. 59–64; and idem, *The Earliest Gospel Manuscript? The Qumran Fragment 7Q5 and Its Significance for New Testament Studies* (Exeter, 1992), pp. 48–52, with plate.

20. An objective case in point is the statement of Émile Puëch, one of the leading members of the official Dead Sea Scrolls editorial team; he is convinced that there are "conclusive reasons" for identifying 7Q4 as a fragment from 1 Timothy: B. Pixner, *Wege des Messias und Stätten der Urkirche,* 2nd enl. ed., ed. R. Riesner (Giessen, 1994), p. 386.

Pixner, in a comment on Puech's statement, notes the chronological problems, by which he probably means the current *communis opinio* among New Testament scholars: 1 Timothy was not written by St. Paul anyway, they say, and it is rather late, perhaps as late as the second century. Apart from the fact that there is a continuous debate about the dating of this epistle and the Pastoral Epistles in general, which is wavering enough to exclude any firm, definitive statements about the earliest possible date, we must keep in mind that St. Paul died in A.D. 64/65, or in A.D. 67 at the very latest—which would give a pupil of his time enough to complete and distribute the letter before it could have reached Qumran by A.D. 68. For the controversy about the date of 1 Timothy, and a reliable summary of arguments for a pre–A.D. 68 date, see D. Guthrie, *New Testament Introduction,* 4th rev. ed. (Leicester, 1990), pp. 607–52.

21. J. O'Callaghan, "1 Tim 3,16; 4,1.3 en 7Q4?," *Biblica* 53 (1972), 362–67.

22. Fragment 20, line 4 (Leviticus 4:27): "If any of the common people sins unwittingly in doing any of the things which *IAO* has commanded not to be done . . ."). See P. W. Skehan, E. Ulrich and J. E. Sanderson, eds., *Qumran Cave 4, IV, DJD IX* (Oxford, 1992), p. 174 and plate 120. For an analysis of the handwriting on pap4QLXXLev^b and its date, see Chapter 5 in this book.

23. S. Brown, "Concerning the Origin of the *Nomina sacra,*" *Studia Papyrologica* 9 (1970), pp. 7–19, here p. 19.

24. Cf. J. O'Callaghan, *"Nomina sacra" in papyris graecis saeculi III neotestamentariis* (Rome, 1970). This book is an indispensable tool for anyone trying to trace *nomina sacra* in the oldest papyri.

25. C. H. Roberts, *Manuscript, Society and Belief in Early Christian Egypt* (London, 1979), p. 46.

26. Ibid.

27. The triangle as a symbol for the Trinity was apparently particularly popular in early northern African Christianity. But there are only a very few traces of it in early Christian inscriptions, etc. This scarcity is accounted for not only by decay, destruction and so on, but also by the doctrine of St. Augustine. He condemned its use, since it had been usurped by gnostic Manichaeans, a sect whose popularity had become dangerous to the Christians in certain regions of the Empire (*Contra Faustum* 20.6). After that, only very few Christian writers dared to use it and write about it. A noteworthy exception is St. (or "Mar") Saba (437–532), whose monastery in the desert near Bethlehem still houses some priceless manuscripts. He wrote a whole treatise about the trinitarian triangle, which has been preserved in a Coptic copy. However, the prevailing influence of St. Augustine prevented its reoccurrence in Christian literature and art until the Middle Ages.

28. Whole bookshelves have been filled with learned debates about the text he might have written (Exodus 23:7, "Have nothing to do with a false charge"?); we just do not know. But there is a minority school of scholars, led by Marta Sordi of the University of Milan, Italy, who think that Jesus actually did write a letter, preserved not in the New Testament but elsewhere. This is the tradition about the historical King Abgar V Ukama of Edessa (A.D. 13–50) and his correspondence with Jesus. Eusebius, the fourth-century church historian, quotes the texts and makes it explicitly clear that he has seen the letters, coming from the royal archives of Edessa (*Church History* 1.13). However, even if we assume that there could have been such a correspondence, we would still not know if Jesus had written his letter in his own hand. Eusebius himself points out that the letters in the Edessa archive were in Syriac, a language no one has so far associated with the historical Jesus. However, this letter of Jesus was so popular that it was copied onto numerous papyri, *ostraca* ("potsherds"), and even on inscriptions and amulets, some of them in Greek, in a version which is different (i.e., independent) from the text transmitted by Eusebius.

29. See also 2 John 12, where parchment and ink are mentioned, and 2 John 13, with a reference to stylus and ink.

30. For an English translation of the fragments, see E. Hennecke, ed., *New Testament Apocrypha*, vol. 2 (London, 1965), pp. 276–322, and M. R. James, *The Apocryphal New Testament* (London, 1924; repr. 1955), pp. 300–36; for a critical edition, see L. Vouaux, *Les Actes de Pierre. Introduction, Textes, Traduction et Commentaires* (Paris, 1922).

31. One commentator, G. Ficker, suggested that this Marcellus was the Granius Marcellus mentioned by Tacitus, *Annals* 1.74: G. Ficker, *Die Petrusakten. Beiträge zu ihrem Verständnis* (Leipzig, 1903), p. 38–39.

32. Needless to say, the mere hint at the thought that St. Peter could have written 2 Peter will cause an outcry of indignation among most New Testament scholars; and this is not the place to take sides. Suffice it to say that the question is still far from being answered conclusively. Two examples may indicate recent flexibilities: E. E. Ellis offered persuasive arguments for a date of St. Jude's letter prior to A.D. 62 ("Prophecy and Hermeneutics in Jude," in idem, *Prophecy and Hermeneutics in Early Christianity* [Tübingen, 1978], pp. 221–36), and J. Crehan argued, on text-critical grounds, for the dependency of Jude on 2 Peter ("New Light on 2 Peter from the Bodmer Papyrus," in *Studia Evangelica*, vol. 7, ed. E. A. Livingstone [Berlin, 1982], pp. 145–49).

Chapter 7: Fragments of the Truth? The Magdalen Papyrus in Our Times

1. J. S. Spong, *Rescuing the Bible from Fundamentalism: A Bishop Rethinks the Meaning of Scripture* (San Francisco, 1992).

2. W. Hamilton, *A Quest for the Post-Historical Jesus* (London, 1993).

3. N. Kazantzakis, *The Last Temptation of Christ* (English translation; Oxford, 1961), p. 9.

4. Cited in M. J. Borg, *Jesus in Contemporary Scholarship* (Valley Forge, Pa., 1994), p. 185; for this debate in general, see S. Neill, *The Interpretation of the New Testament 1861–1961* (Oxford, 1964).

5. Neill, *Interpretation of the New Testament,* p. 4–5.

6. See especially R. Bultmann, *The History of the Synoptic Tradition* rev. ed. (Oxford, 1972).

7. For a fine review of this "third quest" literature, see Borg, *Jesus in Contemporary Scholarship.*

8. See N. T. Wright, *Who Was Jesus?* (London, 1992).

9. Borg, *Jesus in Contemporary Scholarship,* p. 183.

10. See J. P. Meier, *A Marginal Jew: Rethinking the Historical Jesus,* 2 vols. (New York, 1991 and 1994).

11. P. Tillich, *Dynamics of Faith* (London, 1957), p. 51–53.

12. J. Robinson, *Redating the New Testament* (London, 1976), p. 336.

13. Ibid., p. 355.

14. X. Leon-Dufour in *In Search of the Historical Jesus,* ed. Harvey K. McArthur, (London, 1970), p. 61.

15. See, for instance, 1 Corinthians 11:2; 2 Thessalonians 2:15.

16. B. Gerhardsson, *The Origins of the Gospel Tradition* (Philadelphia, 1979), p. 28.

17. Ibid., p. 64.

18. The most recent scholar to develop this line of investigation is R. Riesner, *Jesus als Lehrer,* 3rd ed. (Tübingen, 1989).

19. It is interesting to note how much information the Evangelists took for granted. Mark 1 assumes the reader knows who John the Baptist was; Mark 5 assumes similar knowledge of Pilate.

20. See in particular, R. A. Burridge, *What are the Gospels? A Comparison with Graeco-Roman Biography* (Cambridge, 1992).

21. Ibid., p. 258: ". . . because this is a life of an historical person written within the lifetime of his contemporaries, there are limits on free composition."

22. This is, of course, one of the many ironies of the post-Enlightenment age. Superstitious belief, faith in magic and alleged miracle-working are still prevalent throughout the world—and not only in undeveloped societies. The triumph of rationalism is incomplete. The mythical beliefs of first-century Palestine may be less alien to our own time than we think.

23. Cited in D. Nineham, *The Use and Abuse of the Bible* (London, 1976), p. 62.

24. See E. Auerbach's masterly account of this subject in *Mimesis—The Representation of Reality in Western Literature* (Princeton, 1969).

25. In fact, the writers of the New Testament were well aware of the difference between empirical fact and myth. The careful use of the word "mythos" (1 Timothy 1:4 and 4:7; 2 Timothy 4:4; Titus 1:14; 2 Peter 1:16) makes this very clear.

26. As Robinson argued before him in 1976.

GLOSSARY

Amanuensis: A Latin term for an assistant who takes dictation or assists in the composition of a document, from *a manu,* someone who is at hand. Thus, Tertius (Romans 16:22) was the *amanuensis* of St. Paul, and Silvanus (1 Peter 5:12) that of St. Peter.

Babylonian Talmud: The Talmud ("teaching") consists of the Mishnah ("repetition"), which is the body of Jewish law, and rabbinical comments that often take the form of stories and folklore—also known as the Gemara. The Mishnah was codified in the second century A.D., and the Gemara was collected during the third and fourth centuries. There are two Talmuds: the Jerusalem, or Palestinian, version (Talmud Yerushalmi); and the Babylonian version (Talmud Bavli). It was the latter Talmud that became the authoritative text, comprising thirty-six tractates of about two and a half million words. Daniel Bomberg of Venice, a Christian publisher, printed the first complete edition of the Babylonian Talmud in the 1520s.

Biblical uncial: A technical term used to describe a type of handwriting consisting entirely of capital letters (uncials). It is commonly found in biblical manuscripts traditionally dated to the third to ninth centuries. G. Cavallo and his followers prefer the variant term "biblical majuscule." While this type of handwriting gained currency after the famous fourth-century codices Sinaiticus and Vaticanus, it is of little use in describing the many-faceted manuscripts that predate these official editions. In any case, the Magdalen Papyrus is a precursor of this style of handwriting.

Capsa: A Latin technical term for a transportable, bucket-like container of scrolls, frequently cylindrical in form (cf. the modern English word "capsule"). Murals depicting *capsae* have been found at Pompeii and in the Roman catacombs.

Codex: From the Latin *caudex/codex* ("wooden block" or "tree trunk"), it describes a volume of papyrus, vellum or parchment sheets with writing on both sides, bound together to form a number of single or folded pages like those in a modern book.

Dead Sea Scrolls: This expression commonly refers to the scrolls and fragments of scrolls in Hebrew and Aramaic that were discovered in eleven caves near the settlement of Qumran at the Dead Sea between 1947 and 1956. Its usage, however, is slightly inaccurate, since some of the manuscripts were found elsewhere in the Dead Sea area, for example, in the Nahal Hever and the Wadi Murabba ʿat, and on Masada. We find the first reference to a cave with scrolls in a text by the Christian author Origen at the beginning of the third century A.D.: he informs his readers that he used one such scroll, found in a cave "near Jericho," for the Hebrew text of his edition of the Bible, the Hexapla. It is one of the many mysteries surrounding the Dead Sea Scroll studies that no archaeologist took this information seriously. Instead, it was left to Bedouins accidentally to discover the caves with scrolls. Most scholars assume that the scrolls found near Qumran were written by the orthodox Essene community. There is a consensus that the twenty-five Greek texts—six found in Cave 4 and nineteen in Cave 7—came from outside Qumran. Cave 7, just underneath Cave 4 is an exception because it contains only Greek texts written exclusively on papyrus.

Diacritical signs: Critical or diacritical signs are marks used by scribes or editors to distinguish particular readings or variants and editorial decisions. The obelus (−) and the asterisk (*) are two examples. The system was introduced by Aristarchus at the library of Alexandria in the second century B.C. (Dia)critical signs were also occasionally used to help readers find their way in manuscripts which in antiquity were normally written without spaces between words (*scriptio continua*) and without punctuation marks. Instead, the scribe might use a high point or dot, the *stigme teleía,* to indicate a full stop. A horizontal line under the beginning of a line (*paragraphus*) indicated the end of a passage; and small space (*spatium*), on average between two and nine letters wide, specified the exact place where the passage ended.

Form criticism: The attempt to examine a text and its development on the basis of literary style, its oral predecessors, its literary parts and its *Sitz im Leben* ("setting in the life of a community"). The approach was introduced and developed by the German scholars K. L. Schmidt, H. Gunkel, M. Dibelius, and R. Bultmann.

Gnosticism/gnosis: Derived from the Greek word *gignoskein* ("to know"), these terms cover a whole range of "heretical" movements from the mid-first to the fourth centuries. A common trait of these sectarian groups is that they attempt to gain knowledge of spiritual secrets by mystical and mythological speculation. They can thereby eliminate the role of faith and thus the true nature of God and salvation. Adherents of gnostic teaching thought themselves superior to ordinary, Scripture-oriented Christians. St. Paul attacks gnostic tendencies in 1 Corinthians and other letters. The most important collection of gnostic texts was found by two peasants in Nag Hammadi, Upper Egypt, in 1945.

Häkchenstil: Also called "hooked style" because of the "hooks," or *Häkchen* in German, which characterize letters written in this manner. It is one of many terms used to differentiate between ancient types of handwriting. More often than not, such styles vary, and any one manuscript may present a combination of elements derived from different styles, which we can occasionally attribute to the mannerisms of an individual scribe. However, if not used categorically, these terms help to distinguish between individual hands and their periods. The hooks are indicators of an earlier rather than a later period of biblical uncial papyri.

Herculanean style: A general term similar to *Häkchenstil*, used to describe common characteristics of manuscripts found at Herculaneum. The eruption of Mount Vesuvius destroyed this site in A.D. 79, which is the latest possible date of these texts. Although not all manuscripts discovered at Herculaneum were written there—they could have come from anywhere in the Roman Empire—the term is nevertheless helpful mainly in describing manuscripts collected at a particular place and time.

Membranae: *Membrana* ("skin" or "parchment") was the Latin term for a (parchment) notebook. St. Paul used the term in the Greek transcription in the plural, *membranai* (2 Timothy 4:13), to describe the notebooks he wants Timothy to bring. This is the earliest Greek occurrence of the word. The (parchment) notebooks were precursors of the codex.

Nomen sacrum/nomina sacra: The literal translation is "holy name"/"holy names," and was introduced to describe words like "God," "Lord," "Jesus," "Son," "Spirit" and other words for the persons of the Trinity. These were, as a rule, abbreviated in Christian biblical manuscripts, probably from the introduction of the codex onward. The most common system was the use of the first and last letter, and in some words, an additional middle letter. It seems that Christian scribes and the authorities behind them introduced the *nomina sacra* to emulate the Jewish custom of writing the holy unpronounceable name of God with the Hebrew consonants JHWH, which in Greek manuscripts had the visual effect of an abbreviation.

Ostracon/ostraca: A Greek word to describe potsherds used for writing. Often employed for brief notices, larger pieces sometimes carried whole literary texts. In ancient Greece, such *ostraca* were used to vote on the banishment of people—hence the English word "ostracize."

Oxyrhynchus: One of the Egyptian sites where archaeologists and peasants discovered papyri dating from the early second century A.D. to approximately A.D. 600; other sites include the Fayyûm and Nag Hammadi.

Paleography: From the Greek *palaios* ("old") and *graphe* ("writing"), paleography is the science of studying, analyzing and describing the handwriting in ancient manuscripts.

Papyrology: The study of all ancient texts written on all varieties of materials, except those studied in the science of epigraphy, including stone, cave walls, etc. Literally derived from the Greek words *papyrus* (see below) and *logos*, the modern science of papyrology encompasses a number of related disciplines, such as paleography. For a thorough explanation, see our discussion in Chapter 3.

Papyrus: A tall aquatic plant cultivated, in antiquity, in the Egyptian Nile marshes, and later, during the early Middle Ages, also grown in Palestine, Sicily, and elsewhere. In papyrology, the term refers to the writing material produced from its stem pith. The method was described by Pliny the Elder in his *Natural History*, Book 13, before A.D. 79.

Paragraphus: See "Diacritical signs."

Parchment: A refined form of prepared animal skin used as writing material, developed at Pergamum—hence its name.

Pericope: From the Greek *perikope* ("piece cut out"), which refers to a selected passage from a book. In Christianity, the term described a text set aside for a reading in a service, such as a parable, or in self-contained study.

Philology, classical: The study of the languages and literatures of classical Greek and Latin antiquity, including the New Testament period. For a long time, classical philologists neglected the New Testament documents as much as New Testament scholars neglected the context of non-Christian language and literature.

"Q": An all-encompassing term derived from the German word *Quelle* ("source"), and used to embrace numerous, often conflicting theories about a source or sources behind the Gospels. Thus, if Matthew and Luke used Mark but had material nonexistent in the earliest Gospel, such material could have come from "Q." Any answer to the popular question "Did 'Q' ever exist?" depends on a clear definition. The most likely answer is, of course, that "Q" never existed—and therefore cannot be reconstructed, since there were more than one collection of sayings and other material used by the Gospel writers. St. Luke himself says as much in the prologue to his Gospel (1:2–3), and St. John states that not all the material available to him was incorporated into his Gospel (21:25). Papias, writing in about A.D. 110, refers to *logia* of Jesus collected by St. Matthew in Aramaic. Provided that *logia* here merely means, literally, "sayings," St. Matthew could himself have provided "Q" for his own later, complete Gospel, and for that of St. Luke (which is dependent on Matthew as much as elsewhere on Mark). In any case, no papyrus with any trace of what might be called "Q" has survived.

Quire: From the Latin *quaternio,* a set of four. Four sheets folded to yield eight leaves or sixteen pages.

Qumran: See "Dead Sea Scrolls."

Recto: From the Latin *rectus* ("right"). The right, or front, side of a leaf; in papyri, the side where the fibers run horizontally. Because of the folding system in codices, the text on the verso, or back, sometimes preceded the text on the recto. This is the case with the Magdalen Papyrus.

Scriptio continua: See "Diacritical signs."

Scroll: Preferred to "roll" to describe rolls made of parchment, leather, vellum or papyrus by glueing, occasionally stitching, leaves together and rolling them up. Even though scrolls were often purpose-made, there were limitations to their length; 12 m (39¹/₂ ft.) is considered an above-average length. In the New Testament, the two books by St. Luke, his Gospel and Acts, were published in two scrolls prior to the introduction of the codex, where they would easily fit inside one such "book."

Septuagint: From the Latin *septuaginta* ("seventy"), the term is synonymous with the oldest complete Greek translation of the Hebrew/Aramaic Old Testament of about 250 B.C., including the Apocrypha. The name was derived from the legend that seventy (or rather, seventy-two) scholars translated the texts in seventy days. Its practical purpose was to provide an Old Testament for the growing number of Jews who were unable to read and understand Hebrew. In New Testament times, the Septuagint was used throughout the Roman Empire and was the version quoted in the New Testament. Its common abbreviation is LXX.

Sittybos: Sittybos or *sillybos* is the Greek technical term for a tag, usually made of parchment or papyrus, that was attached to the handle or back of a scroll in order to identify its contents without unrolling it. The name of the work inside, perhaps a short description and—if there was more than one work of the same title (such as *Euangelion,* or *Gospel)*—the name of the author, were written on this *sittybos.* Several ancient examples have survived. For the textual tradition of the New Testament, the common and necessary use of these tags guarantees the correct identification of the Gospel authors during the early stages of the Gospels on scrolls.

Spatium: See "Diacritical signs."

Stichometry: From the Greek *stichos* ("line" or "row"). It describes a line or verse of writing; ancient scribes were normally paid according to the number of *stichoi* they wrote or copied. Stichometry refers to the technique of measuring books. The length of a *stichos* is an important element in the decipherment, identification, and editing of papyri: the average length of a line is a yardstick for the completion of fragmentary lines. Two of the papyri discussed in this book, 7Q5 and Ⴒ⁶⁴, offer far-reaching examples of this procedure.

Synoptic Gospels: In spite of all their differences, Mark, Matthew and Luke share a "common view" (Greek, *syn–opsis*) in the arrangement of their portrayal of Jesus. John, on the other hand, offers a distinctively different approach to the selection of sayings, narratives and chronology. The traditional tendency to prefer the "synoptics" for their historical value had to be abandoned in view of the increasing evidence supporting the accuracy and trustworthiness of John in his own right. It was no longer possible to play them off against each other.

Tachygraphy: From the Greek *tachys* ("sharp") and *graphe* ("writing"), for different systems of ancient shorthand writing common in New Testament times, and before, throughout the Roman Empire.

Torah: From the Hebrew for "precept," "law": the Pentateuch, that is, the five first books of the Old Testament, ascribed to Moses, and, in a more narrow sense, the law of the Old Testament.

Vellum: From the Old French *velin* ("calf"). Writing material made from the skin of young calves and other (often unborn) animals to yield extrafine quality.

Verso: From the Latin *vertere* ("to turn"). The back (or rather, reverse), left side of a leaf, where the fibers run vertically. On parchment, vellum or leather manuscripts, recto and verso refer to the lighter "flesh" side and the darker "hair" side.

Zierstil: German for "decorated style," a term introduced by the German papyrologist Wilhelm Schubart to describe a style of handwriting not unlike the *Häkchenstil*, with decorative roundels and small lines at the extremities of a main stroke in a letter (also called serifs). Schubart assumed that this style was common during the first centuries B.C. and A.D., whereas the British papyrologist E. G. Turner felt that the term was too vague to be useful for dating purposes.

INDEX